# The Code of Trust

# The Code of Trust

## How Cryptocurrency Challenges Power, Redefines Money, and Asks What We Truly Believe

Evelyn Hartstone

Mindful Pages

Published in 2025

ISBN: 9789371777933 (PB)
ISBN: 9789371777148 (eBook)

*Published by*

**Mindful Pages**
*Imprint of Alpha Editions LLC*
312 W. 2nd St #1834
Casper, WY 82601, USA


This book was developed using advanced writing tools to support the drafting and ideation process. All content has been thoughtfully curated, refined, and reviewed to ensure quality and relevance.

# Content

# Introduction
# The Code We Live By

What is money, at its core? Strip away the banknotes, the credit ratings, the gold reserves, the digital balances, and what remains is something far less tangible than we like to imagine: trust. Not the sentimental trust we extend to family or friends, but a colder, systemic kind—a collective agreement that a symbol, a ledger entry, or a string of code can be exchanged for goods, services, or security. Money is not an object; it is a narrative. A code we inhabit, often without questioning.

That narrative is being rewritten.

Cryptocurrency did not begin with a coin, a company, or a marketing campaign. It began with rupture—a fracture in the established consensus of trust. In the aftermath of the 2008 financial crisis, a moment of profound disillusionment, an anonymous entity known as Satoshi Nakamoto released a white paper proposing something radical: a form of money that required neither banks nor governments, nor any trusted intermediary. Instead, governance would emerge from code—mathematics, cryptography, and distributed consensus. Bitcoin was not just a technical innovation; it was a philosophical challenge. It posed a question long avoided: what if we no longer trust the authorities?

In the years since, that question has only intensified. Distrust in institutions is not a fleeting sentiment; it is structural. Financial collapses exposed the fragility of central banks and regulatory bodies. Political scandals revealed the malleability of democracies. Data breaches and the rise of surveillance capitalism made privacy seem almost archaic. In this vacuum, a new kind of faith has emerged—not in people, but in protocols.

This book examines that shift. It is not a manual for trading, nor a primer on blockchain mechanics. It is a philosophical and human exploration of cryptocurrency as a cultural and psychological phenomenon. It investigates not only how crypto works, but why it matters: what it reveals about values, fears, and our evolving relationship with power, identity, and truth.

To understand cryptocurrency, one must first understand what money has always been: a mass hallucination. From cowrie shells to Roman coins, Venetian banknotes to American dollars, and now digital tokens, the principle remains the same. Each represents a collective fiction, a shared belief that something inert gains power when others accept its utility. Money has never demanded intrinsic value; it demands only the illusion of certainty. When that certainty collapses—through hyperinflation, governmental overreach, or loss of trust—people search for new anchors. Cryptocurrency is one such anchor, or at least promises to be.

But the promise is double-edged. On the surface, crypto offers emancipation: control over wealth, protection of identity, bypassing traditional financial gatekeepers. Dig deeper, and ambiguities appear. Mechanisms enabling sovereignty also permit fraud, exploitation, and extremism. The transparency of the blockchain fosters trust, yet it can be unforgiving. Decentralisation protects freedom, but can dilute accountability. Every revolution contains paradox.

A central paradox emerges: can the sovereign individual thrive without the fragile collective?

Crypto is often framed heroically—as rebellion against the state, liberation from fiat, a technological exodus toward freedom. Yet extreme individualism carries risk. Without institutions, who resolves disputes? Without oversight, who safeguards the vulnerable? Without a shared moral framework, what holds communities together when crises strike?

This book navigates those questions without prescribing definitive answers, mapping instead the terrain in which they must be asked. It traces the roots of trust—from ancient trade networks to modern central banks—exploring why scarcity seduces, crowds influence, and rationality so often falters. It scrutinises decentralisation myths, trustless systems, and the tension between code and humanity. It confronts crypto's dark mirror—scams, crimes, and ethical blind spots—and considers the role of law, regulation, and social norms in shaping its evolution.

Yet this is not merely a technological story. It is a story about belief. What do we choose to believe when traditional systems fail? How do we define truth when code replaces law, consensus replaces authority? What does it mean to own something when even the keys to your identity can vanish with a single error?

The answers are complex and context-dependent. For some, cryptocurrency is lifeline—safeguarding against hyperinflation, censorship, or exclusion. For others, it is speculation, a digital casino cloaked in utopian rhetoric. For many, it remains opaque yet compelling. This book is for all of them: the sceptic seeking clarity, the believer seeking grounding, the curious observer sensing that something profound is unfolding beneath the surface of markets and ledgers.

Cryptocurrency is not history's conclusion, nor a panacea for systemic flaws. It is a mirror, reflecting our contradictions: yearning for freedom yet craving stability, desiring autonomy yet longing for safety, distrusting authority yet hoping for order. Crypto exposes these tensions rather than resolving them.

*The Code of Trust* is not a manifesto; it is a map. It guides readers through digital money and decentralised power without dictating a single destination. It asks each reader to consider their coordinates: whom do you trust? What deserves your faith? And are you ready to take responsibility if the code falters?

We enter an era where rules are encoded not only in law, but in algorithms and consensus protocols. Authority can decentralise, yet power may still re-concentrate in subtle forms. Belief becomes programmable; trust is optional—but never obsolete.

The stakes are high, not because crypto is intrinsically virtuous or corrupt, but because it is deeply human. It inherits brilliance and blindness, ingenuity and arrogance. And as we build so-called trustless systems, we must remember who writes the code—and who is left exposed when it fails.

So let us begin—not with blind faith or cynical dismissal, but with attentiveness and reflection. The story of cryptocurrency is far from finished, yet it already asks the most urgent question of our time: what do you truly believe?

# Chapter 1
# The Invention of Trust

Trust, though unseen, is perhaps the most decisive force in human affairs. It builds cities, fuels trade, sustains governments, and silently dictates whether civilisations flourish or collapse. Yet it is so ingrained in the everyday that we mistake it for something solid. We talk of money, contracts, institutions—as though these are objective realities, when in fact they are fragile artefacts of shared belief. Of them all, money stands out as the most universal and least understood example: an illusion with consequences as real as steel and stone.

Long before banks or bonds, people exchanged curiosities that now seem quaint: shells, carved beads, obsidian blades. None carried intrinsic value. Their worth lay in ritual, in repetition, in the collective agreement that this shell or that token could stand in for a debt or a dowry. What mattered was never the object itself, but the invisible rules that governed it—the code, if you will. Those shells and beads were early contracts, whispered stories about value and legitimacy, binding precisely because everyone agreed to honour them.

Modern sensibilities bristle at this idea. We are taught to see money as precise, as neutral—something pegged to labour, commodities, or mathematical calculation. Yet history undermines that neat fiction. Gold, often imagined as the ultimate "real" money, was prized less for utility than for its incorruptibility, its sheen of permanence. Empires stamped emperors' faces into coins not only to stabilise currency but to proclaim political authority. Each coin was a declaration: this ruler guarantees order; trust him, trust his system.

As societies grew more elaborate, their monetary systems had to grow with them. The state became the architect of collective belief. Fiat currency, today's standard, rests on a peculiar act of faith: a piece of paper holds value only because a government says so—and because the people consent to believe it. "Fiat" means "let there be." In this case: let there be value. The dollar, the pound, the rupee—all are stories written not in gold but in law.

But such trust is brittle. When confidence falters, systems unravel. Weimar Germany showed how quickly faith in money can vanish: banknotes worth wheelbarrows one week, scarcely enough for bread the next. Zimbabwe replayed the tragedy in the 2000s, with trillion-dollar bills as useless as confetti. Even in quieter economies, fiat's value erodes under the pressures of inflation, misrule, or political decay. And when belief dissolves, people look for substitutes—foreign notes, barter, or more recently, digital alternatives.

The 2008 financial crisis was one such rupture. Central banks and global institutions, long held as guardians of stability, suddenly appeared complicit, inept, or corrupt. When Lehman Brothers fell, when toxic mortgages dragged economies into chaos, when governments rescued banks with public money, trust collapsed. The curtain was pulled back, and the system was revealed less as a wise guardian than as a stage set propped up by insiders and perverse incentives. Out of this disillusionment came an obscure white paper, quietly proposing a new code of trust.

Satoshi Nakamoto's solution was stark: money without middlemen. A peer-to-peer system where transactions were secured not by banks or states but by mathematics. No central vault, no human guarantor—just cryptographic proof and consensus across a distributed network. The first "Genesis Block" carried a message lifted from that day's newspaper: "The Times 03/Jan/2009 Chancellor on brink of second bailout for banks." It was both a timestamp and a statement of intent: this system is born in response to the failures of the old.

The real novelty of Bitcoin was not technical, but philosophical. It asked whether trust could be shifted from institutions to code, from rulers to rules. Traditional money derives legitimacy from the top down: a monarch commands, a bank certifies, a court enforces. Bitcoin flipped the order. Legitimacy was bottom-up: if the network agrees, if the code validates, the transaction is real. No appeals, no bailouts, no exceptions. A trustless system, paradoxically requiring no trust at all, because no one is asked to act in good faith.

But here lies the deeper question: can trust be outsourced to algorithms? Can lines of code replace the messy, fragile trust that binds people together? Advocates insist yes: humans lie, cheat, and embezzle; code is incorruptible, transparent, immune to favour. But critics point out that code is hardly neutral. It is written, revised, and patched by fallible humans. The infamous DAO hack of 2016 made this painfully clear, as a smart contract flaw drained millions in Ether. The remedy—rolling back the Ethereum chain—wasn't code enforcing purity, but a community deciding collectively to override the machine. Even "trustless" systems, it turned out, still leaned on human judgement.

Why then the faith in code? Because in a world shaken by broken promises, code offered a kind of austerity—rigid rules, untouched by politics, immune to corruption. It appealed to those disenchanted with centralised authority, particularly libertarians and anarcho-capitalists who saw crypto not merely as money, but as revolt: a reclamation of sovereignty by the individual.

Yet this clarity comes at a price. Code cannot sympathise. It cannot weigh mercy against law, or bend rules for the sake of justice. It enforces protocol, not principle. Which means that what is emerging is more than new money—it is a new species of governance, one that seeks to replace discretion with automation, belief with procedure. Whether such a system can hold against the unpredictable mess of human life remains an open question.

The lesson, however, is unmistakable: money has always been a story of trust. From seashells to silver, from paper backed by emperors to digital ledgers humming across the globe, belief has been the constant thread. Fiat may wear the garb of permanence, but its value falters when belief wanes. Bitcoin, by contrast, is backed not by decree or commodity, but by protocol and consensus. Flawed, certainly—but radical in its reimagining of what trust might mean.

What we are living through, then, is not the invention of money out of nothing, but the migration of belief. From the tangible to the abstract. From crown and parliament to protocol and pseudonym. Whether this shift yields resilience or fragmentation, no one yet knows. But one thing is plain: trust is being remade—not as a moral virtue, but as a technological function. And in this remaking, each of us is implicated, whether willingly or not.

## From Cowrie Shells to Central Banks

Money is not what most people think it is. Ask someone to define it, and they may mention coins, notes, or bank accounts—things visible, countable, and seemingly concrete. But these are mere artefacts, surface-level manifestations of something far more profound. Money, at its core, is not a physical object or even a digital ledger—it is a shared belief system. A social contract. One of the most successful and enduring in human history.

This truth is both unsettling and liberating. It means that money, like language or law, is not real in the way a rock or a tree is real. It exists only because enough people agree that it does. The pound in your pocket has no intrinsic value. Nor did the cowrie shells exchanged on African coastlines, or the silver denarii minted in ancient Rome. These forms of currency were not valuable because of their material properties, but because people *acted* as if they were. And once that collective belief took hold, it became self-reinforcing. Money worked because people believed it worked.

The origins of money are frequently misunderstood. Contrary to popular myth, early economies were not driven by barter that eventually gave way to coinage. Anthropological and archaeological research suggests that barter was rare and typically confined to interactions between strangers or enemies. Most early human communities operated on systems of credit and obligation—who owed whom, and for what. These obligations were remembered communally or recorded through tokens, tallies, or ceremonial exchanges. Value was not stored in objects; it was stored in relationships.

When societies grew more complex and strangers began to trade, a more portable and universal symbol of value became necessary. This is where commodity money enters the picture. Cowrie shells, for instance, were used across large swathes of Africa and Asia for centuries—not because they were rare everywhere, but because they were recognisable, relatively durable, and hard to counterfeit. Their value lay not in scarcity alone, but in the stability of belief surrounding them. Similarly, salt bars in Ethiopia, whale teeth in Fiji, and even large limestone discs in the Micronesian island of Yap all served as currency. In each case, their usefulness was secondary to their symbolic role. These objects were tools for representing trust, not storing wealth.

Metals—especially gold and silver—added a new dimension to this dynamic. Their physical properties (durability, divisibility, uniformity) made them well-suited for trade, but their adoption as money was still a matter of consensus. When rulers began to mint coins bearing their likenesses, the coinage served multiple functions: a unit of account, a medium of exchange, and a declaration of sovereign power. To accept a king's coin was to acknowledge his authority. Monetary legitimacy was not derived from the metal, but from the political order that stamped its seal on it.

This convergence of political authority and monetary value laid the groundwork for centuries of state-controlled currency. And with it came the possibility of manipulation. Governments realised they could debase coins—reducing the precious metal content while keeping the face value unchanged. This was not just a technical trick; it was a test of belief. As long as people continued to trust the issuer, they would accept the diluted coins. But if trust faltered, the system would unravel. Throughout history, from ancient Rome to imperial China, this cycle played out repeatedly: overissuance, inflation, loss of confidence, collapse.

What made the modern era different was the emergence of institutional frameworks designed to stabilise that trust. Central banks were not born out of abstract theory; they were created in response to financial chaos. The Bank of England, founded in 1694, was originally a mechanism for managing the Crown's debt. Over time, it evolved into the lender of last resort, charged with maintaining monetary stability. Other nations followed suit, and by the 20th century, most developed economies had established central banks that controlled money supply, set interest rates, and regulated commercial banks.

The shift from commodity-backed to fiat currency—money not convertible into a physical asset like gold—was gradual but decisive. The gold standard, long romanticised as a bastion of stability, was always more fragile than its defenders admit. It required rigid exchange rates and often imposed severe economic constraints. During times of crisis—such as wars or financial panics—governments routinely suspended convertibility. The final break came in 1971, when the United States under President Nixon officially severed the dollar's link to gold. From that moment, money became purely fiat: valuable only because states decreed it so, and because the public believed the decree would hold.

The implications were immense. Fiat currency allowed governments greater flexibility in managing economies—through monetary policy, stimulus spending, and debt financing. But it also introduced new risks. Without a physical anchor, money's value rested entirely on institutional credibility. Inflation, once a technical matter, became a political one. Central banks were tasked with the delicate balancing act of promoting growth while preserving trust. And when that trust wavered—due to hyperinflation, mismanagement, or corruption—the system quickly revealed its vulnerability.

Consider the economic collapse of Argentina in the early 2000s. A currency pegged to the US dollar, unsustainable fiscal deficits, and widespread political instability triggered a crisis of confidence. Bank withdrawals were frozen, savings evaporated, and riots broke out. Or look to Venezuela, where hyperinflation reached surreal levels, rendering the national currency functionally useless. In such cases, the breakdown of monetary trust leads to more than economic disruption—it erodes the very fabric of civic life. People turn to informal barter, foreign currencies, or, more recently, cryptocurrencies, in search of something—*anything*—that can act as a store of value.

It is this historical context that makes the emergence of cryptocurrency so provocative. Bitcoin was not the first attempt at digital money, but it was the first to solve the double-spending problem without requiring a trusted central authority. Its invention was not merely technical; it was ideological. Bitcoin proposed a monetary system that replaced institutional trust with mathematical proof. Transactions would be verified not by banks, but by decentralised consensus. The ledger would be public, immutable, and secure. The money supply would be fixed and transparent, immune to inflationary tinkering. For believers, this was not just a better form of money—it was a form of liberation.

Yet the deeper insight here is not that Bitcoin is superior to fiat currency, but that both are anchored in the same fundamental principle: *collective belief.* The pound sterling works because people believe the Bank of England will manage it responsibly. Bitcoin works because its users believe in the protocol, the rules, and the network effects that support it. Strip away that belief, and both systems collapse—whether the mechanism is a central bank or a decentralised blockchain.

This recognition reframes the history of money as a continuous negotiation between symbols and trust. What counts as money is less about substance than structure. It must be transferable, divisible, scarce, and recognisable—but above all, it must be trusted. That trust can be based on tradition, authority, or code. It can be inherited or engineered. But it must be resilient, or it will be replaced.

Central banks remain powerful precisely because they have mastered the theatre of trust: issuing statements, adjusting rates, signalling intentions. They do not merely manage liquidity; they manage expectations. This performative aspect of monetary policy is increasingly scrutinised in a digital age where transparency is demanded and narrative control is elusive. As trust becomes more volatile—more globalised, more politicised—the question is no longer whether fiat or crypto is "real" money. The question is which system better earns and maintains belief.

From the shells passed hand to hand on coastal trade routes to the cryptographic keys securing billion-dollar transactions today, the story of money is a story of evolving faith. Each era brings new mechanisms, but the essence remains the same. We do not use money because it is valuable. It is valuable because we use it. And once that illusion is broken—whether by inflation, fraud, or technological disruption—the scramble to restore or reinvent belief begins anew. That is the cycle we inherit, and the one we must now learn to navigate with open eyes.

## The Fragility of Fiat

Fiat currency, despite its ubiquity, is a deeply precarious construct. It functions not because it is underwritten by intrinsic value, but because enough people, institutions, and markets *behave* as though it is. This behaviour is not rooted in material reality, but in institutional credibility—faith that the issuing authority will act in a way that preserves the value of the money over time. That trust is not given freely. It is maintained through policy discipline, transparency, legal stability, and, often, the perceived competence of those in charge. When these pillars weaken, fiat becomes brittle. And history shows that they weaken far more easily than the public often assumes.

To understand the fragility of fiat, one must first understand what it actually is. A fiat currency is declared legal tender by government decree, but it has no intrinsic worth and is not convertible into a commodity such as gold or silver. It is, quite literally, a promise backed by a central authority, enforceable by law and sustained by collective confidence. That promise can endure for decades—sometimes even centuries—but it is never immutable. It relies on a precarious equilibrium between economic performance, institutional trustworthiness, and political stability. Break any of these elements, and the currency risks collapse from within.

Inflation is the most widely recognised threat to fiat credibility, yet its roots are often misunderstood. It is not merely the result of increased money supply, but a manifestation of deteriorating trust. When people believe that the issuing authority is losing control—printing too much money, accumulating unsustainable debt, or mismanaging fiscal priorities—they begin to reprice the value of money downward. Prices rise not just because of supply-demand mechanics, but because of anticipatory behaviour. If people expect a currency to buy less tomorrow than it does today, they accelerate spending and demand wage increases, fuelling a self-reinforcing cycle. In extreme cases, this feedback loop breaks into hyperinflation.

The textbook examples are illustrative, but not abstract. In Zimbabwe during the late 2000s, the government's decision to print money to finance deficits, fund patronage networks, and suppress dissent led to a spectacular collapse in the Zimbabwean dollar's value. Inflation rates exceeded 80 billion percent annually, and the currency had to be redenominated multiple times before being abandoned altogether in favour of foreign alternatives. Venezuela offers a more recent and politically complex case, where oil dependency, economic mismanagement, and authoritarian governance have rendered the bolívar virtually worthless. Citizens turned to dollars, barter, and eventually cryptocurrencies—not because of ideology, but necessity. They no longer believed the state could maintain the value of its money, and so they exited the system wherever possible.

Yet fiat does not need to collapse into hyperinflation to show signs of stress. In developed economies, more subtle forms of manipulation and erosion occur. Quantitative easing, negative interest rates, and aggressive fiscal expansions—though often justified as emergency measures—blur the lines between monetary policy and political expediency. Central banks claim independence, but their balance sheets increasingly serve political ends: financing government deficits, propping up asset prices, and preventing market corrections. This blurring raises uncomfortable questions. Who is the fiat system ultimately designed to protect? The citizen, the investor, or the state?

One of the structural vulnerabilities of fiat is its centralisation. Power to create money resides with a small set of institutions—typically central banks, operating under mandates defined by the state. In theory, these institutions are technocratic, rule-bound, and insulated from political influence. In practice, the distinction between policy and politics is porous. Central banks do not operate in a vacuum. They respond to political pressure, market expectations, and media narratives. Their credibility is subject not only to their decisions, but to how those decisions are perceived. When trust in their objectivity erodes, so too does trust in the currency itself.

Consider the case of Turkey in recent years. The Turkish lira has suffered multiple devaluations, not solely because of macroeconomic fundamentals, but due to repeated political interference in monetary policy. President Erdoğan's unorthodox belief that high interest rates cause inflation, rather than curb it, led to the dismissal of several central bank governors and a series of policies that undermined investor confidence. The result was predictable: capital flight, spiralling inflation, and a weakening currency. But the more significant damage was to institutional credibility. Investors and citizens alike began to treat the lira as unstable, not because of external shocks, but because of internal decisions that rendered the money unreliable.

Corruption adds another layer of fragility. Fiat systems depend on a functioning legal and regulatory apparatus to maintain the integrity of the currency and the institutions that support it. When elites use monetary policy for self-enrichment, when regulators fail to prevent financial misconduct, or when the rule of law is selectively applied, the monetary system becomes a tool of exploitation rather than a neutral framework. In such environments, fiat money becomes a symbol not of trust, but of its absence. It is not by coincidence that some of the highest crypto adoption rates globally are found in countries with weak rule of law, high inflation, and low institutional trust.

This brings us to the emerging appeal of cryptocurrency—not as a superior technology, but as an alternative trust architecture. Bitcoin and its descendants propose a radical inversion of fiat logic. Where fiat requires faith in institutions, crypto requires faith in code. The rules of issuance are fixed and transparent. Supply is capped. Transactions are verifiable, immutable, and borderless. No central bank can decide to devalue your holdings. No politician can influence the ledger. In this sense, cryptocurrencies offer what fiat increasingly struggles to provide: *predictability*.

Critics rightly note that crypto markets are volatile, unregulated, and susceptible to manipulation of a different kind. But these critiques often miss the point. For many users, particularly in politically or economically unstable regions, volatility is a feature worth tolerating in exchange for autonomy. Crypto is not a panacea, but it is a powerful hedge against institutional failure. It is a way of opting out—not just from a currency, but from a system that has proven unable or unwilling to protect the integrity of its promises.

Even in stable democracies, the long-term health of fiat is not guaranteed. The COVID-19 pandemic saw governments around the world inject trillions into the economy. While many of these measures were necessary, they also accelerated trends that had been building for years: rising debt-to-GDP ratios, asset price inflation, and growing reliance on central bank interventions. These trends raise uncomfortable questions about the future. If every downturn requires massive stimulus, if monetary expansion is the default response to crisis, what happens when confidence finally runs out? Will fiat survive simply because there is no alternative—or will alternatives, like crypto, become credible enough to force systemic adaptation?

Some defenders of fiat argue that its flexibility is its greatest strength. Unlike hard-capped currencies or algorithmic monetary systems, fiat allows for counter-cyclical intervention, redistribution, and responsive governance. These are fair points. But flexibility is only an asset when it is used judiciously. When it becomes a euphemism for manipulation or negligence, it ceases to be a virtue. The same mechanisms that allow governments to rescue economies can also be abused to serve short-term political goals or entrench elite interests. The public, increasingly aware of these dynamics, is beginning to ask whether the cost of fiat's flexibility is too high.

The deeper issue is not about choosing between fiat and crypto, but about recognising the trade-offs embedded in different trust systems. Fiat asks us to believe in people—technocrats, elected officials, institutional frameworks. Crypto asks us to believe in protocols—mathematical rules, distributed consensus, cryptographic assurance. Neither system is infallible. But the growing appeal of crypto is not rooted in utopianism; it is rooted in disillusionment. It reflects a world where traditional promises are no longer self-evident, and where alternative models—however flawed—deserve consideration because the status quo no longer commands unquestioned loyalty.

The fragility of fiat, then, is not merely a technical concern. It is a philosophical one. It forces us to confront the limits of institutional trust and to consider whether trust can—or should—be rebuilt through other means. The answers are not obvious, and the risks of transition are significant. But the cracks in the old system are widening. And as more people look for exits, the question is no longer whether fiat can survive, but on what terms—and for how long.

## The Genesis Block and the Birth of Bitcoin

The most influential monetary revolution of the 21st century began with a message hidden in a block of code. On 3 January 2009, the pseudonymous creator of Bitcoin, Satoshi Nakamoto, mined the first block of the Bitcoin blockchain—Block 0, later known as the "Genesis Block". Embedded in the coinbase parameter of that block was a short, cryptic sentence: *"The Times 03/Jan/2009 Chancellor on brink of second bailout for banks."* This was no throwaway reference. It was a timestamp, a signal, and a critique rolled into one. It anchored Bitcoin's birth to a precise moment of institutional crisis and made clear that the system being proposed was not just technical, but political. Bitcoin was not merely an invention. It was an indictment.

To grasp the significance of Bitcoin's origins, one must return to the systemic tremors of the 2008 financial crisis. What began as a collapse in the U.S. subprime mortgage market quickly metastasised into a global banking meltdown. Lehman Brothers—one of the most storied financial institutions on Wall Street—filed for bankruptcy. Major banks across Europe and North America were revealed to be undercapitalised and overexposed to toxic assets. Governments scrambled to contain the fallout, injecting billions into the financial system to avert total collapse. Central banks slashed interest rates, extended emergency loans, and deployed unconventional monetary tools that would later become routine. Trust, the invisible infrastructure of modern finance, cracked in real time.

The anger was widespread. In many countries, the public saw institutions that had promised prudence and oversight suddenly revealed as reckless and self-serving. The bailout of banks—perceived by many as a reward for systemic incompetence—fuelled a deep and lasting scepticism. Questions were asked, not just about policy, but about legitimacy. Why were the architects of failure shielded from consequences? Why were citizens asked to absorb the cost? Why was there no alternative?

Bitcoin emerged as a direct response to these questions. Its architecture was designed to eliminate the need for trust in fallible intermediaries. At its core was the idea of *decentralisation*—a network of computers maintaining a public ledger without central control. No government would back it. No central bank could print it. Its supply would be fixed—21 million coins, released on a predictable schedule, immune to inflationary manipulation. Transactions would be validated by cryptographic consensus, not institutional decree. And the rules of the system would be open, transparent, and enforced by code rather than human discretion.

This represented a radical departure from how money had functioned for centuries. The state had always claimed a monopoly on money creation, justified on grounds of economic stability and legal coherence. But Satoshi's white paper, *Bitcoin: A Peer-to-Peer Electronic Cash System*, implicitly questioned whether this monopoly had become a source of systemic risk rather than resilience. By proposing a self-governing monetary protocol, Bitcoin reframed money not as an instrument of statecraft, but as a public utility secured by mathematics.

What made this move intellectually subversive was not just the rejection of centralisation, but the notion that *code could replace institutional trust.* In the traditional financial system, trust is layered and relational: depositors trust banks, banks trust regulators, markets trust central banks, and governments trust one another via diplomatic and financial protocols. Each layer is a potential failure point. Bitcoin proposed a system in which trust was displaced—offloaded onto cryptographic proof, open-source transparency, and game-theoretic incentives. If you followed the rules, the system worked. If you didn't, it ignored you.

The timing was impeccable. Just as trust in mainstream finance was reaching a historic low, Bitcoin offered a plausible, albeit untested, alternative. Its early adopters—often libertarians, cryptographers, and technologists disillusioned with the status quo—saw in it a monetary system that reflected their ideals: sovereignty, censorship-resistance, and predictability. But the network also attracted a broader audience: people in countries with unstable currencies, those excluded from the formal banking sector, and eventually institutional actors looking to hedge against inflation or geopolitical risk.

Bitcoin's pseudonymous creator has never been conclusively identified. The disappearance of Satoshi Nakamoto in 2010 only deepened the mythos. But in a way, that disappearance reinforced the decentralised ethos of the project. There was no leader, no foundation, no corporate structure. Bitcoin became a protocol in the wild—maintained by its users, miners, and developers. Its governance was informal, often contentious, but structurally decentralised. Unlike central banks, which derive legitimacy from law and tradition, Bitcoin derived its legitimacy from continued participation and cryptographic consensus. It was not backed by the state, but by belief—and that belief was, crucially, enforced by code.

This does not mean Bitcoin was perfect or complete. From the beginning, it faced scaling challenges, regulatory uncertainty, energy criticisms, and internal disputes. But these should not obscure the conceptual breakthrough it represented. For the first time in history, it was possible to move value across the globe without relying on banks, payment processors, or governments. This alone was revolutionary. And it posed an uncomfortable question for existing institutions: if trust can be programmed, what happens to the systems built on human discretion?

The Genesis Block's embedded headline was more than a timestamp. It was a statement of purpose. Bitcoin was not created in a vacuum, but in a moment of reckoning—when faith in the traditional financial order was shattered, and alternatives no longer seemed outlandish. The crisis of 2008 was not just about markets. It was about meaning. It exposed how abstract and fragile the entire financial order was, and it invited new narratives to take its place. Bitcoin offered one such narrative: that of a self-regulating, incorruptible financial layer built not on promises, but on protocols.

Over a decade later, the implications are still unfolding. Bitcoin has inspired an entire ecosystem of cryptocurrencies, blockchain projects, decentralised finance (DeFi), and digital asset experimentation. It has forced regulators to confront new realities, pushed central banks to explore digital currencies of their own, and prompted intellectuals across disciplines to rethink foundational concepts: What is money? Who controls it? What constitutes trust in a digital society?

Yet, it is important to resist the temptation to see Bitcoin solely through a technical or financial lens. Its birth was philosophical. It began with a proposition: that money can exist outside the authority of the state, that trust can be decoupled from institutions, and that scarcity can be digitally enforced without violence or decree. These are radical ideas, not because they are anarchic, but because they challenge assumptions so deeply embedded we scarcely notice them.

The financial system that collapsed in 2008 was not merely overleveraged. It was overtrusted. It had substituted complexity for transparency, risk for reward, and growth for resilience. When it failed, the response was to rebuild the same architecture with minor reinforcements. Bitcoin took a different path. It sought to build something altogether new—a base layer not of concrete, but of code.

The Genesis Block was not the beginning of just another payment network. It was the opening of a counter-narrative, one that continues to evolve, challenge, and provoke. To understand Bitcoin is not just to learn about blockchains or mining algorithms. It is to confront a deeper question: *what happens when we stop trusting the centre?*

## Why Code Became King

Trust has always been the fulcrum of human cooperation. Whether in trade, governance, or justice, the ability to rely on others—often strangers—without constant verification is what allows complex societies to function. But trust is expensive. It requires time, institutions, enforcement mechanisms, and reputational collateral. And it fails—often spectacularly. The proposition at the heart of cryptocurrency is that, for certain domains, *we may no longer need trust in people at all.* We may only need code. Specifically, *cryptographic code.* The shift from socially constructed trust to mathematically enforced consensus is not a footnote in the history of money—it is a transformation in how authority is produced and legitimacy maintained in the digital age.

The concept of cryptographic trust begins with a provocative question: what if you could design a system in which trust was not assumed, negotiated, or socially earned, but *engineered* into the architecture itself? The answer, as realised through Bitcoin and the broader blockchain ecosystem, is a system that does not require any participant to be trustworthy. It only requires them to follow the rules—or face automatic exclusion. In this context, trust becomes redundant. The system's integrity no longer hinges on moral character, institutional reputation, or legal enforcement. It is guaranteed, not by oversight, but by mathematics.

This was the philosophical breakthrough behind Satoshi Nakamoto's Bitcoin white paper. The goal was not merely to create a digital currency—it was to create a financial protocol that eliminated the need for trusted intermediaries. Cryptography made this possible. By using digital signatures, hash functions, and consensus algorithms, Satoshi created a system where transactions could be verified by a decentralised network of nodes, each working independently to enforce the same rules. No bank, no central server, no overseer. Only code, running on machines distributed across the globe, reaching agreement through mathematical certainty.

The idea that trust could be replaced with code did not emerge in a vacuum. It was built on decades of development in cryptographic theory and distributed systems. Public-key cryptography, invented in the 1970s, allowed two parties to exchange messages securely without prior contact. Hash functions provided a way to verify data integrity without revealing the data itself. And Byzantine fault tolerance—originally a theoretical model for coordinating consensus in unreliable systems—became the basis for ensuring that distributed nodes could agree on a single version of the truth even if some participants acted maliciously. These components were known, but it was Bitcoin that fused them into a working economic protocol. The genius was not in invention, but in *composition.*

Bitcoin's consensus mechanism, known as proof-of-work, ensures that new transactions can only be added to the ledger if computational effort has been expended. This makes it prohibitively expensive to rewrite history. The longest chain of blocks is assumed to be the valid one because it represents the most accumulated computational work. This mechanism disincentivises fraud not through fear of legal consequences, but through game theory and economic cost. It turns potential attackers into contributors. In effect, it converts distrust into coordination.

Why does this matter? Because trust—especially in financial systems—is often brittle, centralised, and prone to abuse. When we trust a bank, we rely on its solvency, cybersecurity, internal governance, and compliance with regulations. When that trust is breached, the consequences can be devastating. Think of the 2008 financial crisis, where exotic financial instruments and institutional opacity brought global markets to their knees. Or Wells Fargo's fake accounts scandal, where employees, under pressure to meet sales targets, created millions of accounts without customer consent. These failures were not technological—they were failures of human incentives, oversight, and ethical boundaries.

Cryptographic trust reframes the problem. It does not attempt to make actors more trustworthy. It makes trust irrelevant. In a blockchain system like Bitcoin, no node needs to know or trust any other. The system assumes dishonesty, and it is built to withstand it. The integrity of the ledger is not protected by regulation, but by redundancy and consensus. This does not make such systems immune to failure—but it changes *where* failure is likely to occur, and what is required to exploit them.

This shift has far-reaching implications. It enables financial transactions across borders without banks. It allows the issuance and transfer of digital assets without custodians. It enables the creation of decentralised applications—smart contracts—that execute autonomously when certain conditions are met. These contracts do not rely on courts to be enforced. They are *self-enforcing.* Once deployed, they operate exactly as coded, without exceptions, sympathy, or discretion.

Of course, this rigidity introduces its own risks. Code is only as good as the humans who write it, and mistakes in smart contracts can be catastrophic. The 2016 DAO hack on Ethereum, where a vulnerability in the contract code allowed an attacker to siphon off millions in Ether, revealed the limits of relying solely on code.

Ethereum's response—to initiate a controversial hard fork—raised existential questions about immutability and decentralised governance. Was it acceptable to rewrite the ledger to undo a technically valid but ethically problematic transaction? The debate split the community, and ultimately the network. Ethereum and Ethereum Classic were born from that schism.

This tension—between the ideal of trustless code and the reality of human error—cannot be resolved easily. It marks a new philosophical battleground: *is code law*, or is there still a need for interpretive institutions, even in decentralised systems? The answer depends on one's tolerance for ambiguity. Code can automate rules, but it cannot grasp context. It cannot weigh justice or intention. This does not invalidate the promise of cryptographic trust, but it does demand humility about its limits.

Still, the attraction remains strong. In a world of data breaches, surveillance, and regulatory capture, the idea of systems that work without needing to trust anyone—corporate, governmental, or otherwise—is deeply compelling. For individuals living under authoritarian regimes, where banks can be co-opted and financial activity monitored or blocked, the ability to store and transfer value through code is not a luxury—it is a lifeline. For technologists building global infrastructure, decentralised consensus is a path to resilience and censorship resistance.

It also changes the economics of trust. Traditionally, maintaining trust is expensive. It involves insurance, audits, compliance departments, regulators, and layers of bureaucratic oversight. With cryptographic trust, these costs are shifted to computation and network participation. The trade-off is energy consumption, complexity, and sometimes inefficiency. But the gain is *independence*. A system that functions correctly even when participants do not.

There are critics who argue that this model is overhyped—that decentralisation is messy, slow, and difficult to govern. And they are often right. Centralised systems are more efficient. They can make decisions quickly, recover from errors with agility, and enforce policies with consistency. But they also concentrate power. They introduce single points of failure. And they ask for trust that is frequently violated.

This is where code becomes not just a technical tool, but a philosophical stance. It is a statement about how systems should behave—and who gets to control them. By replacing social trust with algorithmic guarantees, blockchain-based systems redefine the boundaries of authority. They disempower gatekeepers and empower users—at least in theory. Whether that power is used wisely is another matter entirely.

The coronation of code did not occur because people stopped believing in one another. It happened because too many of the institutions we were told to trust proved unworthy of it. In response, technologists offered an alternative: a set of protocols where rules cannot be bent, where enforcement is automatic, and where participation is permissionless. It is not a perfect solution. But it is an audacious one. And in many parts of the world, it is the only alternative that has not yet failed.

# Chapter 2
# The Psychology of Value

Value, though central to markets, personal wealth, and economic discourse, is never objective. It is a perception—fluid, contingent, and ultimately psychological. Economists have long sought to quantify it: marginal utility, supply and demand curves, equilibrium prices. Yet time and again, reality intervenes: people invest not with spreadsheets, but with stories, instinct, and emotion. In cryptocurrency, where underlying assets or cash flows are often absent, this truth becomes unavoidable. To understand crypto without grappling with the psychology of value is akin to explaining fire solely through chemistry, ignoring the warmth it imparts.

This chapter examines the subtle and often overlooked forces that shape perception in digital markets: scarcity, social influence, and emotional resonance. Cryptocurrency does not move in orderly increments. Prices surge and plummet in waves, propelled less by underlying technology than by collective belief. One week a token is derided as worthless; the next, it is hailed as a "store of value"; then it is "a bubble"—until somehow, belief shifts once again. The market is not merely reacting; it is narrating itself. Value exists where belief exists—and belief is always vulnerable.

Scarcity sits at the centre of this phenomenon. Humans are wired to prize what is limited. Gold has long enjoyed this status: rare, durable, and culturally resonant. Bitcoin deliberately replicates these dynamics. Its protocol caps supply at 21 million coins, halving issuance roughly every four years. This technical scarcity is designed to mirror the extraction of precious metals, but its psychological resonance is far greater than its mechanics. Fixed supply signals discipline, resistance to inflation, and a kind of digital sanctity. Investors internalise this narrative with near-religious fervour: scarcity becomes value—or at least, it feels as though it should.

Yet scarcity alone is no guarantor. Rarity does not automatically confer worth; it is the human mind that assigns significance. Behavioural economics shows that perceived limitation triggers urgency and accelerates decision-making, often at the expense of rationality. In crypto, such biases are amplified. Token caps, NFT drops, and burn events ignite frenzies not because fundamentals shift, but because scarcity is perceived to rise. Fear of missing out overrides caution. Participation is often reactive, impulsive, and socially contagious.

Emotions in crypto markets are amplified by absence of traditional brakes: no trading halts, no central oversight, minimal regulation. A tweet, a meme, or a rumour can erase billions within hours—or inflate tokens to billion-dollar valuations overnight. Crowds operate at internet speed, carrying all human biases: herd behaviour, confirmation bias, recency effects. Feedback loops magnify each signal. Momentum, in this context, is less rational principle than collective assumption: if others are buying, they must know something I do not. Belief feeds belief until a correction occurs—or chaos intervenes.

The rational actor model—the idea that individuals calculate utility with stable preferences and perfect information—fails spectacularly here. Investors misjudge probabilities, underestimate emotional reactions, and fall prey to heuristics that simplify but distort reality. Crypto does not invent these tendencies; it exposes them. It strips away institutional narrative, revealing the naked interface between human instinct and price.

Information, rather than clarifying, often entrenches bias. With endless analytics and social feeds, investors gravitate toward stories that reinforce prior positions. A rising token is "the future of finance"; a falling one is "manipulated." Communities form around belief rather than evidence; dissent is punished socially. Trading becomes identity formation through capital rather than traditional calculation.

Gamification intensifies these dynamics. Crypto platforms resemble video games more than banking apps: flashing charts, achievement notifications, real-time social feeds. Participation, staking, posting, and evangelising are rewarded with dopamine, not merely financial returns. Tokens are named after memes, animals, and cultural icons. Risk-taking is often framed as play, reward is immediate, and consequences, if abstracted, feel distant.

This evolution is generational. For those raised in digital ecosystems, investment is intertwined with identity and social signalling. Profit remains relevant, but clout, belonging, and narrative dominance are equally prized. Traditional financial education addresses risk, but rarely meaning. In crypto, meaning often outweighs logic.

Yet dismissing these phenomena as irrational misses the point. Human cognition evolved under uncertainty, social competition, and scarcity. These instincts persist, now magnified by high-speed, decentralised markets. Cryptocurrency accelerates the interface between ancient behaviour and modern systems.

This chapter dissects these layers: how scarcity is constructed and weaponised, how collective psychology can override reason, and how platforms exploit these patterns to drive participation. It challenges the myth of the rational investor, arguing that understanding crypto requires understanding the human mind. Ignore psychology, and one misunderstands both the market and oneself.

Ultimately, value exists wherever belief does. But belief is malleable, reactive, and socially contingent. The psychology of value is no side note in the crypto revolution—it is its foundation. To neglect it is to observe the market with one eye closed, mistaking appearance for substance.

## The Scarcity Illusion

Scarcity exerts an outsized influence on the human mind. We are drawn to the rare, the exclusive, the limited—often regardless of whether those things hold any practical utility. This instinct, deeply embedded through evolutionary pressures, governs how we perceive value even in the modern financial landscape. We rarely ask *why* something is scarce; we simply assume that if it is hard to obtain, it must be worth obtaining. But this assumption is not neutral—it is manufactured, reinforced, and often exploited. In the context of money, and especially cryptocurrency, scarcity is less an objective constraint than a *narrative device*. Its power lies not in the actual limitation of supply, but in how that limitation is framed, believed, and acted upon.

Consider gold, the historical benchmark for monetary value. It is chemically inert, relatively scarce in the Earth's crust, and difficult to mine. But these physical properties alone do not explain its centuries-long role as money. Platinum, after all, is even scarcer and has greater industrial utility, yet it has never played a comparable monetary role. The real difference lies in gold's *perceived* scarcity: its visible permanence, its uniform luster, its storied accumulation by monarchs and empires. Gold's value is not intrinsic—it is relational, symbolic, and socially constructed. We believe it is valuable because others believe the same. Its scarcity is important, but only because it maps cleanly onto a psychological craving for certainty in an uncertain world.

Bitcoin inherits and extends this framework. Its capped supply of 21 million coins is not an incidental design feature—it is its central appeal. Introduced in the wake of the 2008 financial crisis, Bitcoin presented itself not just as a decentralised currency, but as *digital gold*—a self-imposed limit in an age of monetary expansion. The appeal was immediate: no more quantitative easing, no discretionary monetary policy, no inflation beyond what was cryptographically preordained. In contrast to fiat currencies, whose supply is governed by central banks responding to political and economic pressures, Bitcoin's supply curve is fixed and predictable. Every four years, the issuance rate halves, gradually approaching zero. This process is called "the halving," and it has become a ritualistic event in the crypto calendar—celebrated, analysed, and mythologised.

But scarcity in Bitcoin is not only technical—it is psychological theatre. It mimics the structure of historical monetary assets while infusing them with algorithmic credibility. No individual or institution can change the 21 million limit without consensus across the decentralised network. That rigidity, interpreted as incorruptibility, becomes its own form of credibility. And this credibility, in turn, breeds value. But here lies the core insight: *Bitcoin is scarce because it says it is, and because enough people believe that claim to be inviolable.* The code enforces the limit, but it is *belief in the code*—and the culture surrounding it—that gives that limit power.

This creates a peculiar situation. The value of Bitcoin, and similar digital assets, is partly derived from a belief in enforced scarcity—yet that scarcity is not grounded in natural limits, but in code. Code can be changed. Networks can fork. Protocols can evolve. What sustains the scarcity illusion is not the absolute immutability of the rules, but the *cost—social, political, technical—of changing them.* This tension between programmability and permanence is what makes digital scarcity so intellectually fascinating. It is a scarcity that exists because we agree to treat it as sacred, even when we know it is, in principle, editable.

The broader market reaction to Bitcoin's scarcity demonstrates the potency of this illusion. Investors cite the 21 million cap as a hedge against inflation, a check on state monetary excess, and a foundation for long-term price appreciation. But none of these outcomes is guaranteed. What *is* guaranteed is that the *narrative of scarcity* acts as a gravitational pull on investor behaviour. It incentivises hoarding, reduces liquidity, and fuels speculative cycles. These behaviours, in turn, reinforce the scarcity story. The less people sell, the rarer the asset appears in circulation, amplifying the perception that "supply is drying up"—even if the actual distribution of coins remains concentrated and illiquid.

The NFT boom of 2021–2022 provides a more recent and extreme example of how digital scarcity can be engineered and monetised. Non-fungible tokens are, at base, lines of code pointing to digital media. Their uniqueness is defined not by content, but by metadata: a token ID, a hash, a link. Yet they fetched millions. Why? Because their issuers claimed they were limited. Ten thousand items in a collection. One of one. First edition. These phrases evoke the scarcity tropes of physical collectibles—fine art, rare books, luxury watches—but within a medium that is infinitely replicable. The JPEG can be copied endlessly, but the token is unique, and it is *that uniqueness, however abstract, that is priced.* Scarcity is simulated, and the simulation is rewarded.

This brings us to the psychological engine behind the illusion: *relative scarcity*. It is not enough that something be scarce in absolute terms. It must also be *scarcer than alternatives*, or at least *appear to be*. The perception of limited supply must outpace the perception of rising demand. Markets do not value things based on total availability—they value things based on *what seems like it will soon be unavailable.* Crypto projects routinely capitalise on this, using token burns, staged releases, and limited-time airdrops to suggest that access is fleeting. These tactics create urgency not through intrinsic value, but through *anticipated regret*—a potent motivator in financial decision-making.

But what happens when artificial scarcity meets infinite replication? This is the paradox at the heart of digital assets. Unlike gold, which requires costly extraction, or oil, which is consumed, digital assets are created with keystrokes and secured by consensus. Their scarcity is not natural—it is *consensual.* And this consensus is fragile. It relies on aligned incentives, on developer integrity, on user loyalty. The moment that consensus fractures—through forks, scandals, or broader cultural shifts—the perception of scarcity can vanish. When new tokens flood the market with similar structures, similar promises, and no clear differentiation, investors begin to ask: *what exactly is rare here?* And when that question lingers, prices collapse.

It is important, therefore, to distinguish between engineered scarcity and economic scarcity. The former is imposed by design—often to induce behaviour. The latter emerges from constraints—physical, technological, logistical. Bitcoin, for all its cryptographic elegance, is a blend of both. Its scarcity is real within the network, but artificial from a geological or resource standpoint. It is not scarce because it must be, but because we have agreed to make it so. This distinction matters, because it affects how we respond to new forms of digital value. Should we treat artificially scarce assets with the same deference as naturally scarce ones? Should we regulate them differently? Should we question their ethical underpinnings, particularly when scarcity is used to justify exclusion, speculation, or exploitation?

The answer depends on whether we view scarcity as a neutral property or a strategic narrative. In traditional markets, scarcity has long been wielded by those in control of production—brands limiting supply to increase prestige, governments restricting money to curb inflation. In crypto, the production is open-source, but the narrative is just as controlled—sometimes by influencers, sometimes by developers, often by unseen networks of early adopters.

Understanding this manipulation is crucial. It is not about rejecting digital scarcity outright, but about approaching it with epistemic humility. Ask not just *how* something is scarce, but *why* it is made scarce—and *who benefits* from that perception.

Scarcity alone does not make something valuable. But *the belief in scarcity* can generate extraordinary value—economic, cultural, and psychological. This belief, however, is not stable. It must be sustained, reinforced, and occasionally defended. As digital systems become more adept at simulating scarcity, our collective challenge will be discerning which scarcities deserve our trust, and which are merely signals without substance. In the world of crypto, where code can make anything appear rare, the scarcity illusion is not just a side effect—it is often the product. Understanding this is not cynicism. It is literacy.

## Fear, Greed, and Herd Behavior

Markets do not run on logic. They run on emotion, narrative, and imitation—particularly in the most volatile corners of finance, like cryptocurrency. While economists have traditionally imagined markets as arenas of rational calculation, behavioural economists have long pointed to the opposite: that investors, especially under stress, are irrational, reactive, and deeply social. Nowhere is this more apparent than in the violent swings of crypto markets, where fear and greed alternate with astonishing speed, and where herd dynamics can inflate or collapse fortunes in hours, not months. These movements are not random. They are patterned. Understanding them requires looking not just at the technologies behind tokens, but at the cognitive and emotional architecture of the people trading them.

Crypto market participants are often described as speculative or impulsive. But such labels, while directionally accurate, miss the deeper mechanics. What defines crypto is not merely volatility—it's the *psychological environment* that volatility creates. Uncertainty, high stakes, fragmented information, and social media amplification converge to produce conditions that magnify cognitive biases. Traditional finance has buffers: institutional investors, regulatory frameworks, long settlement periods, and relatively stable macroeconomic backdrops. Crypto strips these away. It is an unmediated marketplace where behavioural economics plays out in real time, with minimal friction and maximal feedback.

The foundational emotions in this environment are *fear* and *greed*—the twin impulses that behavioural economist Hersh Shefrin famously described as "the most potent drivers of investor behaviour." Greed fuels buying frenzies. It's visible in the euphoric phases of bull runs, when coins with no utility or clear use case rapidly appreciate simply because they *might* become valuable. The key word here is *might.* The mere suggestion of future gains is enough to trigger speculation. When prices rise, new entrants flood in, not because they understand the asset, but because they fear being left out. This fear—known as FOMO, or fear of missing out—is a powerful distorting lens. It causes individuals to abandon caution, to suspend scepticism, and to override previous risk thresholds.

This behaviour is not new, but crypto accelerates it. In traditional markets, due diligence is at least nominally enforced by institutional processes and regulatory standards. In crypto, where barriers to entry are low and hype cycles are driven by online communities, decisions are often made based on tweets, headlines, or the trading patterns of peers. When Elon Musk tweets about Dogecoin, or a Reddit thread drives demand for an obscure altcoin, the market reacts not analytically, but emotionally. Rationality gives way to mimicry.

Fear, by contrast, dominates the other end of the cycle. When prices drop, the absence of anchoring fundamentals means there is no obvious floor. Sellers race to exit before others do, compounding the decline. This phenomenon, known as panic selling, is amplified by liquidity mismatches and cascading stop-loss triggers. A 10% drop quickly becomes a 30% crash—not because of a change in fundamentals, but because of a change in *sentiment.* The volatility is self-reinforcing. And just as greed blinds participants to risk, fear blinds them to opportunity. Assets that were seen as "inevitable" days earlier are suddenly dismissed as scams. It is the same token, the same technology—but a radically different narrative, shaped by market mood rather than intrinsic merit.

The volatility of crypto is not simply a function of low regulation or speculative capital. It is a structural consequence of *herd behaviour*, one of the most studied and misunderstood aspects of financial psychology. Herding occurs when individuals, in the absence of complete information or confidence in their own analysis, default to the actions of others. This is not inherently irrational. In evolutionary terms, imitation is often a sound survival strategy. But in markets, it leads to bubbles and crashes. When everyone is buying because everyone else is buying, prices become disconnected from reality. And when everyone is selling for the same reason, they overshoot on the way down.

Crypto is uniquely fertile ground for herding because it lacks common valuation anchors. Stocks have earnings, bonds have yields, property has rents. Crypto has potential, speculation, and social proof. As a result, narrative becomes the primary valuation tool—and narratives spread virally. Telegram groups, Discord servers, Twitter feeds, and TikTok videos act as accelerants. When a new coin gains traction, it spreads not through institutional research but through memetic virality. The more people talk about it, the more people buy it. The more people buy it, the more it validates the story. This cycle—belief creating price, and price reinforcing belief—is the psychological engine of crypto rallies.

Behavioural economists like Robert Shiller have long pointed to the role of narratives in economic life. In crypto, these narratives are compressed, amplified, and monetised. A single meme or influencer endorsement can function as a catalyst for billions in volume. And the same mechanisms that drive adoption also drive collapse. When sentiment turns, the collective narrative shifts just as quickly. Coins are reclassified from revolutionary to worthless. Communities fracture. Forums that once celebrated exponential growth become arenas of blame and disbelief.

One of the most pernicious cognitive biases at play in these dynamics is *loss aversion*—the idea, popularised by Daniel Kahneman and Amos Tversky, that the pain of losing money is psychologically twice as powerful as the pleasure of gaining it. In crypto, where double-digit swings are common, this leads to erratic behaviour. Investors may hold onto losing positions far longer than is rational, hoping to "get back to even," or they may capitulate too quickly, scarred by previous losses. This behaviour undermines consistent decision-making and creates fragmented, short-term market dynamics where strategy is replaced by reaction.

Another crucial bias is *confirmation bias*—our tendency to seek out information that supports our existing beliefs and ignore evidence to the contrary. In crypto communities, this often manifests as echo chambers. Enthusiasts surround themselves with like-minded participants, filter out scepticism, and reinforce bullish views even in the face of contradictory data. This selective perception can inflate bubbles and exacerbate crashes. It also makes communities more vulnerable to manipulation—by insiders, influencers, or coordinated actors with vested interests in driving sentiment.

Greed in crypto is often framed as irrational exuberance. But it is more nuanced than that. It is frequently linked to identity. Many early adopters are not simply speculating—they are *believers*. Their portfolios reflect not just financial positions, but philosophical commitments to decentralisation, sovereignty, or open finance. This blend of ideology and investment is unique to crypto and intensifies herd dynamics. When a token becomes a symbol of a movement, selling it is not merely an economic decision—it is a betrayal. This emotional attachment can prevent rational reassessment and make markets more brittle in the face of external shocks.

Fear, meanwhile, is exacerbated by the lack of safety nets. Unlike traditional financial markets, which offer regulatory protections, insurance schemes, or institutional interventions, crypto is largely self-custodied and unregulated. There are no circuit breakers, no government bailouts, and limited recourse in the event of fraud or technical failure. This amplifies the stakes of every downturn. The fear is not just of losing money—it is of losing everything, with no one to call. This existential anxiety feeds panic and undermines resilience.

There are those who argue that volatility is simply the price of innovation. That every new market undergoes speculative excess before maturity. This is historically accurate. But it misses the underlying challenge: *how do we build systems that acknowledge human irrationality rather than pretending it doesn't exist?* The answer is not to eliminate emotion from markets—that is neither possible nor desirable—but to design structures that dampen its destructive effects. Some crypto platforms are experimenting with features like time-locked investments, social reputation layers, or algorithmic rebalancing to reduce the influence of herding. Others are investing in financial literacy and behavioural nudges to help users make more grounded decisions.

But much of the responsibility still lies with individuals. Understanding fear and greed is not a matter of avoiding them—it is a matter of *recognising them* as forces that shape perception, behaviour, and ultimately, value. In crypto, where the scaffolding of traditional finance is absent, this self-awareness becomes even more critical. Every buy and sell order is not just a market action—it is a psychological expression, a reflection of internal states projected onto price charts.

Markets, in the end, are mirrors. They reflect back not just economic fundamentals, but collective mood. In the world of crypto, that mood changes fast. Fear and greed are not anomalies—they are constants, oscillating in response to uncertainty and hope. The challenge is not to eliminate them, but to understand them clearly enough to act without being ruled by them.

## The Myth of Rational Actors

For decades, mainstream economics operated under a comforting illusion: that investors are rational, markets are efficient, and decisions in financial contexts are driven by logical calculations aimed at maximising utility. This theoretical construct—the "rational actor"—became the central figure in economic models, policy design, and portfolio theory. It was elegant, predictable, and mathematically tractable. But it was also wrong. Not just occasionally inaccurate, but *systemically misleading.* Markets are not composed of emotionless calculators optimising equations—they are populated by human beings, whose decisions are shaped as much by fear, bias, social dynamics and narrative as by data.

The dissonance between the theory of rational actors and the reality of market behaviour is nowhere more visible than in the world of cryptocurrency. Here, prices swing wildly, driven by speculation, memes, ideology, and misinformation. Investors who claim to be risk-averse regularly pour life savings into untested protocols or tokens with no underlying use case. Others hold assets through catastrophic drawdowns out of loyalty or sunk-cost fallacies. These behaviours do not map onto rational utility maximisation; they reflect *emotionally charged decision-making* under conditions of uncertainty. Crypto doesn't distort human behaviour—it reveals it, in high definition and without filters.

The rational actor model presumes that individuals weigh costs and benefits, update their beliefs in light of new evidence, and seek optimal outcomes based on stable preferences. But decades of behavioural research have shown that this simply doesn't hold. Daniel Kahneman and Amos Tversky, in their landmark work on prospect theory, demonstrated that people value losses more heavily than equivalent gains, a concept known as *loss aversion*. Investors will often go to great lengths to avoid realising a loss, even when doing so would maximise their long-term return. In crypto, this is visible in the "HODL" mentality—a defiant commitment to hold through drawdowns, often as a badge of honour. While it can occasionally be rewarded, it is also frequently irrational, especially when applied indiscriminately across fundamentally weak assets.

Another cornerstone assumption of rational choice theory is that preferences are internally consistent. Yet research into preference reversals shows that choices vary depending on how options are framed. A trader might prefer Asset A to Asset B when shown historical returns, but switch to B if told that A is more volatile—even if both assets have identical expected values. Framing effects, anchoring, and presentation biases consistently alter investor behaviour, especially under time pressure. Crypto trading platforms, which bombard users with real-time data, trending tokens, and performance leaderboards, are environments optimised for *irrational salience*, not cool deliberation.

Consider the phenomenon of *anchoring*. When Bitcoin rose from $10,000 to $60,000 in a matter of months, the new high rapidly became a psychological reference point. Subsequent declines were framed not against long-term value or network fundamentals, but against this arbitrary peak. Investors who entered at $58,000 anchored to that figure, and many refused to sell during the drop to $30,000, believing a "return to all-time highs" was imminent. Others saw $30,000 as a discount, not because of intrinsic valuation, but because of the prior high. This fixation on prior prices—even when they are disconnected from fundamentals—is a recurring behavioural distortion, and it undermines rational re-evaluation.

*Overconfidence bias* is equally corrosive. Studies consistently show that investors overestimate their understanding of complex systems, especially after a few successful trades. In crypto, where fortunes can be made quickly in bull markets, this leads to inflated self-perception. Traders begin to attribute gains to skill rather than luck, ignore downside risks, and double down on leverage or illiquid assets. When corrections inevitably come, these same traders are often unprepared, having discounted the possibility of loss. The rational actor would diversify, limit exposure, and rebalance based on risk tolerance. But most crypto portfolios—especially during hype cycles—resemble gambling strategies, not investment plans.

Herding behaviour further erodes the myth of independent rationality. Individuals, unsure of their own analysis, look to others for cues. This behaviour, while sometimes efficient, often creates bubbles. A token gaining attention on Twitter or trending on CoinMarketCap attracts additional buyers, not because of new information, but because the price is rising. The rationale becomes circular: it is going up because others believe it will go up. In a rational model, market participants incorporate new information into prices in proportion to its value. In reality, they incorporate *signals of social proof*, often disconnected from fundamentals. Social media algorithms, which reward engagement rather than truth, amplify this dynamic and accelerate the formation of consensus—even when that consensus is wildly misguided.

The belief in rationality also fails to account for the emotional architecture of financial decision-making. Emotions are not peripheral—they are central. Anxiety, envy, euphoria, regret, and shame shape how people approach risk. This is especially true in decentralised, permissionless systems like crypto, where participation often reflects broader aspirations—freedom from institutions, technological optimism, or resistance to the status quo. Many holders are not merely speculating—they are *belonging*. Their portfolios are expressions of identity, and their choices are driven as much by *belief affiliation* as by financial logic. This blurs the line between investing and ideology, between price discovery and tribalism.

Take, for instance, the communities around coins like Bitcoin, Ethereum, or Dogecoin. The language of these communities is often evangelical. Terms like "true believer," "diamond hands," or "to the moon" are not financial strategies—they are *morale slogans*. They foster group identity, reinforce loyalty, and insulate participants from critical examination. This is not unique to crypto. Stock market investors have long exhibited confirmation bias and groupthink. But crypto's velocity, youth, and decentralisation supercharge the phenomenon. Once again, the rational actor disappears in the crowd.

Even those trained in economics or finance are not immune. A large body of research shows that financial professionals are just as vulnerable to cognitive bias as laypeople—sometimes more so, because their training gives them an illusion of objectivity. In 2021, major hedge funds entered crypto, some with sophisticated models and risk frameworks. Yet many were caught off guard by retail-led movements, social media coordination, or sudden regulatory shifts. The assumption that institutional capital would "stabilise" crypto markets rested, again, on the flawed belief that rational actors behave as buffers. Instead, they often magnify instability, especially when using leverage or automated strategies triggered by momentum.

To be clear, rejecting the rational actor model does not imply that all behaviour is chaotic or unpredictable. Rather, it acknowledges that investor behaviour follows *patterns*—but those patterns are driven by psychological forces, not just financial ones. Behavioural economics, cognitive science, and even evolutionary psychology offer better tools for understanding these dynamics than neoclassical utility theory. Markets are not just networks of prices—they are ecosystems of human cognition, emotion, and imitation.

Understanding this matters because the assumptions we build into systems shape how those systems evolve. If we design platforms, protocols, or policies based on the idea that users are rational, we leave them vulnerable to exploitation, manipulation, and systemic fragility. If, instead, we acknowledge and design for *bounded rationality*—the idea that humans make the best decisions they can, given limited information and cognitive capacity—we build safer, more resilient financial systems. Crypto, still in its formative years, has a unique opportunity to incorporate this understanding at the protocol level. Some projects already do, with mechanisms that slow trading, prompt reflection, or reward longer-term behaviour. But these are still exceptions, not norms.

The rational actor was always a myth—an elegant simplification that made economics easier to model but harder to understand. As crypto forces open the black box of investor psychology, it is time to retire that myth for good. In its place, we must reckon with a more accurate portrait: *investors are not computers—they are people.* And people are messy, inconsistent, emotional, and social. Any market that pretends otherwise is not realistic. It is just unprepared.

## Gamification of Wealth

Finance, once the domain of spreadsheets, institutional gatekeepers and late-night earnings reports, has become *fun.* Or at least, it has been made to feel like it. Crypto exchanges, meme coins, and NFTs have blurred the lines between investment, entertainment, and identity in ways that legacy markets could never imagine—nor, arguably, replicate. This isn't simply about accessibility or decentralisation. It's about design. *The financial experience itself has been transformed into a dopamine-driven interface*, engineered to trigger emotion, reward compulsive behaviour, and convert participation into loyalty. The result is a new species of financial engagement: part trading floor, part video game, part social network—wrapped in speculative adrenaline, and often divorced from economic fundamentals.

The rise of gamified finance isn't accidental. It is a design philosophy imported from behavioural psychology and honed by the digital economy. Traditional trading platforms were built for utility; they presented data, executed orders, and recorded outcomes. They assumed users were informed, rational actors. By contrast, crypto platforms have taken their cues from mobile gaming, social apps, and behavioural finance. Their interfaces are *not* passive; they are persuasive. Price charts bounce with animation. Portfolio gains light up in green. Losses blink in red. Leaderboards rank traders. Flash sales and token airdrops simulate scarcity and urgency. There is no time to reflect—only time to act, before the next opportunity disappears.

The central mechanism here is *variable reinforcement*, a principle well understood in the world of casinos and gambling. When rewards are unpredictable, intermittent, and potentially large, users are more likely to stay engaged. In crypto, the entire experience is structured around this principle. Prices move constantly, often irrationally. A token bought for £5 could be worth £50 tomorrow—or worthless. These extremes are not bugs; they are features. The volatility *is* the appeal. Traders aren't just managing risk; they are chasing a high. And the platforms—whether centralised exchanges or decentralised protocols—are built to keep them chasing.

Consider Binance, one of the largest crypto exchanges in the world. Its interface includes not only standard trading tools, but futures, leverage, staking pools, quizzes for token rewards, and rotating promotional events. These are not mere financial instruments—they are *gamified products*, designed to encourage repeat interaction. Robinhood, while primarily stock-focused, pioneered the gamification trend with features like confetti animations and commission-free trading, enticing a generation of users to treat investing as play. But crypto has taken it further. Here, entire economies are built around speculation. Tokenomics is not simply about supply and demand—it's about *incentive engineering.*

Meme coins like Dogecoin and Shiba Inu exemplify this dynamic. These tokens were never designed with robust utility in mind. Their value is driven by community enthusiasm, virality, and performative loyalty. Price movements follow cultural momentum more than technical merit. Buying a meme coin is not just a bet—it's a statement, a joke, a meme in itself. Traders use humour to mask risk, but the financial stakes are real. Some win big, others are left holding digital assets with no liquidity or long-term vision. The irrationality is part of the game. And because the rules are social, not economic, price discovery becomes performance: a theatre of belief played out on Twitter threads and Telegram channels.

NFTs pushed this boundary even further by redefining what it means to own something online. Suddenly, a JPEG of a cartoon animal could sell for hundreds of thousands of dollars—not because of its artistic merit or utility, but because of its *narrative, provenance, and meme potential.* Ownership became a game of prestige. Wallets were public scoreboards. The rarest tokens were badges of status, often flaunted as profile pictures or staked in lending protocols. The market turned speculative collectibles into cultural currency. And yet, beneath the glamour and tribalism, NFTs were also delivering the same intermittent reinforcement: surprise mints, gas wars, whitelist lotteries. Investors became players. Art became a leaderboard.

Gamification operates not only through design but through *identity mechanics.* Crypto participation is not just about making money—it's about being *seen* doing it. Social trading platforms, Discord communities, influencer endorsements and viral YouTube content have transformed financial decisions into expressions of personality and alignment. People do not just buy tokens; they join tribes. Being early in a project confers clout. Posting gains attracts followers. Exit strategies are discussed less than *exit narratives*: how to sell without betraying the community, how to explain a loss as part of a longer game. Investment is no longer private judgement—it is *public performance.*

This dynamic introduces complex ethical and psychological risks. Gamification can encourage engagement, but it can also *normalise addiction.* Studies on financial behaviour and neuroeconomics show that frequent exposure to high-risk, high-reward scenarios activates the same dopaminergic pathways as gambling. The brain learns to crave the stimulation, not the outcome. In the absence of regulation or self-limiting design, users can spiral into compulsive behaviours—refreshing charts obsessively, entering trades out of boredom, or "revenge trading" to make up for losses. Unlike traditional gambling, which is often constrained by physical venues or legal thresholds, crypto is accessible 24/7, on any device, with no oversight. The barrier to self-harm is low—and the incentives to keep playing are high.

Moreover, the consequences of gamified wealth are not confined to the individual. They ripple outward. Retail investors borrowing against inflated assets to fund lifestyle upgrades. Young traders ignoring diversification principles in pursuit of 100x returns. Vulnerable users entering Ponzi-like DeFi schemes disguised as yield farms. The gamification aesthetic—fun, colourful, meme-driven—conceals the reality that real money is at stake, and real people get burned. The narrative of "financial empowerment" often masks predatory design. When users lose, they are told it's their fault for not playing the game correctly. But *who designed the game?* And who profits when players lose?

Some defenders argue that gamification democratises finance. That it brings engagement, participation, and agency to groups historically excluded from elite financial circles. There is some truth to this. Crypto does open access. It allows anyone, anywhere, to participate in global capital markets with a smartphone. But access without literacy is not empowerment—it is exposure. And when the tools are designed to optimise for user retention rather than user wellbeing, participation becomes risk by design.

Not all gamification is harmful. Used thoughtfully, it can encourage learning, discipline, and community accountability. Platforms that reward long-term behaviour, transparency, or risk management can reshape the crypto experience in healthier ways. But these are exceptions. The dominant model is still based on acceleration: more trades, more users, more hype, more noise. Until the incentives shift—either through design reform or regulation—the industry will continue to blur the line between innovation and exploitation.

Ultimately, the gamification of wealth in crypto is not a side effect. It is a feature—one that reflects deeper cultural shifts. In a world where economic systems feel distant, manipulated, or out of reach, gamified finance offers immediacy, agency, and spectacle. But it also asks us to make serious trade-offs: between engagement and clarity, between accessibility and safety, between fun and responsibility.

Understanding this tension is not just important for investors—it is essential for anyone trying to build a future where digital finance is not just *exciting*, but *equitable*. In crypto, the game is always on. The question is whether we know we're playing—and at what cost.

# Chapter 3
# Decentralisation: The Beautiful Lie

Few concepts in the crypto discourse carry as much weight—or as much ambiguity—as decentralisation. It is the banner under which cypherpunks rally, the ethical justification invoked by blockchain evangelists, and the implicit virtue embedded in nearly every white paper published over the past decade and a half. At its loftiest, it promises a redistribution of power: from the few to the many, from centralised hierarchies to distributed networks, from opaque bureaucracy to transparent, open-source governance. It hints at a world in which individuals transact, organise, and even legislate without intermediaries. In its idealised form, decentralisation transcends mere technical architecture; it is political philosophy, social reform, and, for some, a near-spiritual aspiration.

Reality, however, is rarely so neatly aligned with ideology. Beneath the rhetoric lies a more complex, often contradictory landscape: decentralisation frequently reproduces the very power concentrations it claims to dismantle. What appears horizontal may conceal vertical structures. What is marketed as egalitarian can mask subtle forms of control. Mining pools dominate network hashrates. Core development teams steer protocol roadmaps with limited formal accountability. Token distribution schemes concentrate wealth into a handful of wallets. Network effects, though framed as organic, can entrench incumbents and stifle competition. In practice, decentralisation sometimes functions less as a structural safeguard than as branding: a narrative of neutrality covering real hierarchies.

This chapter interrogates that tension. It does not dismiss decentralisation as a failed experiment; rather, it situates it in a contested space—where technical possibility, ideological ambition, and economic gravity intersect. Declaring a system decentralised is easy. Sustaining it in a way that is resilient, equitable, and transparent is far more difficult. True decentralisation depends not merely on node counts or governance mechanics, but on incentive alignment, power distribution, and genuine access to influence. Without attention to these factors, the decentralisation thesis risks becoming what this chapter calls a beautiful lie: persuasive, seductive, and ultimately misleading.

To understand the stakes, we must return to the founding mythos of crypto. Bitcoin proposed electronic cash that required no trust in intermediaries. Ethereum offered decentralised computation capable of hosting applications free from censorship or downtime. These were serious ambitions, born from financial crises, mass surveillance, and institutional disillusionment. The appeal was clear: systems resistant to corruption because they relied on protocol, not people; infrastructures that were borderless, neutral, and permissionless; individuals empowered as custodians of their own data, wealth, and identities. Let code, not politics, govern the digital commons.

But growth brought unforeseen consequences. In Bitcoin, mining power—once dispersed among hobbyists—coalesced into industrial-scale operations with cheap electricity and specialised hardware. Today, a few pools control most of the network's hashrate, raising questions of collusion and censorship at the consensus level. Ethereum, though more developer-centric, exhibits similar centralising tendencies: a small core group controls the reference client, and decisions, while ostensibly discussed publicly, remain concentrated. Even decentralised autonomous organisations, or DAOs, often hinge on large token holders or charismatic founders.

This is not necessarily failure; it is path dependency. Power centralises because scale favours coordination, and coordination favours efficiency. The problem arises when systems pretend otherwise. When protocols claim community governance while critical decisions occur in private chats. When tokens are distributed under democratic pretences but hoarded by insiders. When founders assert neutrality while wielding informal vetoes. These contradictions are structural, not marginal—and they undermine the legitimacy of trustless systems.

Technology does not eliminate power; it redistributes it. Unless that redistribution is explicit and transparent, decentralisation risks creating new oligarchies. Token economies make this visible: early access, ICOs, liquidity mining, and venture-backed launches concentrate wealth and influence before public participation. The rhetoric remains revolutionary, even as economic reality mirrors traditional finance.

Network effects further complicate matters. Open systems are prone to winner-takes-most dynamics. Protocols with substantial adoption become entrenched—not necessarily due to superior design, but because they boast more users, liquidity, and integrations. Ethereum's dominance in smart contracts, Bitcoin's symbolic primacy as digital gold: these outcomes are momentum-driven. Protocol-level decentralisation does not prevent ecosystem-level centralisation.

Compounding the challenge, decentralisation is often elevated from technical goal to moral ideal. Projects are judged less on functionality than on perceived decentralisation. The term becomes talismanic—invoked in marketing, governance debates, and online communities—but rarely rigorously defined. Node counts, token distribution, voting mechanics: which measure truly matters? Ambiguity allows nearly any system to claim legitimacy while obscuring critical evaluation.

This ambiguity has tangible consequences. Projects asserting decentralisation often resist regulation. Yet, when hacks, losses, or forks occur, human intervention reappears: developers patch, foundations issue statements, leaders rally the community. Authority reasserts itself without accountability. Decentralisation becomes a shield for power, not a check against it.

This chapter does not reject decentralisation; it interrogates it as a contingent reality, one that must be continually negotiated and redesigned. What does decentralisation protect us from? What does it cost? Who benefits, and who is marginalised? Can decentralisation coexist with scale, usability, and efficiency, or is compromise inevitable? There are no fixed answers, but these questions are essential to move beyond slogans and build systems worthy of their ideals.

Decentralisation must be understood as a spectrum of trade-offs, a framework for evaluating risk, and a design challenge without easy solutions. Its promise lies in reimagining coordination and power in the digital era; its peril lies in myth-making and self-deception. Between these extremes lies the truth—a truth that must be earned, not assumed. This chapter begins that reckoning.

## The Promise of Peer-to-Peer Power

Decentralisation did not originate as a technical configuration—it began as a political aspiration. Beneath the architectural blueprints of blockchain lies a deeper, older yearning: to reclaim control from distant authorities, to transact and communicate without surveillance, and to assert personal agency in a world increasingly mediated by opaque institutions. The dream of peer-to-peer power is not merely about efficiency or innovation; it is about *liberation.* It responds to the long-standing human desire to escape imposed trust, eliminate unnecessary gatekeepers, and participate in systems that are fair because they are open. It is a vision animated by a simple but radical premise: that individuals, given the right tools, can govern themselves.

To understand why this vision took hold so powerfully in the digital age, one must first consider the erosion of confidence in traditional intermediaries. Financial institutions failed to protect the public during the 2008 crisis. Tech platforms, once hailed as engines of openness, now trade user data as their primary currency. Governments, in many parts of the world, have weaponised information infrastructure for control and repression. Across these domains, the trend has been clear: centralisation tends to accumulate power, and power, once concentrated, tends to be abused. Against this backdrop, decentralised systems emerged not just as alternatives, but as forms of resistance.

Bitcoin's introduction in 2009 was a milestone, not simply for its technological novelty, but for its foundational ethos: *a trustless currency that operated without a central bank or state.* Its architecture was explicitly peer-to-peer—nodes validated transactions independently, and users could hold, send, or mine value without permission. For the first time, ownership of money could be separated from the banking system. This was not a technical footnote; it was a political act. Bitcoin's pseudonymous creator, Satoshi Nakamoto, embedded in its genesis block a reference to a Times headline: "Chancellor on brink of second bailout for banks." This was no coincidence. It was a declaration.

The promise of peer-to-peer systems extends well beyond finance. It reimagines coordination itself. File sharing platforms like BitTorrent decentralised data distribution. Encrypted messaging apps decentralised communication. Mesh networks challenge the monopoly of telecom infrastructure. Each of these tools seeks to dissolve the dependence on central points of failure—not just for efficiency, but for resilience. In a decentralised model, *control is not seized by one party, it is diffused across many*. This diffusion not only mitigates censorship and manipulation, it also enhances fault tolerance. If one node fails, the system endures. If one authority is corrupted, the rest remain intact.

Within this paradigm, *censorship-resistance* is not an optional feature; it is a fundamental design goal. In centralised systems, the ability to revoke access, freeze funds, or rewrite history lies with a single authority—or is at least within reach of coercion. In decentralised systems, such capabilities are deliberately engineered out. Once a Bitcoin transaction is confirmed, it cannot be undone. Once a smart contract is deployed to Ethereum, it operates as written—automated, immutable, and beyond rollback. This creates a new class of autonomy: one enforced by code rather than policy. It also redefines responsibility. The user becomes not just a participant, but a sovereign actor.

This vision is particularly potent in regions where access to stable financial infrastructure or political freedoms is limited. For citizens in Venezuela, Zimbabwe, or Turkey, decentralised currencies have functioned not as speculative assets, but as practical tools for survival amid hyperinflation and capital controls. For dissidents, whistleblowers, and activists, decentralised platforms offer communication channels that are harder to monitor or disrupt. In such contexts, the liberating potential of peer-to-peer systems is not abstract—it is *existential*.

But the appeal of decentralisation is not confined to those under duress. For a growing number of users in liberal democracies, it represents a philosophical choice: to opt out of surveillance capitalism, to reject custodial dependence, and to experiment with new forms of coordination. Decentralised Autonomous Organisations (DAOs), for instance, propose a model of governance in which rules are encoded transparently, decisions are executed automatically, and participation is open. The ideal is not merely to disintermediate—but to redesign authority itself.

Yet even as it inspires, this vision invites scrutiny. Peer-to-peer power is not without trade-offs. Autonomy demands competence. Responsibility for one's private keys means there is no one to call when funds are lost. Censorship-resistance can enable free speech—but also hate speech and fraud. Code-based enforcement eliminates discretion, but also nuance. These challenges are not incidental; they are structural. Decentralised systems cannot rely on the oversight mechanisms that centralised ones can. This is part of their strength—and part of their risk.

Moreover, the idea that decentralisation equals freedom assumes a kind of rational self-governance that is aspirational at best. *Not every user wants radical autonomy. Not every community thrives without leadership.* Coordination is hard, incentives can misalign, and protocol governance often devolves into social politics by other means. The dream of decentralisation can become a burden if it assumes a level of competence, engagement, and integrity that users are unwilling—or unable—to sustain. In this light, peer-to-peer power is as much a cultural challenge as a technical one.

Even so, it would be reductive to judge the decentralised vision purely by its present limitations. Every transformative system begins as a minority movement, rough around the edges and full of contradictions. The real question is not whether decentralisation has flaws—it does—but whether it opens new possibilities for human coordination, especially in domains where current systems have failed. And here, the answer is unmistakably yes. The very existence of trustless payment systems, censorship-resistant applications, and autonomous coordination tools suggests that *something novel has been unlocked.*

Peer-to-peer power is not a finished project. It is a provocation—a call to rethink how trust, authority, and value can be organised without coercion or monopoly. It is also a mirror, reflecting both our hopes for emancipation and our reluctance to relinquish the comforts of control. As such, its future will be shaped not only by cryptographic breakthroughs, but by our collective willingness to embrace complexity, tolerate friction, and reimagine the social contract.

This article begins a deeper exploration into the gap between decentralisation's idealism and its implementation. It will interrogate where power hides in supposedly flat systems, how scale introduces hierarchy, and why decentralisation has become both a design principle and a moral narrative. But it begins with the promise—the powerful, imperfect, and still unfinished promise—that peer-to-peer technology can do more than optimise systems. It can *liberate people.* Whether that promise is realised—or betrayed—depends not only on the protocols we write, but the values we encode within them.

## Hidden Centralisations

Decentralisation, when stripped of its idealistic sheen, reveals a more uncomfortable truth: while distributed systems may flatten certain power structures, they do not eliminate power itself. In fact, they often recreate it—less visibly, more insidiously, and sometimes with even fewer accountability mechanisms than the centralised regimes they aim to replace. Beneath the rhetoric of peer-to-peer sovereignty lies a complex web of concentrated influence, exercised not through legislation or policy but through control of infrastructure, technical expertise, and financial leverage. These are *the hidden centralisations*—the quiet return of hierarchy in systems designed to resist it.

The myth of pure decentralisation often begins with mining. In theory, Bitcoin's proof-of-work consensus allows anyone with computational resources to participate in securing the network and earning rewards. In practice, however, mining has become a specialised industry dominated by a small number of large entities. These mining pools coordinate vast amounts of hash power—aggregating thousands of machines, sometimes spread across continents, under unified operational control. As of recent data, fewer than five pools control the majority of Bitcoin's total mining output. This concentration poses an existential risk: if a few entities can collude to control over 50% of the network's computational power, they could, at least temporarily, rewrite transaction history or censor transactions altogether. This is not hypothetical—it is structurally plausible, and on several occasions, dangerously close.

The reasons for this centralisation are economic, not ideological. The proof-of-work model rewards scale. Larger operations enjoy efficiency gains, reduced costs, and more predictable returns. Hardware manufacturers cater preferentially to institutional buyers, creating barriers to entry for hobbyists or smaller miners. Energy costs further skew the playing field—regions with cheap, abundant electricity become hotspots for industrial-scale mining, often under the tacit approval or direct involvement of state actors. What emerges is not a decentralised collective of equals, but an oligopoly of infrastructure gatekeepers whose incentives may not align with the broader network.

Beyond mining, centralisation reappears in the governance of protocols themselves. Open-source projects like Bitcoin and Ethereum are maintained by small, highly technical groups of core developers. These individuals are not elected, nor are their decisions subject to binding community vote. They are often volunteers, yet wield enormous influence over which code changes are implemented, which vulnerabilities are prioritised, and how forks are handled. Their power is informal but profound—what they merge becomes canonical; what they reject may never see daylight. While they may act in good faith, the lack of formal checks and balances raises a critical question: *Who watches the coders?*

This dynamic became glaringly visible during contentious forks in major blockchains. The Bitcoin vs. Bitcoin Cash split in 2017, and the Ethereum vs. Ethereum Classic divide in 2016 following the DAO hack, both exposed how ideological disagreements, developer influence, and community inertia interact to produce schisms—not through democratic consensus, but through narrative control and coordination power. In both cases, technical leadership framed the debate, steered public perception, and ultimately catalysed irreversible divergence. Code was not neutral; it was the product of human decision-making—opinionated, selective, and shaped by politics as much as logic.

Further compounding these issues is the role of *whale investors*—individuals or entities that hold disproportionately large amounts of a given token. In networks where one token equals one vote, whales exert significant influence over governance outcomes, market dynamics, and public sentiment. They can move prices with a single transaction, sway community votes with large stakes, or destabilise ecosystems by exiting positions en masse. Their identities are often unknown, their motives opaque, and their accountability nonexistent. They operate within systems designed to prevent overt domination, yet exercise control through sheer magnitude. This financial asymmetry undermines claims of egalitarianism within decentralised networks.

Liquidity provision and venture capital also play a centralising role. In the early stages of many crypto projects, funding comes from a small circle of investors who receive favourable allocations before public launches. These early holders not only capture disproportionate upside, but often dictate strategic decisions, tokenomics, and narrative framing. As the line between protocol and product blurs, early-stage investors increasingly function like shadow governors—unofficial, but highly influential. The claim that decentralisation distributes power equally falters when one analyses the cap tables and governance participation rates of supposedly decentralised projects.

Even decentralised finance (DeFi), which prides itself on eliminating intermediaries, is rife with re-centralisation. DeFi protocols are governed by DAOs—Decentralised Autonomous Organisations—that theoretically allow token holders to vote on proposals. Yet these votes often suffer from low participation, skewed quorums, and token concentration among insiders. Moreover, smart contracts underpinning DeFi platforms are frequently upgradeable by a small group of administrators or multisig signers. This creates a paradox: the front end is decentralised, but the backend is not. Trustlessness becomes a user illusion—one contingent on the honesty and competence of an invisible managerial class.

The persistence of hidden centralisations should not be seen purely as a failure of technology. It is, rather, a reflection of human tendencies: the drive to optimise, consolidate, and simplify; the natural emergence of expertise hierarchies; the tendency for early movers to accrue advantage. These are not pathologies—they are properties of complex systems. Even in biology, decentralisation gives way to organisation; even in democracy, leaders emerge. The problem arises when the rhetoric of decentralisation obscures its practical limits—when power is denied rather than disclosed.

The solution is not to abandon decentralisation as an aspiration, but to interrogate it more rigorously. *Where does power really reside? Who controls infrastructure, incentives, and interpretation?* Transparency, not purity, must be the new ideal. Protocols must surface—not conceal—the real sources of influence. Governance frameworks should account for information asymmetries and economic concentration. Users must be educated to understand that decentralised systems are not magic—they are architectures of trade-offs. And power, when it exists, must be named, scrutinised, and—where possible—diluted.

There is still profound value in decentralised architectures. They offer new modalities of coordination, resist certain types of coercion, and introduce novel economic models. But the idea that they are *intrinsically* immune to centralisation is empirically false and intellectually lazy. If the crypto movement is to mature, it must shed its naive metaphors and embrace the hard work of structural analysis. Decentralisation is not a binary state but a gradient—and the degree to which a system is decentralised must be continuously measured, challenged, and recalibrated.

Ultimately, the test of a decentralised system is not whether it claims to be leaderless, but whether it is *resilient* in the face of concentrated influence. Can it survive the corruption of a developer group? The exit of a major miner? The collapse of a whale's holdings? If not, then decentralisation is not a safeguard—it is a slogan. Recognising hidden centralisations is the first step toward building systems that are not just ideologically compelling, but structurally robust. It is a call not for purity, but for realism—because only when we see the system clearly can we design it wisely.

## Network Effects and the Tyranny of Scale

Decentralisation promises a flattening of power—an architectural antidote to hierarchy. Yet, the moment a network begins to function at scale, the promise collides with a stubborn paradox: decentralised systems tend to recentralise through mechanisms that are neither conspiratorial nor malicious, but mathematical and behavioural. Network effects and scale, often celebrated as engines of success in technological ecosystems, carry with them an embedded gravity. Once a decentralised system reaches critical mass, its dynamics can produce new bottlenecks of influence and entrenched incumbents. The tyranny lies not in overt coercion, but in the quiet compulsion to centralise for the sake of efficiency, speed, or survivability.

Network effects describe a phenomenon where the value of a product or service increases as more people use it. In the context of digital platforms—social media, operating systems, communication protocols—this feedback loop generates explosive growth and strong winner-takes-most dynamics. The same holds true in blockchain ecosystems, where user adoption, developer tooling, liquidity, and infrastructure deepen a protocol's defensibility. Once a chain like Ethereum achieves a threshold of decentralised applications, developer talent, and community capital, it becomes increasingly difficult for new contenders to displace it—not necessarily because it is the best designed, but because it is the best populated.

This self-reinforcing advantage is not neutral. It favours early adopters disproportionately, especially those with the foresight, capital, or proximity to engage with the system in its infancy. In Bitcoin's case, early miners and believers acquired coins at a fraction of current valuations, giving them not just wealth but lasting influence over the ecosystem's narrative and governance. In Ethereum, early token buyers, developers, and insiders became de facto stewards of its evolution. Their positions are often unassailable—not through malicious design, but because the inertia of network effects cements their status.

Such dynamics challenge the idea that decentralised systems offer equal access or opportunity. In reality, participation comes in layers:

those who shape protocols, those who build atop them, and those who merely use them. The higher up the stack one sits, the more leverage one holds. And as the stack matures, it calcifies. New entrants must overcome not just technical hurdles but social ones—navigating established norms, reputational hierarchies, and dense ecosystems of existing power. Decentralisation, then, is less an even field than a slowly hardening stratigraphy of influence.

Technology itself contributes to this centralising pull. Blockchain infrastructure is complex and demanding. Running a full node in many systems requires considerable storage, bandwidth, and technical know-how. Participating in consensus mechanisms—whether proof-of-work or proof-of-stake—involves economic and logistical commitments that are not feasible for most users. As a result, services emerge to abstract and simplify these tasks: staking pools, RPC providers, API gateways, managed wallets. While these services improve usability, they also create dependency. Few users run their own nodes or manage their own keys; most outsource trust to a small number of infrastructure providers. These intermediaries, though technically optional, become de facto gatekeepers, concentrating critical functionality in the hands of the efficient few.

Consider the case of Infura, a popular backend infrastructure service for Ethereum. Though Ethereum is decentralised in architecture, a significant portion of its traffic routes through Infura's servers. During high-profile outages, large swathes of the Ethereum ecosystem have been rendered temporarily unusable—not because the chain failed, but because reliance on a centralised provider introduced a single point of failure. This fragility is not unique. Block explorers, data aggregators, wallet providers, and bridges all exhibit similar characteristics. Decentralisation at the protocol level does not guarantee decentralisation at the experiential level. Users interact with interfaces, not source code—and those interfaces are often controlled by a handful of well-funded entities.

Economics exacerbate this trend. Building and maintaining infrastructure at scale requires capital. Venture-funded startups enter the space not as ideological actors, but as economic ones—seeking returns, market share, and defensibility. Their incentives align with centralisation: optimise for performance, capture users, reduce friction. Token incentives may claim to democratise access, but often do little to address underlying concentration. Early token holders and founding teams frequently retain control of governance levers, while public distributions remain thin or skewed toward insiders. Over time, the economic scaffolding of decentralised projects can begin to resemble the venture-backed hierarchies they claim to transcend.

This is not to say decentralisation is meaningless. Rather, it is not automatic. Without deliberate design choices, checks on concentration, and cultural commitments to openness, decentralised systems gravitate toward centralised outcomes. The tyranny of scale is subtle: it arrives not through coercion but through convenience, not through conspiracy but through complexity. It whispers that speed matters more than sovereignty, that scale is synonymous with legitimacy, and that central coordination is the price of coherence.

There is an enduring tension between decentralisation and usability. Decentralised systems demand more from their users: more responsibility, more understanding, more patience. Yet users often demand simplicity. The result is a delegation of power—not in the form of state authority, but to technical specialists, infrastructure providers, and early-adopter elites. The ideological purity of decentralisation bends under the weight of market pragmatism. To scale is to compromise.

History offers ample precedent. The early internet was decentralised in structure, composed of autonomous nodes and open protocols. But as it scaled, it centralised: search consolidated under Google, social interaction under Meta, commerce under Amazon. Each phase of consolidation brought efficiency, but also risk: surveillance, manipulation, and monopoly. Blockchain networks may follow a similar arc unless course corrections are made. The technical architecture permits decentralisation, but the socio-economic reality often does not reward it.

This is why it is essential to distinguish *permissionless* from *decentralised.* A network can allow anyone to join and still evolve into a hub-and-spoke model dominated by a few large players. Permissionless entry does not guarantee pluralistic power. Nor does open source prevent capture; many open-source projects are steered by small teams whose strategic decisions shape the future path. Transparency is not the same as dispersion.

Still, resistance is possible. Protocol designers can embed limits on concentration, whether through stake caps, quadratic voting, or randomised validator selection. Communities can foster norms of inclusivity and transparency, countering the rise of opaque leadership. Users can be educated to scrutinise dependencies and demand alternatives. But these are choices, not defaults. The gravitational pull of scale must be actively countered. Otherwise, decentralised ecosystems will find themselves reconstituting the very asymmetries they sought to dissolve.

The challenge is not to prevent scale, but to manage it wisely. Scale enables resilience, reach, and robustness. It allows protocols to serve millions, attract builders, and integrate with the wider economy. But scale must be decoupled from dominance. The future of decentralisation depends on our ability to design systems that grow without concentrating control—systems where network effects empower communities, not corporations.

In this light, decentralisation is not a destination but a discipline. It requires continual vigilance, honest reflection, and institutional innovation. The beauty of peer-to-peer networks lies not in their romantic potential, but in their capacity to resist ossification—to evolve without calcifying, to scale without succumbing. That capacity, however, is fragile. It must be cultivated, not presumed. Only then can decentralised systems truly offer an alternative to centralised power, rather than its digital reincarnation.

## Decentralisation as a Moral Narrative

Decentralisation, once a technical design choice aimed at removing single points of failure, has evolved into something far more emotionally charged and ideologically freighted. For many within the crypto ecosystem, it is no longer just an architectural principle or a governance model—it is a creed, a declaration of belief in how power *should* be distributed and how societies *ought* to be structured.

In this transformation from code to conviction, decentralisation has become, for some, a moral absolute rather than a practical framework. It functions less as a flexible tool to be judiciously applied than as a quasi-religious narrative: unquestioned, defended, and sanctified.

This moral elevation is not accidental. It speaks to a profound disillusionment with existing institutions. For decades, individuals have witnessed state actors abuse power, corporations extract value while externalising risk, and media gatekeepers curate reality in ways that seem more ideological than objective. In this context, decentralisation offers a seductive promise: a system where no single entity controls the levers, where no authority can censor or confiscate, and where individuals, not intermediaries, make the rules. It is not merely a technical fix—it is, for many, a form of ideological refuge.

But like any ideology, when decentralisation is elevated from principle to dogma, it begins to lose nuance. Its practitioners start to believe that any system not fully decentralised is inherently suspect, and that decentralisation, by its mere presence, guarantees fairness, freedom, and justice. Such assumptions are not only unproven—they are actively dangerous. Systems do not become ethical simply by distributing control. They do not become resistant to abuse merely by removing central nodes. In fact, decentralised systems can obscure responsibility, evade accountability, and entrench new forms of power behind the veil of openness.

Consider the reverence many in the crypto community hold for decentralised autonomous organisations (DAOs). The idea that rules encoded in smart contracts can supplant human discretion is often held up as a moral improvement over traditional governance. Yet real-world DAO experiments frequently reveal significant limitations: voter apathy, manipulation by insiders, plutocratic influence from large token holders, and a lack of recourse when things go wrong. Despite these shortcomings, the narrative endures: *at least it's decentralised.* The implicit suggestion is that process matters more than outcome—that structural purity trumps practical results.

The roots of this moralisation can be traced to broader historical currents. Throughout modernity, revolutions have often coalesced around structural critiques of power: monarchies replaced by republics, centralised religions by individual spirituality, top-down media by peer-to-peer platforms. Decentralisation, in this lineage, presents itself as the next frontier—a techno-political reformation, breaking down the papacy of banks and governments in favour of a flatter, freer society. The rhetoric mirrors that of past movements: transparency, sovereignty, liberation. Yet as with past movements, the risk of disillusionment looms large when idealism meets operational complexity.

One of the dangers of decentralisation as moral narrative is that it masks its own blind spots. Systems that claim to be decentralised are often nothing of the sort. Power concentrates through less visible channels—core developer influence, liquidity dominance, social capital within communities, and gatekeeping by exchanges and media platforms. But so long as the underlying protocol avoids explicit centralisation, the community often turns a blind eye to these informal but consequential hierarchies. The myth of decentralisation creates a false sense of equality and fairness, even as systemic advantages persist.

Moreover, the moralisation of decentralisation has led to a rhetorical rigidity that stifles healthy debate. Critics who raise valid concerns about scalability, governance, or user experience are often met with accusations of being anti-crypto or pro-centralisation—as though pragmatism were a betrayal. This kind of dogmatic purity does not advance the ecosystem. It impoverishes it. By turning decentralisation into a sacred cow, we lose the ability to evaluate it critically, apply it selectively, or refine it intelligently.

Decentralisation is a powerful idea—but power requires stewardship. In mature societies, power is not abolished; it is constrained, distributed, and made accountable. The best democracies do not operate without leaders—they operate with checks, balances, and institutions. Likewise, the most effective decentralised systems will not eliminate all forms of hierarchy. They will make those hierarchies visible, contestable, and replaceable. That requires more than decentralisation—it requires thoughtful governance, cultural humility, and a willingness to evolve.

A useful analogy may be drawn to the early days of the internet. In the 1990s, the internet was hailed as a radically decentralised medium. It would democratise information, empower creators, and dismantle corporate monopolies. The reality turned out to be more complex. Over time, network effects and convenience drove consolidation. Today, a handful of companies mediate vast portions of the digital experience. The original vision was not wrong—but it was incomplete. The same may be said for blockchain. Without intentional design, decentralised systems may re-centralise in new forms—opaque, unaccountable, and harder to reform.

There is also an uncomfortable truth within this narrative: many who proclaim the virtues of decentralisation do so selectively. Projects tout their decentralised nature while quietly maintaining central control over treasury decisions, roadmap priorities, or branding. Influencers promote decentralised ideals while wielding disproportionate power over discourse. Exchanges celebrate decentralised finance while gatekeeping access through listings and liquidity. This gap between rhetoric and reality undermines trust and weakens the moral force of the decentralisation argument.

Yet all of this should not be read as a rejection of decentralisation. Rather, it is a call to de-mystify it—to bring it down from the clouds and subject it to the same scrutiny we apply to any other institutional framework. Decentralisation is not a get-out-of-jail-free card for ethical complexity. It is not a substitute for trust, responsibility, or legitimacy. In many cases, it requires *more* ethical engagement, not less—because distributed systems lack the central chokepoints where accountability naturally accrues. In decentralised networks, everyone is a stakeholder—and everyone is also a potential vector for harm.

The future of decentralisation depends on whether its community can transition from moralism to maturity. Can it move beyond the binary of centralised = bad, decentralised = good? Can it develop nuanced standards for legitimacy that account for power, access, and impact—not just architecture? Can it balance openness with curation, resilience with usability, sovereignty with safety? These are not technical questions. They are moral and political ones. And they demand answers more thoughtful than ideological purity can provide.

Ultimately, the value of decentralisation lies not in its symbolism but in its capacity to enable new forms of cooperation. Its promise is real, but its realisation will not come from chanting slogans. It will come from doing the hard work of design, governance, and ethical reflection. Only by letting go of decentralisation as a sanctified ideal can we begin to build systems where its practical benefits are felt—not just proclaimed. And only then will decentralisation cease to be a beautiful lie and become, instead, a useful and lived truth.

# Chapter 4
# The Anatomy of Trustless Systems

Trust has always been the scaffolding upon which societies are built. Banks, courts, governments, notaries, legal contracts—all exist because human behaviour cannot be predicted or enforced with certainty. We create layers of bureaucracy, not for elegance, but as a hedge against deceit, error, and coercion. In other words, trust is indispensable; civilisation leans upon it. Blockchain technology, and decentralised systems more broadly, propose a radical departure: a world in which trust is no longer placed in people or institutions, but in code, mathematics, and protocols. Hence the term "trustless." Yet the concept is riddled with tension: can a system be truly trustless when humans, fallible and biased, build, maintain, and interpret it?

The allure of trustless systems lies in technological self-enforcement. Smart contracts do not negotiate—they execute. Blockchains do not forget—they record. Code becomes the ultimate arbiter, both the rule and its enforcer. This vision has a potent appeal for those disillusioned by opaque institutions, political capture, and delayed justice. Yet it also poses uncomfortable questions. What if the code contains a flaw? Who bears responsibility when outcomes deviate from intention? And, fundamentally, can trust ever be eliminated—or is it merely displaced?

The DAO hack of 2016 exemplifies this fragility. A vulnerability in the code was exploited not through breaking the rules, but by adhering to them more cleverly than the developers anticipated. The Ethereum community faced a stark choice: honour the principle that "code is law" or intervene to reverse losses, undermining immutability. They chose intervention, resulting in a hard fork that split Ethereum. The incident illustrated a crucial lesson: even in ostensibly autonomous systems, human judgement remains unavoidable.

This lesson repeats itself across the decentralised ecosystem. From bridge hacks to oracle failures, governance exploits to treasury drains, the "trustless" infrastructure often relies on implicit trust. Oracles, which feed smart contracts with external data, introduce vulnerabilities—they can be manipulated, delayed, or corrupted. Cross-chain bridges, designed to move assets between blockchains, frequently centralise authority in a handful of validators, creating targets for attackers. The 2022 Ronin bridge hack, which siphoned over $600 million, was less a failure of decentralisation than a failure to recognise its limits.

DAOs—Decentralised Autonomous Organisations—offer another dimension. Held up as exemplars of on-chain governance, they often reveal a more complicated reality. Voter turnout is low. Power consolidates among whales or venture-backed insiders. Proposals are poorly drafted, coordination costly, and remedies for failure inadequate. The lesson here echoes across all trustless promises: decentralisation does not obviate the need for leadership, governance design, or legitimacy.

The human factor remains central. Smart contracts do not self-write; they are designed, coded, and deployed by people. Reliability depends on assumptions about users, markets, and adversaries. When these assumptions fail, the code performs "as designed," but not as intended. Bugs, once deployed on immutable chains, can be extremely difficult to rectify. Audits mitigate risk, formal verification promises security, yet both are imperfect. In the end, trusting code is to trust the coder—reintroducing subjectivity the system sought to remove.

User interfaces add another layer. Most people do not run full nodes or manually sign transactions. They rely on MetaMask, Etherscan, Infura, and similar tools—centralised gateways in a decentralised ecosystem. These intermediaries can fail, go offline, or impose restrictions. In effect, the belief in a fully trustless system masks new dependencies, subtle forms of re-centralisation.

Philosophically, the insight is clear: trust is never binary. Cryptography does not eliminate it; it transforms it. In "trustless" systems, faith shifts from institutions to software, from discretionary judgement to deterministic rules. But this migration is neither complete nor absolute. New vulnerabilities emerge, new loci of control appear, and accountability must be continually reasserted.

Trustless does not mean trust-free—it means trust has moved. And like all trust, it must be earned, scrutinised, and managed.

This chapter examines these dynamics, not as abstractions, but as concrete realities. Where do smart contracts succeed? Where do they falter? How do bridges, oracles, and APIs introduce risk? How do DAOs, despite their promise, sometimes reproduce hierarchy and stagnation? And crucially, how does perfectly executed code still rest upon fallible assumptions? The aim is not to dismiss trustless architectures, but to illuminate their boundaries and interrogate their implications.

Ultimately, trust is coordination. Decentralised systems are not about abolishing trust—they are about redistributing it, constraining it, and designing for resilience. Achieving this requires more than elegant code; it demands clear intent, thoughtful design, and, above all, humility about the limits of automation in a world that remains profoundly human.

## Code is Law?

It is a radical proposition: that legal contracts, which for millennia have relied on human interpretation and institutional enforcement, can be replaced by lines of code. Immutable, self-executing, and incorruptible, smart contracts promise to enforce agreements without need for courts, lawyers, or regulators. This is not merely an efficiency gain; it is a philosophical leap. It suggests that trust—once embedded in relationships, reputations, and systems of accountability—can now be engineered. The rallying cry "code is law" reflects this belief: that we can write rules in software and let those rules enforce themselves automatically. But as with many utopian slogans, the clarity of the phrase belies a world of complexity, risk, and unintended consequences.

Smart contracts are powerful precisely because they do not rely on discretion. Once deployed, they operate exactly as programmed, unaltered by emotion, politics, or personal judgment. This rigidity is often presented as a virtue: no backroom deals, no selective enforcement, no delays. Yet the very feature that makes smart contracts compelling also makes them brittle. Unlike human judges, software cannot weigh context. It cannot infer unstated intentions or adjust to evolving norms. When reality diverges from assumptions—as it often does—the code executes regardless. It does not ask whether it *should*, only whether it *can*. And this distinction is not merely theoretical; it has played out in financial losses, community splits, and existential dilemmas across the crypto ecosystem.

The DAO hack of 2016 remains the most iconic case study in the risks of rigid logic. A decentralised venture capital fund built on Ethereum was drained of $60 million worth of ether through a recursive call exploit in its smart contract. The attacker did not "hack" in the traditional sense. They simply invoked the code in a way that was permissible but unforeseen. According to the literal code, their actions were valid. According to the community's ethical standards, they were theft. Ethereum developers faced a moral and practical crisis: do they honour the code or reverse the loss? The decision to fork the chain and restore funds was pragmatic—but it shattered the illusion that code could replace law. It proved that, ultimately, humans still arbitrate meaning, even in systems designed to eliminate discretion.

To understand the limits of "code is law," we must distinguish between two types of trust: *functional* and *intentional*. Functional trust is about reliability—can a system do what it claims? Smart contracts excel here. Intentional trust is about alignment—does the outcome match the parties' shared understanding? This is where smart contracts struggle. Consider a simple employment contract: it involves expectations around quality, time, conduct, and discretion—none of which are easily reduced to deterministic code. Attempting to automate such nuance often leads to false precision: technically correct but substantively wrong. This misalignment is not a software bug—it is a human reality that code struggles to capture.

The challenge extends beyond isolated bugs. It is structural. Code reflects the assumptions, incentives, and blind spots of its authors. Even when those authors act in good faith, they cannot foresee every possible future state. Economic conditions shift. Political landscapes evolve. Users behave in novel, often irrational ways. A contract that functions elegantly today may collapse under tomorrow's complexity. Moreover, in decentralised environments, upgrading or patching deployed contracts is notoriously difficult. Immutability, while touted as a guarantee of integrity, becomes a liability when it freezes flaws in place.

Even the most well-intentioned and audited contracts have failed. Compound's protocol, for example, once mistakenly awarded millions in tokens due to a faulty governance proposal. The protocol worked precisely as coded—yet the result was disastrous. Similarly, the DeFi platform bZx suffered multiple attacks through flash loan exploits, despite its code passing multiple reviews. These incidents underscore a critical truth: self-enforcing contracts may remove traditional gatekeepers, but they introduce new ones—developers, auditors, oracles, and governance participants. The chain of trust has not disappeared; it has merely migrated, often to parties less visible and less accountable than their traditional counterparts.

Another dimension of risk arises from user interface design. Most participants in decentralised systems do not interact directly with raw contracts. They rely on front-end applications, wallets, and APIs that interpret and broadcast transactions on their behalf. These interfaces can be misleading, buggy, or even malicious. If the front end misrepresents what the contract will do—or is manipulated—the user's intent is distorted before it even reaches the chain. A contract might enforce terms flawlessly, but if the user was deceived into signing it, can we still claim justice was served? The answer depends on whether one values form over substance—an old legal debate reanimated in digital form.

There is also the question of jurisdiction. Code may be borderless, but human disputes are not. If a contract on Ethereum violates consumer protection laws in France, which system prevails? Who is liable? Where is redress? Courts are already wrestling with these questions. In some cases, smart contract terms are overridden by local statutes. In others, users discover that technical enforceability offers no real recourse. Regulators have begun issuing guidance, but the global nature of blockchain creates jurisdictional ambiguity. Legal pluralism collides with technological absolutism. And for all the rhetoric about self-sovereignty, when things go wrong, users still look for someone to hold accountable.

There are domains where smart contracts shine. Escrow services, token swaps, and automated auctions benefit from deterministic execution. These functions have clear parameters and minimal ambiguity. But even here, failure can occur at the edges: a misconfigured gas fee, a reorg of the blockchain, or a manipulation of time-stamped data. More complex applications—insurance, employment, credit, dispute resolution—remain heavily reliant on subjective interpretation. Attempts to codify such relationships risk producing either overly simplistic or dangerously rigid outcomes. No matter how elegant the code, it cannot yet encode empathy, judgement, or forgiveness.

The idea that "code is law" also risks importing a dangerous form of techno-authoritarianism. When law is automated, discretion disappears. This may sound desirable in corrupt regimes—but it is equally dangerous in systems that lack appeals, nuance, or proportionality. A frozen account, an erroneous liquidation, or a rejected transaction may have irreversible consequences, even if the user acted in good faith. Code does not distinguish between a malicious actor and a user who mistyped a decimal point. Unlike a human judge, it cannot offer leniency or interpret extenuating circumstances. The brutality of perfect enforcement is often celebrated by those not on the receiving end of its failures.

Still, dismissing smart contracts outright would be equally unwise. They offer extraordinary benefits when used appropriately: reducing costs, increasing transparency, and enabling new economic primitives. They can facilitate global collaboration among strangers, bootstrap new institutions, and decentralise power away from gatekeepers. But they are not a panacea. They are tools—potent, yes, but also prone to misuse, misunderstanding, and overreach. Their success depends less on technical perfection than on institutional design, user literacy, and social norms. In the end, trust is not eliminated; it is redistributed. The real task is not to ask whether code can replace law, but to determine *where* it should—and *how* we govern the consequences when it does.

Rather than embracing "code is law" as dogma, we must view it as a proposition to be interrogated. Law is not just about execution; it is about meaning. Contracts are not just about enforcement; they are about relationships. And systems are not just technical—they are social. A future built on smart contracts must recognise this complexity. It must balance the efficiency of automation with the ethics of interpretation. It must complement code with context. Only then can we build systems that are not only trustless, but truly trustworthy.

## Oracles, Bridges, and the Fragile Middle Layer

In blockchain architecture, the promise of decentralisation is often rooted in purity: a network of nodes, distributed governance, trustless computation, and the elimination of single points of failure. But as the space has matured beyond native token transfers and speculative trading, the complexity of use cases has exposed a critical architectural paradox. In practice, decentralised systems rarely function in isolation. They need inputs from the outside world—prices, timestamps, weather data, sports results, exchange rates. They also need to interact with one another across blockchain boundaries. These two functions—bringing off-chain data into on-chain environments and facilitating cross-chain communication—fall to oracles and bridges. These mechanisms, despite their apparent auxiliary nature, are not peripheral. They are foundational. And yet, they are also the most structurally vulnerable elements in the supposedly "trustless" ecosystem.

Oracles are services that supply external data to smart contracts. Without them, blockchains would be blind to the real world. A decentralised insurance platform, for example, must know whether it rained in London. A derivatives contract must track the price of gold. Oracles serve as these sensory organs—but the irony is striking: while smart contracts are designed to eliminate trust, oracles reintroduce it. Even decentralised oracle networks such as Chainlink rely on mechanisms that are not provably trustless. They aggregate data from multiple sources, apply weighting formulas, and distribute incentives—but they are still subject to manipulation, latency, and dependency risks. A single inaccurate feed can trigger a cascade of unintended consequences, as contracts execute automatically based on faulty data.

The significance of this vulnerability is not hypothetical. In April 2022, the stablecoin protocol Beanstalk was exploited through a flash loan attack that manipulated its governance mechanism via an oracle feed. The attacker gained enough voting power to pass a malicious proposal, draining tens of millions of dollars. The exploit did not target a smart contract bug; it targeted the oracle system. Similarly, in the 2020 bZx attack, the attacker used manipulated price feeds from an oracle to exploit the lending platform. These events illustrate that even if the underlying contract logic is sound, the system is only as robust as the data it consumes. Garbage in, disaster out.

Bridges, meanwhile, are designed to facilitate the transfer of assets and data between distinct blockchain ecosystems. Given the proliferation of Layer 1 and Layer 2 solutions—Ethereum, Solana, Avalanche, Arbitrum, and others—interoperability has become essential. Bridges promise this connectivity. But they too introduce complexity and attack surface. Unlike oracles, which focus on data, bridges manage value. Their role is to lock assets on one chain and issue a synthetic representation on another. This process often involves multi-signature wallets, validator quorums, and off-chain coordination. Each of these components becomes a potential target.

Some of the largest heists in crypto history have targeted bridge infrastructure. The Ronin Bridge, used by the popular play-to-earn game Axie Infinity, was exploited in 2022 for over $600 million due to compromised validator nodes. Wormhole, another high-profile bridge, lost $320 million after an attacker forged a message to mint wrapped ether without collateral. Harmony's Horizon Bridge was drained of $100 million by exploiting its multisig architecture. The common denominator is not esoteric zero-day vulnerabilities but structural centralisation in the very components meant to support decentralisation. These systems often rely on a handful of operators, or fail to design robust redundancy mechanisms, undermining the ethos they are built upon.

Part of the issue is conceptual. The blockchain ecosystem celebrates permissionless design and decentralised control, yet it simultaneously relies on middle layers that are neither permissionless nor decentralised. This dissonance is often glossed over in white papers and marketing decks. Developers speak of "trust minimisation," but oracles and bridges routinely operate on trust assumptions that are opaque or oversold. The community accepts this compromise in the name of functionality—but the consequences are severe. Every time a major oracle or bridge is compromised, the narrative of decentralised invincibility suffers. Worse still, retail users bear the brunt while institutional actors increasingly demand insurance and regulatory protections, diluting the principle of self-sovereignty.

Efforts to decentralise the oracle layer are ongoing. Chainlink's DONs (Decentralised Oracle Networks) and newer players like UMA, API3, and Band Protocol aim to distribute the data sourcing and validation process. Some systems use cryptographic proofs to verify data integrity, while others introduce economic staking mechanisms to penalise bad actors. These are commendable innovations—but they cannot eliminate all forms of risk. Ultimately, someone chooses the data source. Someone calibrates the aggregation logic. And someone maintains the infrastructure. These are not trivial decisions, and they involve trade-offs that must be scrutinised, not abstracted.

The same applies to bridges. Projects such as Cosmos's Inter-Blockchain Communication (IBC) protocol and Polkadot's cross-chain message passing aim to achieve more native, protocol-level interoperability. These models reduce reliance on third-party validators or wrapped tokens, embedding security into the chains themselves. Yet even these systems are not immune to scale-related complications, latency, and governance bottlenecks. As with oracles, the question is not whether these tools can be built. It is whether they can be trusted to operate reliably under pressure, at scale, and in adversarial conditions.

The implications extend beyond technical architecture. They touch on governance, incentives, and accountability. If an oracle feed delivers corrupted data, who is liable? If a bridge is hacked, who absorbs the loss? Traditional finance, for all its faults, has frameworks for resolution, remediation, and insurance. Decentralised systems often do not. Users may be left with nothing but a vague tweet, a retroactive governance vote, or a hard fork proposal. This fragility reveals that, despite claims of autonomy and transparency, the system retains centralised decision-making at critical junctures—it just wears a different badge.

Moreover, the fragility of the middle layer has broader economic implications. If developers must routinely build backstops for bridges and oracles, decentralised systems become more costly and complex. This raises barriers to entry, favours larger players with infrastructure resources, and discourages experimentation. The end result is a concentration of influence—not at the protocol level, but at the infrastructural level. This is a new kind of centralisation: invisible, under-discussed, but deeply consequential.

One possible future is the rise of hybrid models. Systems that use oracles and bridges, but with formal verification layers, auditing incentives, dispute resolution protocols, and even integration with legal frameworks. This does not mean abandoning decentralisation, but rather rethinking what it requires. Pure code is insufficient. So are reputational networks. What is needed is an architecture that acknowledges the grey zones between binary states: between on-chain and off-chain, between trustless and trusted, between immutable and adaptable.

The middle layer—where oracles and bridges reside—is not a temporary patch. It is a permanent feature of real-world decentralised systems. As such, it deserves deeper attention, greater investment, and more critical scrutiny. Rather than treating these components as secondary, we must centre them in discussions of security, resilience, and governance. After all, the strength of a decentralised system is not determined solely by the cryptographic purity of its core. It is tested at the seams—where it touches the world beyond the chain, and where the illusion of trustlessness must reckon with the reality of complexity.

## Human Governance in DAO Experiments

The allure of decentralised autonomous organisations—DAOs—is rooted in a profound philosophical wager: that technology can succeed where traditional hierarchies fail. By encoding governance into code and distributing decision-making power across token holders, DAOs promise a future free from the frailties of bureaucracy, the corruption of centralised control, and the inefficiencies of top-down management. But in the years since their emergence, DAOs have revealed something deeper than just technical complexity—they have exposed how inescapable human nature remains, even within structures designed to minimise it. When governance becomes a function of tokens, screens, and smart contracts, it doesn't transcend human tendencies. It distills them.

At their best, DAOs represent an innovative reimagining of collective action. Projects like MakerDAO have demonstrated how community-led financial infrastructure can manage billions in stablecoin issuance and collateral governance. Gitcoin has shown how decentralised funding can support public goods, distributing grants without centralised gatekeepers. ConstitutionDAO briefly galvanised a global community to bid on a rare copy of the US Constitution, showcasing coordination at speed and scale. Each of these examples was widely celebrated as a breakthrough—not just for what was achieved, but for what it symbolised: the emergence of coordination without centralised coercion.

But these successes are often brittle. ConstitutionDAO collapsed almost as quickly as it rose, crippled by ambiguity about fund refunds and plagued by logistical confusion. MakerDAO, while operationally resilient, has struggled with prolonged governance fatigue, low voter turnout, and dominance by large stakeholders. Gitcoin has faced challenges in Sybil attacks, coordination complexity, and disagreements over funding criteria. These problems are not marginal. They speak to a central contradiction at the heart of DAOs: *while the architecture is decentralised, the behaviour within it remains profoundly human.*

The notion that code can replace trust misunderstands what trust entails. Governance, even when mediated by smart contracts, is not just about execution—it is about judgment, deliberation, compromise, and leadership. DAOs routinely face disputes over proposals, friction in consensus, and debates over vision that no algorithm can resolve. The original DAO—the infamous experiment on Ethereum in 2016—was hacked not due to a flaw in Ethereum, but because of a vulnerability in its governance contract. The community was then forced into an existential decision: accept the theft as part of "code is law," or intervene via a hard fork. The majority chose the latter, splitting Ethereum in two. That choice, though technical in nature, was fundamentally political. It exposed the fiction of pure autonomy. In reality, *every decentralised system eventually encounters a moment where human discretion reasserts itself.*

One persistent challenge is the problem of plutocracy. In most DAOs, voting power is tied to token ownership. This aligns with the economic logic of "skin in the game," but it undermines egalitarian governance. The wealthy vote more. Often, a few large holders—so-called whales—can unilaterally swing votes or suppress proposals. This dynamic mirrors traditional shareholder governance in corporations rather than the democratic ideals many DAOs claim to embody. The result is disillusionment among smaller participants and the gradual centralisation of influence. Projects like Compound and Uniswap, while technically decentralised, have seen governance proposals dominated by a handful of powerful delegates or VC-backed entities.

Low participation is another critical vulnerability. Token holders frequently abstain from voting, leading to decisions made by a vocal minority. In some cases, voter turnout falls below 5%. Unlike political democracies, there is often no civic culture, no sense of duty, and no reputational cost for disengagement. This apathy can paralyse decision-making or allow bad proposals to pass due to inertia. Some DAOs have introduced delegation mechanisms to address this, enabling users to entrust their votes to more active participants. While this improves efficiency, it introduces a new layer of representational complexity—one that increasingly resembles traditional politics.

Coordination costs are also significant. Designing and implementing effective governance structures requires more than code. It requires process, norms, and institutional memory. DAOs often struggle with continuity, role clarity, and accountability. The absence of formal leadership may sound liberating, but it often leads to ad hoc committees, shadow hierarchies, or charismatic individuals who informally steer direction without formal mandate. Without clear boundaries and responsibilities, decision-making becomes muddled. Disputes over scope, authority, and ownership proliferate. Even trivial issues can devolve into prolonged debates, draining energy and resources.

Moreover, culture matters. DAOs are as much social organisms as they are technical constructs. Community norms, expectations, and unwritten rules shape behaviour in profound ways. In highly idealistic communities, dissent may be stigmatised. In more cynical ones, free-riding and extractive behaviour dominate. Some DAOs attract ideologues, others speculators. Some optimise for long-term mission alignment, others chase short-term returns. The code may be immutable, but the community is not. Human personalities, histories, and conflicts shape how governance actually unfolds.

Attempts to address these issues are evolving. Some DAOs are experimenting with non-token-based governance models, such as quadratic voting or conviction voting, which aim to amplify collective intelligence and reduce plutocratic influence. Others are introducing "meta-governance" structures, where governance frameworks themselves are subject to periodic review and revision. There is also a growing interest in hybrid systems that blend smart contract automation with off-chain deliberation, recognising that *code can execute, but humans must interpret.*

Even so, hard problems remain. Who resolves disputes when consensus fails? Who manages onboarding, education, and community health? What happens when interests diverge irreconcilably? Traditional organisations rely on boards, regulators, and courts. DAOs, by contrast, often rely on social consensus and ad hoc conflict resolution. This flexibility is powerful—but it is also fragile. Without robust mechanisms for dissent, reform, and exit, DAOs risk becoming either authoritarian or incoherent.

The deeper insight is that governance is not just a technical challenge. It is an existential one. Building a DAO is not merely about writing smart contracts—it is about cultivating a shared vision, managing collective identity, and designing for the messiness of human behaviour. DAOs expose a tension between aspiration and execution, between idealised decentralisation and the actual dynamics of group decision-making. *The dream is noble—but the implementation is always political.*

None of this renders DAOs a failure. Rather, it reveals that they are not post-political technologies. They are political in a new form. Their potential lies in making power explicit, contestable, and programmable—but not in eliminating it altogether. The goal is not to escape governance, but to make it more transparent, participatory, and accountable. To achieve that, the DAO community must embrace complexity, not deny it.

There is no perfect governance model. But there are better and worse ones. The next generation of DAOs will not be defined by how much code they automate, but by how well they align human incentives, resolve conflicts, and adapt to change. *Trustlessness may be the promise of the protocol, but governance is always a human act.* Recognising this is not a concession—it is a design principle. One that must sit at the heart of any DAO that aspires to endure.

## The Fallibility of Code Writers

A system is only as trustless as the humans who build it. That is the paradox at the heart of all software, but it cuts deepest in the world of cryptocurrency and decentralised finance, where code is routinely positioned as the final arbiter of truth. Blockchain networks promise mathematical certainty, incorruptibility, and immutable rules—yet their foundations are still written, audited, and maintained by fallible human beings. The more we lean on code to replace institutional trust, the more critical it becomes to reckon with the vulnerabilities introduced not by systems, but by their authors.

The belief that "code is law" collapses when law itself is flawed. While code can execute instructions with machine-like fidelity, it cannot determine intent, anticipate edge cases, or negotiate ambiguity. The DAO hack of 2016 is perhaps the most iconic example: an elegant but naive smart contract intended to decentralise venture capital ended in catastrophe, not because the system was broken in its infrastructure, but because its creators misunderstood the creative ingenuity of adversaries. An attacker exploited a recursive call vulnerability, draining over $60 million in ether. Technically, the contract did what it was programmed to do. Ethically, it broke every expectation of fairness. The ensuing hard fork that split Ethereum and Ethereum Classic was not a triumph of code, but a reminder that *human intervention remains the ultimate failsafe in a supposedly autonomous world.*

Programming is not merely a mechanical task. It is a cognitive and ethical act. Developers write code under conditions of uncertainty, with incomplete knowledge and bounded rationality. Even in the most security-sensitive environments, errors are not just possible—they are inevitable. Bugs hide in the interplay of modules, emerge under rare execution paths, or manifest only in production. Open-source codebases, even when audited, are susceptible to subtle flaws. A single misplaced line or unanticipated dependency can trigger financial chaos. Consider the Poly Network breach in 2021: a cross-chain interoperability protocol was exploited due to a smart contract vulnerability, leading to over $600 million in tokens being siphoned out—later returned, not due to the strength of the system, but at the discretion of the attacker. The most advanced cryptographic architecture cannot account for the psychological or moral intentions of those who engage with it.

Audits, while helpful, are not infallible. Many prominent DeFi hacks have occurred in audited codebases. Auditing itself depends on the skill, time, and scope of human reviewers. It is a snapshot in time, not an ongoing guarantee. Moreover, as systems grow more complex, the interdependencies between contracts, libraries, and protocols become increasingly difficult to reason about holistically. The mental model required to fully grasp an ecosystem like Ethereum or Solana is beyond what any single developer—or even team—can maintain without error. The modularity that makes code composable also makes it fragile. *Composability amplifies not only utility but also the surface area of risk.*

Human error is not the only concern—malicious intent is equally corrosive. Insider threats, rug pulls, and deliberately obfuscated backdoors have plagued the crypto space since its inception. The promise of decentralisation has too often masked centralised control by founding teams or protocol maintainers who wield significant, often unaccountable power. In some cases, critical upgrade privileges lie in the hands of a single multi-sig wallet or even one developer. This is not theoretical. In 2022, the Solana-based DeFi protocol Mango Markets was drained of over $100 million due to a price manipulation attack that relied on a known oracle weakness—and the attacker publicly argued that he had simply "used the protocol as designed." The ambiguity between hack and feature is a recurring theme in crypto. And it is always a human judgement call.

Even well-intentioned teams face moral dilemmas. When bugs are discovered post-deployment, developers must choose whether to patch them silently or disclose publicly—risking panic and exploitation. When forks are proposed, communities must decide whether to prioritise immutability or pragmatism. When upgrades are necessary, decentralised protocols often find themselves relying on the very forms of off-chain coordination they claimed to transcend. Governance crises, factional splits, and accusations of betrayal frequently follow. *Code does not remove politics. It merely moves the battleground to GitHub and Discord.*

The tension between deterministic execution and social legitimacy is especially acute in smart contracts. These contracts are not contracts in the legal sense—they are programs that cannot understand context, fairness, or force majeure. A traditional contract allows for judicial interpretation. A smart contract does not. This rigidity is both its strength and its flaw. In markets where billions are at stake, users expect not just predictability, but justice. Yet, smart contracts have no concept of equity. They are blind to asymmetric information, coercion, or unforeseen use. What happens when a bug benefits one party unfairly? Who decides whether to intervene, and on what basis?

Several high-profile protocol failures illustrate this dilemma. The bZx lending protocol suffered multiple flash loan exploits due to flawed logic in price feeds. The Yam Finance launch was famously derailed by a critical bug in its rebasing mechanism. The Cream Finance exploit resulted in a loss of over $130 million due to flaws in its flash loan implementation. These were not isolated incidents—they reflected systemic challenges in smart contract engineering, often exacerbated by rushed timelines, copy-pasted code, and market hype. Even the most careful projects are haunted by the complexity of their creations.

This complexity breeds opacity. For non-technical users, the "trustless" label may imply reliability, but few actually read smart contracts, let alone understand them. In practice, most users rely on interfaces, influencers, or community sentiment—hardly a radical departure from traditional finance. The supposed trustlessness of code is often replaced by a new kind of trust: *trust in anonymous developers, trust in audit firms, trust in rapidly shifting narratives*. That trust, once broken, is difficult to restore. And when exploits happen, the decentralised nature of most systems offers no insurance, no recourse, and no regulator to appeal to.

The fallibility of code writers also exposes deeper philosophical questions about responsibility. If a smart contract malfunctions and causes financial loss, who is liable? The developer who wrote it? The DAO that deployed it? The auditor who approved it? Legal systems worldwide have yet to catch up with these questions. In the meantime, users are left navigating a world where trust is displaced, not eliminated—where the risk of human error, negligence, or malice is not removed but *abstracted into the codebase.*

To move forward, the crypto community must embrace a more realistic view of code. Rather than idolising immutability or fetishising decentralisation, protocols must design for resilience. This includes multi-layered defences: rigorous testing, formal verification where feasible, multiple rounds of peer review, and contingency plans for failure. More fundamentally, it requires cultural maturity—a willingness to prioritise long-term integrity over short-term velocity, to acknowledge uncertainty rather than mask it in technical jargon.

Some projects are beginning to embed this thinking. Ethereum's move toward modular rollups and client diversity reflects a desire to reduce single points of failure. Formal methods are being applied more widely, especially in high-value systems. Progressive decentralisation frameworks allow governance power to transition gradually rather than abruptly. But none of these measures eliminate the core truth: *software reflects the assumptions, limitations, and biases of those who write it.* Trustless systems are only as robust as the humans behind them.

To speak of "perfect code" is to invoke a fantasy. All software has seams. Every system harbours assumptions that may fail under pressure. As long as people write the code—and people always will—the potential for unintended consequences remains. The goal, then, is not perfection, but transparency. Not utopia, but accountability. And above all, the humility to admit that *even in a world of decentralised ledgers and cryptographic certainty, the most persistent risk is not the machine—it is ourselves.*

# Chapter 5
# Wallets, Keys, and Personal Sovereignty

Possession in the digital currency era is not a matter of who holds the object in their hands, but of who controls the cryptographic keys. In this landscape, keys are authority, and sovereignty begins not in lofty ideals but in the cold mechanics of infrastructure. The refrain—"not your keys, not your coins"—is so often repeated in crypto circles that it risks sounding trite, yet its urgency has rarely felt sharper. What hangs in the balance is the individual's true position in a financial order that preaches disintermediation even as it tempts people back toward convenience and delegation. Here lies a tension both quiet and profound: while the founding vision of cryptocurrency was one of personal sovereignty, the instruments designed to realise it are, for many, too unforgiving, too obscure, too hostile to be genuinely liberating.

For the ordinary user, the freedom of self-custody comes at a punishing cost. Forget a seed phrase and you've effectively bricked your fortune. Misplace a private key and it's gone, irretrievable. The permanence of the blockchain, celebrated as incorruptible record-keeping, is at the same time merciless. In the traditional world, we are cushioned: a bank will reset your password, a card company will cancel the stolen piece of plastic, an institution will restore your access. The decentralised world does none of this. Irreversibility is its doctrine. Admirers call it a feature. To most, it feels like a perilous balancing act between empowerment and ruin. Sovereignty here demands total responsibility, and that is a burden few are eager—or able—to shoulder.

The irony is almost painful. In their flight from the custodians of old, users have rallied to a new class of intermediaries. Centralised exchanges, hosted wallets, slick apps that promise to tame the unruly machinery of crypto—these are the bridges people actually walk across. Coinbase, Binance, and their kin succeed not because they are decentralised, but because they remove the headaches of key management. Yet this very ease is a trap. What arrives as friendly design smuggles back the vulnerabilities that crypto was meant to abolish: the reappearance of counterparty risk, surveillance, regulatory choke points, and failure-prone hubs of power. Convenience masquerades as safety, while undermining the founding ethos.

The uncomfortable truth is that users are not wrong to recoil at the weight of pure responsibility. Most are not engineers. They cannot think in hashes and hexadecimal addresses, nor should they be expected to. People crave interfaces that forgive mistakes, safety nets to catch the inevitable slip. And crypto—at least in its raw form—provides none. Wallets today are stripped-down, brutalist contraptions, exposing technical scaffolding without translating it into concepts ordinary minds can hold. A seed phrase is no more meaningful to the average user than a string of hieroglyphs; a wallet address inspires little trust as a badge of identity. Instead of empowerment, the prevailing emotional state is one of low-level dread.

This mismatch between sovereignty and usability is perhaps the sharpest thorn in crypto's side. Hardware wallets may be secure, but they intimidate. Software wallets are only as safe as the laptops and phones they reside on—devices riddled with vulnerabilities. Browser extensions, mobile apps, and web-based portals all introduce their own trade-offs, balancing control against convenience, and often leaving both compromised. This is not simply a technical shortcoming but a philosophical one. The infrastructure has been built to flatter ideology rather than to embrace human frailty.

There is, moreover, a psychological gravity at work. A private key is not only a password—it is an identity. Losing it is not a minor setback, but an erasure of self in the digital realm. The analogue world offers buffers: customer support lines, legal recourse, institutional mediation. Here, the silence is absolute. For the technically adept, this silence feels liberating. For everyone else, it is paralysing.

But paralysis need not be the endpoint. The challenge is not to discard the principle of self-custody but to reshape it for actual human beings. This requires thinking less about technical elegance and more about behavioural reality. It means recognising that people forget, err, and panic—and designing systems that cushion those moments without sacrificing the integrity of true ownership. Sovereignty will not spread by dogma. It will spread through design that meets people where they are.

New approaches offer promising hints. Social recovery schemes, where a circle of trusted peers can collectively restore access, allow safety without surrender. Smart contract wallets, with programmable rules—multisigs, time delays, spending caps—bring subtlety to what has so far been a binary choice. Thoughtful use of biometrics, with privacy preserved, could spare users the tyranny of long strings of random words. Even small gestures—a name instead of an address, warnings that are genuinely comprehensible—can tilt the balance from fear to confidence.

Yet the sticking point is not purely technical. It is also ideological. Absolute sovereignty, though exalted, is not something most people actually crave. Few want to be their own bank in the strictest sense. They want control, yes—but with the reassurance of recourse. They want freedom, but tempered by support. They want responsibility, but buffered by protection. The self-custody versus custodial dichotomy is simply too crude for reality. What is needed is a spectrum, allowing users to progress from assisted autonomy to complete independence at their own pace.

This discussion is not about taking sides between custody models. The more pressing task is to expose what is at stake. Who holds the keys is not a technicality—it is the essence of the matter. Sovereignty cannot be real if it is inaccessible to the very people it is supposed to empower. If systems trumpet independence while ignoring usability, they merely replicate the old patterns of dependency, dressed in new rhetoric. True liberation will come only when sovereignty is not just technically sound, but humanly possible.

Responsibility for this does not rest with end users alone. It rests with the architects of these systems—to create wallets that educate without intimidating, that protect without condescension, that forgive errors without hollowing out the principles they enshrine. The aim is not a trade-off between security and autonomy, but a marriage of the two.

In this chapter, we will trace these paradoxes of key ownership: why the majority still choose intermediaries, why today's wallets are so alienating, and how more human-centred design might narrow the gap between ideological purity and lived experience. At its core lies a single, insistent question: if sovereignty is meant to be the cornerstone of crypto, why does it remain so distant for those it was built to serve?

## Not Your Keys, Not Your Coins:

The phrase *"Not your keys, not your coins"* is not simply a clever meme—it is the distilled ethos of the crypto movement, a warning and a principle embedded in four blunt words. It captures the radical promise and sobering responsibility of digital ownership in decentralised finance. At its core, this maxim asserts a simple but uncompromising truth: if you do not hold the private cryptographic keys to your assets, you are merely renting your wealth from a custodian who can deny you access at any time. Sovereignty, in this new monetary paradigm, is no longer conferred by institutions but encoded in mathematics. And yet, most users, overwhelmed by the practical burden of key management, continue to delegate control to the very intermediaries that blockchain technology was designed to replace.

To understand why key ownership matters so deeply, one must grasp what a private key is and what it represents. A private key is not merely a password—it is the singular credential that authorises control over a blockchain wallet. Possession of that key means exclusive access to the associated funds. Lose the key, and the funds are irretrievably lost. Share the key, and you relinquish security. Delegate it to a custodian, and you inherit their risk profile, legal obligations, and business continuity. This is not theoretical. It is brutally practical. Crypto's ledger is immutable, its rules inflexible. There is no customer service line, no bank manager, no safety net. *Control is binary: either you have it, or you don't.*

Historically, the financial system has relied on trusted intermediaries to manage and safeguard assets on behalf of individuals. From banks and brokers to pension managers and clearing houses, we have built an architecture of trust atop a foundation of institutional hierarchy.

Crypto was conceived in rebellion against that dependency. Bitcoin's original whitepaper, published under the pseudonym Satoshi Nakamoto, outlines a system where value transfer requires no central authority—no bank, no government, no corporation. Yet as crypto has gained popularity, many users have found themselves reverting to old habits, parking their funds with exchanges and wallet services for the sake of convenience. They have recreated the old world within the new, often without realising it.

The preference for custodianship is not just a matter of laziness or ignorance. It is, more fundamentally, a usability failure. Self-custody in crypto is intimidating. It requires understanding key phrases, backup procedures, and hardware wallets—none of which are intuitive to the average person. The anxiety of losing access, coupled with the irreversible nature of blockchain transactions, makes self-custody feel like walking a tightrope without a harness. In traditional systems, mistakes are reversible. In crypto, they are permanent. This unforgiving design deters many would-be adopters from assuming control over their keys.

The case of QuadrigaCX illustrates the danger of misplaced trust. When the founder of the Canadian crypto exchange died unexpectedly in 2018, he took with him the private keys to over $190 million in user funds. Clients who believed they were accessing a secure, reputable platform instead discovered they had been operating under a centralised honeypot, with no recourse once access vanished. The same structural vulnerability has appeared in less dramatic, but equally instructive forms: exchange hacks, exit scams, regulatory seizures. Time and again, the lesson is repeated—custody is a point of failure, and decentralisation is not something one can outsource.

But even self-custody carries risks, particularly for users unequipped to manage complex security protocols. One wrong click, one phishing email, one lost device, and the consequences can be financially catastrophic. The Parity multisig wallet hack in 2017, which froze over $150 million in Ether, was the result of a subtle code flaw that rendered funds permanently inaccessible. More recently, stories of individuals misplacing seed phrases or being coerced into revealing them under duress have become cautionary tales. The purity of cryptographic sovereignty must be tempered with a realistic understanding of human fallibility.

In practice, this has given rise to a growing tension between usability and security. On one end of the spectrum are hardcore crypto-anarchists who argue that true sovereignty requires uncompromising self-custody. On the other are mainstream users who want exposure to digital assets without the cognitive overhead of personal key management. Between these poles lies a space for innovation—tools that can abstract complexity without reintroducing centralisation. Multi-signature wallets, social recovery mechanisms, hardware-enforced protections, and biometric interfaces all attempt to bridge this divide. Yet each solution comes with trade-offs, and no consensus has yet emerged on what "humane" custody looks like.

This is not merely a technical issue—it is philosophical. At stake is the very definition of ownership in the digital age. In Web2, users are accustomed to licensing access, not owning property. Your movies on Netflix, your songs on Spotify, even your emails on Gmail—none of them belong to you in any enforceable sense. You are granted temporary use, conditional upon terms you cannot negotiate and policies that can change at will. Crypto, by contrast, offers an uncompromising promise: true, final, non-repudiable ownership. But it asks something in return—*the willingness to bear responsibility for your own access.*

Why, then, do so many users resist this? Part of the answer lies in behavioural psychology. We are conditioned to prefer convenience over control, especially when the cost of a mistake feels intolerable. The psychological comfort of a "forgot password" link is hard to surrender. Platforms that offer frictionless onboarding, easy interfaces, and recovery options will always attract users who are more interested in speculative upside than in sovereignty. This is not a failure of character—it is a predictable outcome of incentives and interface design. But it raises a difficult question: *Can the ideals of decentralisation survive mass adoption if users consistently opt out of their own agency?*

Some argue that the emphasis on private key custody is doctrinaire—that it prioritises purity over practicality, and alienates non-technical users. Others maintain that any compromise on key ownership fatally undermines the decentralised architecture that gives crypto its transformative potential. These are not trivial disagreements. They touch on the identity of the entire movement. Is crypto a technology platform, or a political revolution? Is it a speculative asset class, or a redefinition of economic agency? The way we answer these questions will shape the infrastructure we build—and the behaviours we normalise.

Importantly, not all custodians are created equal. There is a spectrum between full self-custody and full third-party custody, with hybrid models and programmable constraints offering creative middle grounds. Some wallets, like Gnosis Safe or Argent, implement multisig or social recovery, enabling users to delegate partial control in ways that remain transparent and non-custodial. These innovations suggest that trustlessness need not mean user-hostility. But they also require careful scrutiny: *Who sets the rules? Who has the power to change them? And what assumptions are being made about user behaviour, incentives, and technical literacy?*

Ultimately, "Not your keys, not your coins" is not a slogan of exclusion. It is an invitation to engage with the foundational questions of digital ownership. It challenges users to think beyond convenience and to consider what autonomy truly entails. It demands literacy—not just in the mechanics of key management, but in the politics of infrastructure. In a financial world increasingly defined by opaque algorithms, automated enforcement, and programmable assets, control over your keys is not a technical detail. *It is the difference between freedom and dependence.*

If crypto is to fulfil its emancipatory potential, key ownership must be made not only possible, but desirable—and not only desirable, but viable. That means designing systems that acknowledge human limitation without surrendering to paternalism. It means educating users without overwhelming them. It means recognising that sovereignty is not a default—it is a discipline. And discipline, like code, can be learned, shared, and refined. But it must begin with a simple, uncompromising truth: *if you do not hold the keys, you do not hold the future.*

## The Custodial Temptation:

The foundational premise of cryptocurrencies was disintermediation—the radical idea that individuals could transact, store value, and secure assets without relying on central authorities. Bitcoin's genesis block carried a message referencing bank bailouts, a subtle indictment of institutional trust. Ethereum introduced programmable contracts that promised to replace human arbiters with immutable logic. Yet, despite the ideological architecture of decentralisation, the everyday behaviour of crypto users reveals a stark contradiction. A majority continue to entrust their assets to centralised exchanges, custodial wallets, and third-party platforms. The decentralised dream, it seems, has encountered an ancient seduction: convenience. The custodial temptation is real, persistent, and structurally embedded in the ecosystem—and its implications are more than philosophical. They are systemic.

At the surface, the appeal is obvious. Centralised exchanges offer user-friendly interfaces, instant liquidity, and seamless fiat integration. They abstract away the complexities of seed phrases, gas fees, and wallet protocols. Platforms like Coinbase, Binance, and Kraken have onboarded millions precisely by making crypto feel familiar—more like online banking than cypherpunk rebellion. For newcomers, this is a feature, not a flaw. But beneath the surface, custodial services recreate the very power dynamics decentralisation sought to dismantle. By holding users' private keys, they become gatekeepers to assets that were supposed to be unmediated. Control, access, and trust are once again centralised—not by necessity, but by design.

This design has consequences. When users forfeit their keys, they inherit the platform's risk profile—technical, legal, financial, and even geopolitical. The collapse of FTX in 2022 was not merely a story of corporate mismanagement. It was a catastrophic demonstration of how custody, when abused or inadequately regulated, can vaporise billions in customer funds. Users who believed they owned their coins discovered, too late, that they were unsecured creditors in a failing institution. The lessons were painful but not new. Mt. Gox, Cryptopia, QuadrigaCX—each case a variation on the same theme: when you do not control your keys, you do not control your wealth.

The irony is that custodianship in crypto thrives not despite decentralisation, but because of its current limitations. Self-custody remains technically daunting, especially for those unfamiliar with cryptographic principles. Secure storage of private keys, safe handling of backups, and the ability to transact without making irreversible mistakes are not trivial demands. Moreover, human error is unforgiving in blockchain systems. There is no undo button, no call centre, no recovery hotline. Custodial platforms exploit this gap by offering ease-of-use in exchange for trust—a trade that many users, rationally or otherwise, are willing to make.

But this trade is not neutral. Custodial services often impose withdrawal limits, freeze accounts, comply with arbitrary regulations, or become inaccessible due to legal action or technical failure. These risks are not speculative. They are documented and recurring. In times of financial stress, when access to assets matters most, custodians have historically become bottlenecks rather than bridges. Even well-meaning platforms can be compromised, co-opted, or compelled. When custody centralises, so does vulnerability.

What's more, the scale at which custodians operate introduces systemic fragility. When a handful of platforms control the majority of retail crypto holdings, the ecosystem becomes interdependent in ways that contradict its decentralised foundations. A regulatory action against one major exchange can ripple across liquidity pools, trading volumes, and even token prices. The architecture becomes brittle, sensitive not to code but to corporate decisions, legal jurisdictions, and political winds. And while decentralisation theoretically distributes power, custodial concentration reaggregates it under new banners—logos, servers, and CEOs.

Some argue that custodianship is a transitional phase—that users will migrate to self-sovereign solutions as tools become more user-friendly. This narrative is both comforting and flawed. Technological progress does not automatically produce behavioural change. People will not adopt harder systems simply because they are philosophically purer. They need incentives, safeguards, and intuitive design. Without these, the gravitational pull of custodianship will persist. Worse, it will be normalised.

Consider the growing prevalence of custodial staking services, where users delegate their coins to platforms like Lido or Coinbase to earn yields. While technically efficient, these services compound centralisation by aggregating voting power and protocol influence into fewer hands. In proof-of-stake systems, this undermines the decentralised consensus that secures the network. The more we trust custodians to manage our assets and participate on our behalf, the less decentralised these systems become in practice—even if their architecture remains nominally distributed.

Custodianship also distorts user incentives. When ownership is abstracted, users engage with assets differently. They are less vigilant, less informed, and less empowered. They are renters, not stewards. This psychological shift has profound implications for governance, security, and education. It creates a passive user base that relies on platforms rather than participating in them. The idea of a "sovereign individual," so central to the crypto ethos, becomes a rhetorical artefact rather than a lived reality.

And yet, custodianship is not inherently malicious. There are contexts—enterprise storage, multi-party escrow, regulatory compliance—where third-party custody may be appropriate or even necessary. The issue is not whether custodians exist, but whether users understand the trade-offs they are making. Transparency, auditability, and user control must be the baseline, not afterthoughts. Platforms that position themselves as custodians should disclose their security models, their legal exposure, and their contingency planning. Users, in turn, must develop the literacy to assess these structures—not with blind trust, but with informed scrutiny.

The question, then, is not how to eliminate custodianship, but how to rebalance power. What does responsible custody look like in a decentralised context? Can we design systems where users retain ultimate authority, even when delegating certain operational tasks? Emerging models like non-custodial multisig wallets, smart contract vaults, and programmable escrow offer promising directions. These tools can provide convenience without surrendering control—*but only if their incentives, governance, and codebases are transparent and verifiable.*

At its core, the custodial temptation is a test of values. It asks whether we are willing to endure some friction in exchange for freedom—or whether we will sacrifice autonomy for the illusion of safety. The answer is not binary. It will vary by context, by user, by purpose. But it must be intentional. A decentralised system cannot remain resilient if its users consistently opt into centralised dependencies. The infrastructure will not matter if the behaviour does not align.

The allure of convenience will not disappear. Nor should it. But it must be met with a parallel commitment to education, design, and structural accountability. If the crypto movement is to live up to its rhetoric, it must confront the silent drift toward centralisation that custodianship represents. Not with dogma, but with design. Not with purity tests, but with usable alternatives. And not by punishing users for their choices, but by offering them better ones—choices that respect their agency, safeguard their assets, and preserve the decentralised principles upon which this ecosystem was founded.

## The UX Barrier to True Ownership:

The foundational promise of cryptocurrency was empowerment: a digital architecture in which individuals could own and control their assets without reliance on intermediaries. That promise hinges on a deceptively simple premise—*you control your keys, you control your coins.* Yet for all its ideological clarity, the path to true ownership is littered with friction, confusion, and irreversible loss. What stands in the way is not a lack of interest or technical capability, but the cumulative weight of poor user experience design. Interfaces confuse more than they clarify, instructions presume a level of literacy most users do not have, and the stakes of even minor errors are disproportionately high. In short, the UX of crypto actively obstructs the very sovereignty it aims to deliver.

The contrast with traditional finance is telling. Losing access to your bank account is inconvenient, but rarely catastrophic. There are helplines, reset options, even human managers to speak with. By contrast, losing the private key to your crypto wallet is tantamount to burning cash—without the fire. There is no undo function, no institution to appeal to, and no mechanism of recourse. The ethos of "be your own bank" may sound liberating, but it imposes a cognitive load most users are unprepared to carry. *True ownership in crypto demands a level of operational competence that is both unfamiliar and unforgiving.*

This gap between promise and practice has become one of the most persistent challenges in the ecosystem. Wallet interfaces—be they hardware, software, mobile or browser-based—often fail the most basic usability tests. Seed phrases must be transcribed and stored without error. User interfaces rely on technical jargon that is opaque to newcomers. And visual feedback, when it exists at all, does little to communicate the irreversible nature of actions like signing transactions or transferring assets. For users outside the technocratic core, crypto often feels not like emancipation, but like exposure.

These problems are not accidental. They are design artefacts of systems built by developers for developers, with user safety as an afterthought. Security is prioritised, understandably, but often at the cost of usability. This creates a paradox: *users must navigate highly technical processes precisely because the system is designed to protect them from themselves.* The result is a landscape in which power users thrive while average users tread carefully, or opt out altogether.

Consider the experience of setting up a self-custodial wallet. The process usually begins with a randomly generated 12- or 24-word seed phrase. The user is instructed to write this down, secure it offline, and never share it. There is rarely guidance on how to store the phrase securely, how to avoid phishing attempts, or what to do if the phrase is lost. The user interface may include a perfunctory warning—"if you lose your seed phrase, your funds are gone forever"—but few systems provide tools to mitigate this risk. For a first-time user, the process is anxiety-inducing at best, paralysing at worst.

Even experienced users make catastrophic errors. Ethereum Classic suffered a blockchain reorganisation due to insufficient confirmation policies. Solana-based wallets like Slope were compromised not by protocol-level flaws, but by insecure seed management practices. Millions have been lost to simple mistakes: copy-pasting the wrong address, misunderstanding gas fees, signing malicious contracts. These are not edge cases. They are structural failures in the way crypto UX is conceived, built, and deployed.

The industry's attempts at improvement have been piecemeal. MetaMask, the most widely used browser wallet, has made strides in education and interface clarity, yet still presents users with critical security decisions during initial setup. Hardware wallets like Ledger and Trezor improve security, but add layers of friction and often confuse non-technical users. Multisig wallets, while more resilient, demand coordination across multiple parties and are impractical for most individual users. Smart contract wallets and social recovery mechanisms—such as those pioneered by Argent or Safe—represent a step forward, but adoption remains limited.

The deeper issue is philosophical. Much of crypto UX is still built on the assumption that users should adapt to the system, rather than the system adapting to the user. This mindset reflects a broader tension between ideological purity and mass adoption. Purists argue that any attempt to abstract away complexity undermines sovereignty; that responsibility must accompany freedom. But this binary framing misses the point. *Designing for usability is not antithetical to decentralisation—it is essential to it.* If systems are so brittle that only experts can use them safely, they are not decentralised in any meaningful sense. They are exclusionary by design.

The cost of this exclusion is measurable. Billions in value have been lost due to misplaced keys, forgotten passwords, and failed backups. Studies suggest that up to 20% of all Bitcoin in circulation may be inaccessible due to lost credentials. These are not the consequences of adversarial hacks. They are the by-product of bad UX—a silent erosion of confidence that undermines public trust in self-custody. When users fear their own tools more than external threats, the promise of sovereignty becomes hollow.

More subtly, poor UX reshapes behaviour. Faced with cumbersome wallets and unforgiving recovery systems, many users migrate to custodial platforms—not out of ignorance, but out of rational self-preservation. Exchanges like Binance and Coinbase have become default wallets for millions not because users prefer centralisation, but because the alternatives feel too risky. *When decentralised systems are too difficult to use, users do not remain ideologically loyal—they migrate to systems that work.*

Addressing this barrier requires more than interface tweaks. It demands a complete rethinking of design priorities. Wallets must offer safety nets—intelligent defaults, layered permissions, and recovery pathways that respect both autonomy and fallibility. Educational content must be integrated natively, not relegated to blogs and FAQs. Transaction signing should be transparent and explainable, with context-aware warnings that make sense to lay users. And perhaps most importantly, the language of crypto needs reform. Technical jargon may impress, but it excludes. Clear, intuitive language must become a design standard, not a luxury.

There are encouraging developments. Projects experimenting with account abstraction on Ethereum are attempting to separate ownership from operational complexity. Features like biometric authentication, session keys, and rate-limited withdrawals are being explored to bridge the gap between usability and control. Newer wallets are building human-centric onboarding flows, and community-driven standards for wallet UX are emerging. But these advances remain uneven, siloed, and often too late for users already burned by bad design.

The challenge is not merely technical—it is cultural. Developers, product designers, and security experts must collaborate with educators, psychologists, and users themselves to build systems that respect both the power and the limits of human cognition. Complexity cannot be eliminated entirely, but it can be managed, abstracted, and explained. The bar is not perfection; it is comprehensibility. Users should not need a degree in cryptography to participate safely in a decentralised economy.

Ultimately, the UX barrier to true ownership is not just a usability problem—it is a civilisational one. At stake is the question of who gets to participate in the next phase of digital finance. Will it be limited to the technically literate, or extended to the billions who need it most? Will tools be designed for real people, or will they remain the preserve of enthusiasts and early adopters? The answers will shape not just adoption rates, but the moral architecture of decentralised systems themselves.

Crypto cannot afford to ignore this challenge. A system that offers sovereignty in theory but punishes users in practice will not scale ethically or practically. If the goal is to build a new financial order—one that is inclusive, resilient, and free from centralised coercion—then user experience is not peripheral. *It is the battleground upon which the promise of decentralisation will be won or lost.*

## Designing for Human Error:

For all its ideological commitment to individual sovereignty, the crypto ecosystem remains profoundly brittle in the face of human fallibility. One mistyped address, one misplaced seed phrase, one phishing link clicked—and what was intended as financial empowerment turns instantly punitive. There are no chargebacks, no customer service reversals, and no room for redemption. The architecture is elegant, but the lived experience can be brutal. The system, by design, has little forgiveness. This rigidity might be tolerable in low-stakes experimentation, but when financial futures, livelihoods, or even collective treasuries are on the line, the absence of safety nets is neither noble nor sustainable. *True self-sovereignty requires tools that protect users not only from others, but from themselves.*

Designing for human error is not an admission of weakness in decentralised finance—it is a recognition of the human condition. The foundational assumption of self-custody, "you control your keys, you control your coins," is deceptively simple. But what if you lose your keys? What if you misinterpret a prompt? What if your wallet interface fails to warn you of a malicious smart contract? The system responds with silence. It assumes that users are infallible executors of perfect decisions. But *users are not machines.* They are distracted, anxious, under-informed, and frequently operating under conditions of cognitive overload. Any system that fails to acknowledge this will fail its users.

What makes this particularly urgent is not just the possibility of error, but the severity of consequences. In traditional systems, financial infrastructure is built around redundancy and recovery. Banks require multiple authorisations. Credit cards offer fraud protection. Passwords can be reset. Crypto, by contrast, is built for finality. Transactions are irreversible. Credentials, once lost, are unrecoverable. This may be technically impressive, but it is a nightmare for usability. Designing humane wallet systems means shifting the question from *How do we enforce perfect security?* to *How do we minimise irreversible failure when security inevitably falters?*

One promising direction is layered authentication—systems that separate ownership from execution. In traditional crypto wallets, the private key confers absolute authority. Lose it and you lose everything. But what if different keys or authorisations were required for different types of actions? Daily spending could be governed by one key, high-value transactions by another, and recovery functions delegated to a trusted quorum. This idea, often implemented via *multi-signature wallets* or *smart contract wallets*, creates a graduated model of control. Users can act autonomously for low-risk activity but are insulated from catastrophic error through built-in friction for high-risk moves.

Another vector for human-centric design lies in *social recovery*. The principle is simple: if you lose access to your wallet, you can regain it through the cooperation of pre-designated guardians—trusted friends, family members, or even institutional entities. Implemented thoughtfully, this restores a layer of social trust without undermining decentralisation. Tools like Ethereum's ERC-4337 and wallet projects like Argent or Safe have begun experimenting with this paradigm. The model is not perfect—it depends heavily on guardian trustworthiness and proper onboarding—but it represents a tangible response to the realities of human memory and vulnerability.

Critically, these solutions must be *invisible until needed*. One of the fatal errors of crypto UX is frontloading complexity. Users are often introduced to seed phrases, gas fees, and public-private key architecture before they have any sense of what these things mean. The result is not empowerment—it is alienation. Good design hides complexity until it is relevant. It guides the user with progressive disclosure: the right information at the right moment, no more, no less. *Interfaces must be literate in user psychology, not just protocol logic.*

Wallets also need to do more to explain *intent.* When a user signs a transaction, they are often confronted with hexadecimal gibberish, inscrutable contract calls, and irrelevant technical data. What's missing is context: What are you authorising? What will happen if you proceed? Can it be undone? MetaMask and others have begun incorporating transaction previews and warnings, but the ecosystem as a whole remains primitive. If we can't explain a transaction's implications in plain language, we shouldn't expect the average user to authorise it intelligently.

Another overlooked domain is *error prevention.* Wallets could, for example, detect unusually large transfers and prompt a secondary confirmation. They could flag known scam addresses, simulate smart contract execution before it occurs, or notify users when interacting with unusually permissive approvals. These are not speculative capabilities—they already exist in isolated tools and extensions. The issue is not feasibility, but integration. Humane design means embedding these protections natively into the experience, not outsourcing them to power-user plugins.

Beyond the technical, there is a cultural layer to this challenge. The crypto community often romanticises the idea of radical responsibility—of users becoming fully sovereign entities who read smart contracts, audit wallets, and air-gap their devices. But this vision is aspirational at best and exclusionary at worst. It privileges the technically fluent and leaves the rest behind. Designing for human error is a way of *democratising access* to decentralised finance. It recognises that participation should not require mastery of cryptography or constant vigilance. Systems must earn users' trust by being not only secure, but survivable.

That does not mean reverting to full custodianship or centralised backdoors. The goal is *resilience without dependency.* A well-designed wallet should tolerate mistakes, not punish them. It should allow for recovery paths that maintain user autonomy. It should anticipate user confusion and offer clarity. It should act not as a silent executor of commands, but as an intelligent companion—always vigilant, occasionally insistent, and never inscrutable.

Some of the most compelling prototypes draw from safety-critical fields. Aviation systems, for example, are designed to prevent single-point human failures. They rely on redundancy, checklist workflows, and constant feedback. Medical interfaces assume that operators may be under stress or distraction. They colour-code vital actions, use audible warnings, and enforce verification protocols. Crypto designers would do well to study these fields—not for their constraints, but for their methods. *Error-tolerant systems are not softer—they are smarter.*

Ultimately, humane wallet design is a litmus test for the maturity of the crypto ecosystem. If decentralisation is to scale beyond ideological circles, it must grapple honestly with the limits of human cognition. The alternative is stagnation: systems that are theoretically sound but practically unusable, promising sovereignty while delivering anxiety. The tools must meet users where they are—not where we wish they were.

The future of decentralised finance depends not only on protocol innovation but on interface innovation. Governance models, consensus mechanisms, and zero-knowledge proofs may capture the headlines, but it is wallet design—quiet, mundane, unglamorous—that will determine whether crypto remains a niche experiment or becomes a public good. That means designing systems that assume mistakes, that survive accidents, and that restore power without exacting punishment. Not because users are weak, but because they are human. And in a system that claims to liberate individuals, respecting their fallibility is not just a design choice—it is a moral imperative.

# Chapter 6
# The Dark Mirror: Crime, Scams, and Shadows:

If technology serves as a mirror to society, cryptocurrency holds up one of the clearest—and most unforgiving—reflections. It reveals our aspirations: autonomy, transparency, fairness. But it also exposes our pathologies: greed, deception, and opportunism that thrives in the shadows of ambiguity. Nowhere is this duality more visible than in the darker corners of the crypto world: the scams, schemes, and shadow economies that have proliferated alongside innovation. This chapter confronts that mirror, not to sensationalise, but to understand—structurally, psychologically, and ethically.

Critics have long portrayed crypto as a haven for wrongdoing. While this claim is often exaggerated, it is not entirely baseless. Ransomware groups demanding Bitcoin, darknet markets trading Monero, decentralised mixers shuffling illicit funds—these are not hypothetical anomalies but enduring realities. Chainalysis estimates that illicit crypto transactions surpassed $20 billion in 2022 alone. Yet such figures can mislead, conflating anonymity with lawlessness, decentralisation with chaos, and novelty with inherent risk. The pertinent question is not whether criminals exploit crypto—clearly they do—but why the architecture of crypto both enables innovation and facilitates abuse, and what that duality reveals about human systems more broadly.

Cryptocurrency does not generate crime; it transforms the terrain on which certain crimes operate. Money laundering predates blockchains; Ponzi schemes predate the internet. What crypto contributes is a new affordance: programmable value. This programmable layer, for all its promise, also permits criminal sophistication at unprecedented scale. Smart contracts can automate fraud. Decentralised exchanges can obscure trails. Flash loan exploits, Sybil attacks, rug pulls—these are native features, not aberrations. The question becomes whether these risks are inherent to the technology itself, or symptomatic of an unregulated frontier.

Consider ransomware. Before Bitcoin, extortionists faced a practical problem: how to collect payment safely. Cryptocurrency solved this with pseudonymity and frictionless, borderless settlement. A victim in New York could pay an attacker in Lagos within minutes, each party oblivious to the other's identity. The innovation was not merely concealment—it was the removal of procedural friction. Crypto didn't just make crime harder to trace; it made it easier to execute. And that, more than mere anonymity, is the challenge that regulators, law enforcement, and users must confront.

Yet crypto crime is not confined to shadow networks. It sometimes appears respectable, adorned with conference panels, media coverage, and sponsorship deals. The 2017 ICO boom illustrates this perfectly. Projects without product, team, or accountability raised millions on the strength of a whitepaper alone. Investors, caught up in the same speculative euphoria that inflates every historical bubble, were complicit. The predictable result: evaporating wealth, collapsing trust, and belated regulatory scrutiny. Worse, the cycle repeated with NFTs, DAOs, and meme coins—the vehicles changed, but the behavioural patterns remained.

At the core of many such schemes is the enduring logic of the pyramid. Modern Ponzi structures don't hawk seminar tickets—they sell tokens. Unlike their predecessors, they can scale globally overnight. Projects such as BitConnect, OneCoin, and Forsage leveraged the rhetoric of decentralisation to disguise centralised profiteering. Promises of algorithmic returns, community ownership, or revolutionary applications masked a simple truth: early adopters profited at the expense of later ones. The blockchain did not prevent the fraud; it merely concealed it—until exposure was unavoidable.

These scams flourish not because people are foolish, but because human behaviour is predictable. Greed, fear of missing out, herd mentality, overconfidence—these cognitive levers are expertly manipulated by those designing financial traps in digital clothing. Technology amplifies weakness rather than eliminating it, accelerating both opportunity and deception. And because crypto operates without traditional gatekeepers, discernment is left almost entirely to the individual. This is simultaneously liberating and perilous.

Calls for regulation present their own dilemmas. Who governs a decentralised network? Who enforces laws across borderless protocols? Jurisdiction blurs; accountability diffuses. Applying conventional legal frameworks often produces awkward compromises or chilling effects. Curtailing anonymity may reduce crime, but it also threatens legitimate privacy. Blacklisting wallets might block stolen funds, but risks ensnaring innocent actors. The trade-offs are complex, rarely binary. Regulation is not a panacea—it is a negotiation between freedom and control, prevention and permission.

Platforms that profit from chaos compound the problem. Exchanges listing dubious tokens, influencers promoting unvetted projects, venture capitalists flipping allocations for quick returns—all reinforce a feedback loop where grift becomes normalized and short-term gain is incentivised over enduring value. This tolerance is not cost-free: credibility erodes, careful participants are discouraged, and critics gain ammunition to call for wholesale suppression rather than reform.

Yet focusing only on malfeasance misses the broader lesson. Criminal exploitation does not invalidate cryptocurrency—just as phishing does not discredit email, or cash transactions do not discredit currency. Instead, these episodes illuminate the system's stress points, revealing vulnerabilities that must be addressed both technologically and ethically. What is at stake is not merely crypto's reputation, but the very architecture of financial agency in a digital era.

This chapter does not catalogue every scam nor vilify every misstep. Its aim is more precise: to dissect the anatomy of abuse in decentralised systems. To understand how it arises, why it persists, and what interventions might reduce harm without extinguishing the radical potential that crypto embodies. Each fraud, each exploit, each regulatory blind spot serves as a diagnostic signal in the ongoing evolution of a system built to operate without conventional oversight.

Ultimately, the future of crypto—whether it becomes a liberating force or a lawless carnival—depends less on what the technology permits and more on what culture allows. And unlike code, culture cannot be audited; it must be shaped. That shaping begins with clear-eyed understanding, not moral panic or naive optimism. The chapters ahead aim to provide exactly that: rigorous analysis, uncomfortable truths, and an honest appraisal of the darker potentials inherent in a system designed to trust no one.

## Crypto as Crimeware:

The greatest technological disruptions don't just reinvent markets; they also reshape the architecture of crime. Cryptocurrency, often lauded for its potential to decentralise finance and empower individuals, has simultaneously become a preferred tool in the digital criminal's toolkit. It offers something unprecedented: programmable, permissionless, pseudonymous value transfer. For bad actors, that is not just convenient—it is structurally enabling. The point is not that crypto causes crime. Rather, it *radically optimises* the mechanics of illicit behaviour. Understanding how—and separating legitimate concern from moral panic—is critical to evaluating the technology's systemic risk.

In 2013, when U.S. federal agents shut down the Silk Road, the first major darknet marketplace, they seized 173,991 bitcoins—then worth around $33 million, now worth billions. That event marked a watershed moment: not just in law enforcement, but in public perception. Bitcoin, long hailed in niche circles as an escape from central banking, was suddenly synonymous with narcotics, hitmen, and cybercriminals. Politicians and pundits painted crypto as a digital Wild West. That caricature persists to this day. But the reality is more complex. While cryptocurrency can be used for crime, its most powerful role is not concealment—it's *efficiency*. It replaces cash not because it's invisible, but because it's *faster*, *frictionless*, and increasingly global.

Ransomware is the clearest—and most destructive—example. Before crypto, digital extortion was clumsy. Attackers had no reliable way to collect money from victims across borders without exposing themselves. Cryptocurrency changed that calculus. Now, a ransomware operator in Eastern Europe can encrypt the medical records of a hospital in California, demand payment in Bitcoin or Monero, and vanish with near impunity. In 2021 alone, the FBI received reports of ransomware payments exceeding $600 million, with the actual figure likely much higher due to underreporting. Groups like REvil, DarkSide, and Conti operated like decentralised franchises, offering "Ransomware-as-a-Service" to affiliates and splitting the profits. Cryptocurrency didn't invent extortion—it *commercialised* it.

Yet it would be a mistake to blame the tool rather than the trade. Fiat currency is still used in the vast majority of global criminal activity. What crypto does is make some crimes scalable, automated, and hard to reverse. The very features that make it revolutionary—censorship resistance, final settlement, and programmability—can also be weaponised. Smart contracts can encode fraud. Mixers like Tornado Cash can obscure transaction trails. Decentralised exchanges offer no gatekeepers, making it difficult to impose sanctions or compliance checks. But even this infrastructure is a double-edged sword. Transparency, paradoxically, is both an asset and a liability. Blockchain forensics firms like Chainalysis and Elliptic have become invaluable to regulators, tracing flows that traditional finance would never reveal. Most ransomware payments *are* tracked. What's missing is often the legal or diplomatic machinery to act on those insights.

Darknet markets offer a different lens into crypto's criminal applications. Sites like AlphaBay and Hydra built reputations for customer service, escrow systems, and reputation scores—mimicking legitimate marketplaces like eBay or Amazon, but for illegal goods. These platforms weren't just criminal—they were *sophisticated.* They used Bitcoin and, later, privacy coins like Monero to reduce traceability. But even the best-laid opsec (operational security) has cracks. AlphaBay's founder was eventually arrested due to poor digital hygiene. Hydra, the largest Russian darknet market, was shut down in 2022 through a coordinated effort involving German and U.S. authorities. Here again, the tension is instructive: crypto enables a new class of decentralised black markets, but it also leaves digital breadcrumbs. Crime is easier to conduct, but not always easier to hide.

Money laundering in crypto is also misunderstood. Critics often assert that crypto enables "perfect laundering." This is technically incorrect. Every transaction on a public blockchain is traceable. The problem lies in the *conversion points*. Criminals exploit weak Know Your Customer (KYC) enforcement on exchanges, or use decentralised platforms with no KYC at all. They may also leverage "layering" tactics: using multiple wallets, tokens, and services to obfuscate origin. Still, the blockchain provides something traditional financial surveillance lacks: immutable logs. These logs can be analysed retroactively, enabling law enforcement to reconstruct illicit flows in minute detail. In many cases, it's *easier* to track laundered funds on-chain than through offshore bank accounts. The difference is not invisibility—it's *jurisdictional evasion*. Criminals don't need untraceable funds; they need systems that can't or won't prosecute them.

This raises the broader issue: fear-mongering often outpaces evidence. Media coverage of crypto-related crime tends to sensationalise. A single darknet drug bust or ransomware incident becomes emblematic of the entire ecosystem. Meanwhile, systemic fraud in traditional finance—Wells Fargo's fake accounts, HSBC's laundering for drug cartels, or the 2008 global meltdown—rarely provokes the same existential scrutiny. The question is not whether crypto is used for crime, but whether its *proportionate risk* justifies its *disproportionate stigma*. So far, criminal activity in crypto represents a small fraction of total volume. According to Chainalysis, illicit addresses accounted for just 0.24% of all cryptocurrency transactions in 2022. That's not an exoneration—but it is a necessary calibration.

Still, systemic risk does exist—and it's often overlooked. The real danger is not individual crimes, but *infrastructure exposure*. If a protocol is widely used and becomes vulnerable to attack—whether via a software bug, economic exploit, or governance failure—the impact can cascade across users, platforms, and even industries. Think of what happened to Wormhole, a cross-chain bridge that lost over $300 million due to a smart contract exploit. Or Ronin Network, whose breach—linked to the North Korean Lazarus Group—cost over $600 million and affected millions of gamers using Axie Infinity. These aren't niche events. They are structural stress tests.

And they expose how brittle some supposedly "trustless" systems remain.

What's often missing in debates about crypto and crime is a coherent moral framework. Is privacy a right or a liability? Should anonymity be regulated or respected? Is censorship resistance a feature or a flaw? Different jurisdictions answer these questions differently. China has cracked down on all crypto activity, citing financial stability and criminal abuse. The U.S. has taken a fragmented approach—aggressive enforcement by the SEC and OFAC, but little legislative clarity. Europe, through MiCA (Markets in Crypto-Assets), is attempting to walk a regulatory tightrope: enabling innovation while policing abuse. Each approach reflects competing values, but none fully resolve the tension between freedom and control.

Ultimately, the future of crypto will hinge not just on its technological merit, but on its moral resilience. The ecosystem must grapple with the fact that its most cherished principles—decentralisation, anonymity, autonomy—are also its most exploitable. That doesn't mean abandoning them. It means *designing around their misuse*. Privacy-preserving tools like zero-knowledge proofs, decentralised identity frameworks, and audit-friendly mixers represent one path forward. Another lies in robust self-regulation: industry standards, code audits, ethical disclosures, and reputational deterrents. Law enforcement, too, must adapt—not just with better tools, but with deeper fluency in decentralised architecture.

To see crypto solely as crimeware is to fall into a trap of intellectual laziness. To ignore its criminal potential is to fall into a trap of ideological naivety. The truth lies between these poles. Cryptocurrency is a mirror—sometimes dark, sometimes clarifying. The challenge is not to break the mirror, but to see clearly what it reflects. And to build systems that are not merely powerful, but worthy of the trust they ask us to place in code, in markets, and ultimately, in one another.

## The ICO Bubble and Financial Theater:

There are few episodes in financial history that so vividly combine technological optimism, speculative euphoria, and human credulity as the 2017 Initial Coin Offering (ICO) boom. At its peak, ICOs were being launched daily—often with nothing more than a white paper, a website, and a token ticker. Within that digital theatre of disruption, billions of dollars changed hands, countless investors were burned, and regulators worldwide were caught flat-footed. The rise and fall of ICOs did not just reveal a failure of oversight; it exposed a deeper vulnerability: the human tendency to believe in innovation as a kind of salvation, particularly when dressed in the language of decentralisation, blockchain, and programmable money.

The term "ICO" itself was a deliberate mimicry of the more regulated "IPO"—Initial Public Offering. But unlike traditional equity markets, ICOs bypassed institutional gatekeepers. Instead of filing with securities commissions or undergoing due diligence, ICO projects turned to global crowdfunding. Investors, often retail participants with little experience, would send cryptocurrency—most commonly Ether—to a project's smart contract and receive freshly minted tokens in return. The pitch was usually vague but compelling: reinvent finance, decentralise identity, disrupt gaming, build a new internet. In many cases, the tokens had no working product, no business model, and no clear legal status. Yet that did little to slow the flow of capital. According to data from CoinDesk and TokenData, ICOs raised more than $6 billion in 2017 alone. By mid-2018, that figure had surpassed $20 billion.

Why did this frenzy capture the imagination of so many? Part of the answer lies in timing. The price of Bitcoin had climbed from under $1,000 in January 2017 to nearly $20,000 by December. Ethereum, which underpinned most ICOs via its ERC-20 token standard, saw similar meteoric gains. Against this backdrop, ICOs offered a kind of digital lottery—a chance to invest early in "the next Ethereum." Influencers on YouTube and Twitter hyped presales and private allocations. Telegram groups became hotbeds of speculation and conspiracy. White papers mimicked academic language but often offered little substance. Investors—many of whom had missed out on earlier crypto gains—were gripped by FOMO: fear of missing out. That emotional state was expertly manipulated by project founders, who promised revolutionary change while delivering vaporware, or worse, outright fraud.

Consider the infamous case of Plexcoin. Marketed as "the next cryptocurrency for the masses," Plexcoin promised 1,354% returns. The U.S. Securities and Exchange Commission intervened, labelling it an outright scam and freezing $15 million in assets. Then there was BitConnect, which offered investors guaranteed daily returns via a mysterious "trading bot." BitConnect collapsed in early 2018, wiping out billions in value and leaving behind a legacy of meme-worthy absurdity and financial devastation. These were not anomalies—they were emblematic. According to a 2018 study by Satis Group, approximately 80% of ICOs launched in 2017 were scams, while a further 10% failed outright. Only a small fraction delivered any usable product at all.

Yet not every ICO was fraudulent. Projects like Ethereum itself had originated through a token sale. Other major platforms—Tezos, Filecoin, Polkadot—also used ICO-like models to bootstrap development. But even these legitimate efforts suffered from poor investor protections, unclear token economics, and speculative bubbles that distorted their mission. The problem wasn't just bad actors—it was structural. The very design of the ICO model lacked the institutional scaffolding that traditional capital markets rely on: disclosures, accountability, lock-up periods, anti-fraud protections. In its absence, financial theatre filled the void. Stage-managed token launches, celebrity endorsements, and countdown clocks created an illusion of momentum. It wasn't investing—it was theatre masquerading as capital formation.

Regulatory response was, initially, disoriented. Jurisdictions struggled to determine whether ICO tokens were securities, commodities, or something entirely new. In the U.S., the SEC applied the Howey Test—originally developed in the 1940s—to determine whether a token qualified as a security. In most cases, the answer was yes. But enforcement was selective and reactive. In Asia, responses varied: China banned ICOs outright in September 2017, while Japan attempted a more permissive but monitored framework. The European Union, as with much of crypto policy, adopted a fragmented stance. This global inconsistency created a kind of regulatory arbitrage, where founders would incorporate in one jurisdiction, market in another, and raise funds from a third—often with little regard for investor protection in any.

The ICO bubble also revealed profound gaps in financial literacy. Many investors did not understand tokenomics, governance rights, or even the difference between utility and security tokens. Nor were they equipped to evaluate technical claims. Projects would boast of hash rates, consensus mechanisms, or scalability breakthroughs that were either impossible or irrelevant. Terms like "decentralised autonomous organisation" or "smart contract insurance" were invoked not as technical realities but as rhetorical flourishes—used to dazzle, not explain. This obfuscation was not always malicious, but its effect was the same: retail investors placed real capital into speculative ventures with little or no grasp of what they were buying. The ICO boom did not just expose a lack of oversight—it revealed a widespread illusion of understanding.

At the heart of this mania was a peculiar form of faith: that technology alone could override centuries of institutional knowledge about finance, governance, and law. The mantra of "trust the code" displaced hard questions about accountability. Token distribution was often skewed heavily toward insiders, creating perverse incentives. Founders could raise millions before writing a single line of code. And once tokens were liquid—often via decentralised exchanges—there was no incentive to build anything of value. The ICO model made it possible to extract value *before* creating it. That inversion remains one of the most corrosive legacies of the bubble.

However, the post-ICO reckoning also seeded a more mature ecosystem. The failures of 2017–2018 led to the rise of alternatives like Initial Exchange Offerings (IEOs), Security Token Offerings (STOs), and later, more structured forms of decentralised fundraising such as launchpads and IDOs (Initial DEX Offerings). While many of these inherited similar problems, they also experimented with mechanisms to reduce fraud: KYC requirements, vesting schedules, and third-party audits. More importantly, they rekindled an essential question: how can capital formation be democratised without descending into chaos? The ICO boom was a test case—and a cautionary tale—for that inquiry.

The lessons of the ICO era remain relevant today. Speculative manias are not unique to crypto. From the South Sea Bubble to the dot-com crash, financial history is a cemetery of collective delusions. What makes ICOs distinct is the speed, scale, and accessibility with which they unfolded. A high-school student in Ohio could send Ether to a smart contract operated by pseudonymous founders in Singapore, based on a white paper written in broken English—and do so in under five minutes. That level of frictionless exposure is both revolutionary and dangerous. It is the financial equivalent of removing every guardrail from a highway and assuming drivers will self-regulate.

Ultimately, the ICO boom was not just a bubble in asset prices—it was a bubble in *belief*. Belief that decentralisation was inherently good. Belief that code could replace governance. Belief that early participation guaranteed later rewards. These beliefs were not always wrong, but they were almost always underexamined. In that sense, the ICO frenzy was less about technology than about psychology. It was an experiment in collective financial storytelling—a grand, decentralised narrative about the future of money, acted out on an unregulated stage.

Its aftermath leaves us with two enduring imperatives: first, to design systems that reward value creation over speculation; and second, to ensure that the next wave of innovation does not mistake exuberance for legitimacy. The ICO era may have closed, but the questions it raised remain unresolved—and perhaps more urgent than ever.

## Ponzi Schemes in Digital Clothing:

The promise of financial autonomy offered by cryptocurrency has a dark twin: the persistent rise of decentralised Ponzi schemes disguised as innovation. These schemes do not merely replicate the frauds of the past; they modernise them. With flashy user interfaces, pseudonymous teams, algorithmic wrappers, and marketing jargon steeped in the language of disruption, digital Ponzi schemes embed themselves into the very infrastructure of crypto ecosystems—leveraging blockchain transparency as a cover for deeply opaque financial logic. Their emergence is not an aberration; it is a structural vulnerability born of unchecked speculation, technological opacity, and human credulity.

At the heart of any Ponzi scheme lies a simple mechanism: old investors are paid with the money from new investors. There is no genuine profit generation—only the illusion of yield, sustained by constant inflows. Traditionally, such schemes have relied on interpersonal trust or charismatic leadership. In the crypto world, that trust is increasingly offloaded onto code, smart contracts, and decentralised applications. This shift creates a psychological sleight of hand: if the payout is governed by software, and not by a person, it *feels* less fraudulent. Yet the underlying mechanics remain unchanged—fragile, extractive, and ultimately destined to collapse.

Consider the case of BitConnect, one of the most infamous examples of a crypto-era Ponzi. Launched in 2016, it promised guaranteed daily returns through a "trading bot" that supposedly leveraged volatility for profit. Users would lock up their Bitcoin and receive BitConnect tokens in return. The longer they locked in, the higher their returns. It operated like clockwork—until it didn't. When regulators in the U.S. and UK issued warnings, confidence evaporated, the price collapsed, and the exit door slammed shut. At its peak, BitConnect had amassed billions in market capitalisation; its sudden implosion left a trail of financial wreckage and set a precedent for how deceptive such schemes could become under a veneer of digital sophistication.

The same playbook was seen, with subtle variations, in the case of PlusToken—a Chinese-origin scheme that lured users with a wallet application offering high yields. Its operators allegedly stole more than $2 billion in user funds. The scheme unravelled only after arrests were made and on-chain analysis revealed how the stolen funds were being laundered through mixers and decentralised exchanges. PlusToken didn't just represent individual fraud; it became a systemic risk, influencing Bitcoin price movements as large quantities of illicit assets were moved through the network.

These examples illustrate a critical dynamic: *the decentralised nature of blockchain does not eliminate Ponzi dynamics; it automates and amplifies them.* Where once fraudsters needed to cultivate personal trust, today they launch smart contracts. Where once exit scams required secrecy, today they are celebrated in Telegram groups, only to vanish weeks later. The proliferation of DeFi (Decentralised Finance) platforms has accelerated this trend. Many so-called "yield farming" or "staking" protocols function as quasi-Ponzi mechanisms, offering unsustainable APYs (Annual Percentage Yields) with no underlying revenue model. As long as token prices rise and new capital enters, returns seem real. But when inflows slow, liquidity dries up, and the protocol implodes—leaving late participants with nothing but worthless tokens and a hard lesson in financial physics.

The problem is not solely technological. It is deeply psychological. Humans are hardwired for optimism and pattern recognition. When early adopters profit handsomely, others rush to follow, believing they have decoded a hidden system. Greed overrides caution. Community becomes cult. Discord servers are flooded with memes, token price speculation, and moral justifications for why "this time is different." Ponzi schemes thrive in these conditions not just because they are technically viable, but because they are socially contagious. Crypto, in its speculative form, has become an accelerant for this contagion.

Some defenders argue that users willingly participate in these schemes and should bear responsibility for their decisions. "Do your own research" has become a cultural mantra within crypto circles—a warning and a disclaimer rolled into one. But this ethos overlooks a fundamental asymmetry: the informational and cognitive gaps between project creators and retail participants. Most users are not software engineers, financial analysts, or game theorists. They cannot audit smart contracts, decode tokenomics, or spot subtle indicators of Ponzi dynamics. Instead, they rely on social signals—Twitter influencers, Reddit upvotes, community size—many of which are easily manipulated or entirely synthetic.

This points to a deeper philosophical tension: *is trustlessness a sufficient substitute for trustworthiness?* In the case of digital Ponzi schemes, the answer is clearly no. The ability to deploy a smart contract that governs fund flows without human intervention is not the same as creating a fair, sustainable, or ethical financial system. Code can execute logic, but it cannot guarantee legitimacy. It has no conscience, no empathy, no ability to say: "this is exploitative." Without social norms, oversight, or incentives for honest behaviour, trustlessness becomes a façade—one that malicious actors are increasingly adept at exploiting.

The emergence of "Ponzinomics"—a term now used semi-ironically to describe the token distribution and incentive structures of many crypto projects—further blurs the line between innovation and grift. Projects often launch with tokenomics designed to benefit early adopters disproportionately, rewarding those who stake early or refer others. These systems mimic network effects but are functionally indistinct from pyramid schemes. The token price rises not because of product-market fit, but because of scarcity-driven speculation. The moment the music stops, latecomers are left holding the bag. The damage is not merely financial—it erodes public trust in the legitimacy of decentralised finance itself.

Attempts at self-regulation have emerged, but they remain fragmented. Token audits, KYC onboarding, decentralised reputation systems, and even rating platforms like DeFi Safety or RugDoc aim to reduce risk. But none have solved the core problem: the low cost and high speed at which new Ponzi schemes can be created, marketed, and scaled. The architecture of Web3 enables rapid experimentation, but it also enables rapid exploitation. Until there are systemic disincentives for predatory behaviour—or mechanisms for collective redress—the cycle will repeat. The tools of decentralisation cannot be neutral if their dominant use-case is extraction.

At a policy level, regulators face a dilemma. Heavy-handed enforcement risks stifling legitimate innovation. But passive observation allows harm to metastasise. Some jurisdictions have begun targeting individuals involved in fraudulent DeFi launches, but enforcement lags behind the technology. Others have focused on regulating centralised on-ramps—exchanges and stablecoins—but these actions only partly address the decentralised core where many of these schemes are incubated. The challenge lies in *designing legal frameworks that are proportionate, technologically informed, and globally coordinated.* Anything less simply incentivises fraudsters to relocate, rebrand, and relaunch.

The persistence of Ponzi schemes in crypto is not merely a cautionary footnote—it is a mirror. It reflects back the vulnerabilities of human psychology, the design flaws of permissionless systems, and the inadequacy of both community norms and regulatory frameworks. If decentralisation is to fulfil its promise of a fairer, more transparent financial future, it must reckon with the ways in which its very affordances can be weaponised against the vulnerable. Transparency alone is not enough. Community is not a substitute for accountability. And trustlessness, while elegant in theory, cannot compensate for a vacuum of moral responsibility.

There is nothing inherently Ponzi-like about crypto. But there is something deeply human about our susceptibility to illusions of easy wealth, particularly when wrapped in the language of progress. The task ahead is not to abandon decentralised finance, but to ensure it is built on foundations that reward long-term value over short-term hype. That means aligning incentives, elevating real use cases, enforcing ethical standards, and confronting—without euphemism or evasion—the parasitic schemes that continue to masquerade as innovation.

Until then, the line between breakthrough and betrayal will remain dangerously thin.

## Moral Hazard and the Lawless Frontier

The libertarian dream at the heart of cryptocurrency—an economic system unfettered by institutional control—is often framed as a moral good: transparency over bureaucracy, autonomy over surveillance, decentralisation over centralised abuse. But when freedom is defined as the absence of external constraints, a disturbing paradox emerges. *What mechanisms prevent freedom from devolving into lawlessness?* What stops liberation from becoming licence? These questions, once philosophical, now have material consequences. As the crypto ecosystem grows in size, complexity, and influence, its most passionate advocates are being forced to confront what they long resisted: the reality that systems designed to minimise trust in institutions may also minimise protection for individuals.

Moral hazard arises when actors take on excessive risk because they do not bear the full consequences of their actions. In traditional finance, it is typically used to describe situations where bailouts, insurance, or state guarantees remove disincentives to reckless behaviour. But in the decentralised world, the moral hazard takes a more perverse form: *the absence of enforcement itself becomes the incentive.* Projects can launch anonymously, solicit millions in capital, and disappear overnight without consequence. Platforms can engineer unsustainable yield schemes or manipulate tokenomics to enrich insiders while exposing retail investors to asymmetrical downside. If the game has no referee, then only those willing to bend or break the rules will dominate it.

Take the phenomenon of rug pulls—projects that attract capital under the guise of innovation, only to be deliberately abandoned. In 2021 alone, rug pulls accounted for over a third of all crypto-related scam revenue. Many of these schemes used audited smart contracts and polished user interfaces. The manipulation didn't happen in the code; it happened in the incentives, the narrative, and the governance (or lack thereof). The actors weren't hackers—they were founders. And in jurisdictions with no applicable securities laws, no KYC requirements, and limited recourse mechanisms, these exits were not illegal. They were *simply unregulated.*

This is where decentralised systems confront their own mythology. The idea that trustlessness eliminates the need for rules collapses the moment economic self-interest diverges from communal good. Without accountability, power doesn't disappear—it migrates. Often, it concentrates in the hands of those most willing to exploit opacity. The rhetoric of "financial freedom" becomes a cover for financial manipulation. And the insistence that users must "do their own research" becomes a cultural shield for avoiding institutional responsibility. *The lawless frontier, in this form, does not liberate the many—it empowers the few who understand how to extract value from confusion.*

The response from the crypto community is frequently ambivalent. On one hand, there is pride in the speed and openness with which innovation occurs. On the other, there is unease at how easily that same openness can be hijacked by bad actors. This ambivalence often manifests as calls for "self-regulation"—a paradoxical term that implies decentralised systems should somehow police themselves without sacrificing their decentralised essence. In practice, self-regulation has meant whitepapers of dubious origin, code audits that fail to catch social engineering, and governance tokens that promise voice but rarely deliver accountability. *The very tools intended to decentralise control are repurposed to obscure who, if anyone, is actually responsible.*

The 2022 collapse of Terra/Luna offers a textbook case of decentralised moral hazard. Billed as a stablecoin ecosystem backed by algorithmic mechanisms, its growth was fuelled by unsustainable yields through the Anchor protocol. Users flocked to deposit their assets in exchange for what appeared to be safe, high returns. Warnings about systemic fragility were dismissed or drowned out by maximalist narratives and cult-like enthusiasm. When the peg broke, over $60 billion in value was wiped out in days. The ecosystem's defenders claimed no fraud had occurred—only market failure. But to critics, the entire architecture of Terra was a pyramid of financial theatre that relied on user belief, not economic fundamentals. *And when the collapse came, there was no central body to absorb the shock—only victims, forums, and silence.*

Regulatory response to these dynamics has been predictably reactive. In the United States, the Securities and Exchange Commission has pursued enforcement through litigation, often years after harm has occurred. In Europe, the MiCA framework aims to establish pre-emptive guidelines, particularly for stablecoins and asset-backed tokens. But these initiatives face a double-bind: regulate too early and risk stifling the industry's potential; regulate too late and inherit a landscape littered with fraud and disillusionment. Moreover, *jurisdictional arbitrage remains the default escape hatch for projects unwilling to engage with any form of oversight.* Launch in one country, register in another, deploy code globally, and operate anonymously. Enforcement mechanisms rooted in nation-states struggle to map onto systems that are borderless by design.

Yet the question is no longer whether regulation will arrive—it is what form it will take, and who will shape it. Will governments impose top-down controls that replicate the very centralised systems crypto was meant to escape? Or will the crypto community participate in constructing frameworks that preserve decentralisation while protecting against abuse? These are not technical questions—they are political, ethical, and philosophical. And they require more than whitepapers. They demand consensus, compromise, and moral clarity.

Critics of regulation often invoke the risks of state overreach: censorship, surveillance, and financial exclusion. These are not hypothetical threats. Around the world, centralised institutions have a well-documented history of using control over money to suppress dissent, limit civil liberties, and reinforce existing power structures. But *resisting centralisation cannot mean tolerating predation.* There is no moral high ground in a system that celebrates sovereignty while enabling theft, obfuscation, and harm to the unsuspecting.

What is needed, then, is a redefinition of freedom—one that understands freedom not as the absence of constraints, but as *the presence of safeguards that enable meaningful agency.* In a truly free system, users must not only have the right to participate but also the right not to be exploited. That means designing protocols with built-in guardrails, disclosure requirements, and redress mechanisms. It means recognising that "code is law" is insufficient if the law rewards malice and punishes ignorance. And it means understanding that *freedom without responsibility is not innovation—it is negligence.*

There are promising signs. Decentralised identity systems, zero-knowledge proofs, and cryptographic attestations offer new ways to balance privacy with accountability. DAOs exploring reputational staking and incentive alignment are experimenting with governance mechanisms that resist capture and manipulation. Some protocols have begun integrating community insurance funds or social recovery mechanisms, recognising that no system is ever truly immune from failure or bad actors. These are not panaceas—but they are steps toward a future in which decentralisation and safety are not in conflict.

Ultimately, the lawless frontier is not a destination—it is a phase. A necessary period of creative chaos in which the boundaries of possibility are tested, stretched, and often broken. But it cannot last forever. *A system that cannot protect its participants cannot scale. A system that celebrates its freedom but disavows its consequences cannot endure.* The question is not whether regulation will kill crypto. It is whether crypto can evolve fast enough to avoid killing itself.

To build durable trust, crypto must move beyond the adolescent thrill of defiance and toward the mature task of governance. That means rejecting the false dichotomy between total freedom and total control. It means embracing complexity, ambiguity, and the hard work of accountability. And it means recognising that *the true test of any decentralised system is not how well it avoids regulation, but how well it sustains fairness when no one is watching.*

# Chapter 7
# Regulation: The Paradox of Control

If cryptocurrency was conceived as an act of defiance, regulation represents its long-foreseen reckoning. From the earliest days, Bitcoin and its progeny cast themselves in opposition to state-sanctioned systems: central banks, financial surveillance, legal tender laws, and intermediated trust. Their ideological foundation rested on cryptographic autonomy—a vision in which mathematics enforces rules more reliably than courts, and code supplants bureaucracy. Yet as crypto matured from a fringe experiment to a multi-trillion-dollar infrastructure, the question evolved: not if governments would intervene, but how—and with what ramifications. Regulation is no longer a hypothetical threat whispered among cypherpunks; it is a structural force, asserting itself through sanctions, statutes, licensing regimes, and surveillance mandates. Its hand is already shaping the trajectory of digital assets.

And yet, for all its inevitability, regulation in this domain is riddled with contradiction. Governments seek to harness innovation without relinquishing control. They demand transparency for law enforcement, yet expect privacy for citizens. Compliance is required, but universal rules remain elusive. The outcome is a fractured global patchwork: China enforces outright bans, India oscillates between taxation schemes, the European Union experiments cautiously under MiCA, while the United States pursues a dual-track approach of regulation-by-enforcement and persistent uncertainty. In this ambiguity, a paradox emerges: regulating decentralised systems can inadvertently centralise power in unforeseen—and potentially hazardous—ways.

At its most constructive, regulation clarifies expectations, mitigates systemic risk, and shields consumers from fraud. At its most corrosive, it becomes a tool wielded by incumbents to stifle competition under the guise of public interest. The challenge is not merely how to regulate crypto, but how to prevent the regulatory apparatus itself from being co-opted by those it was meant to constrain. Nowhere is this tension more evident than in the arena of Know-Your-Customer (KYC) and Anti-Money Laundering (AML) mandates—legal instruments intended to curb illicit flows yet routinely encroaching on privacy and financial autonomy. As decentralised finance grows, states confront a fundamental dilemma: can civil liberties coexist with total traceability?

Consider the FATF "Travel Rule," which obliges Virtual Asset Service Providers to share customer information for transfers exceeding defined thresholds. Ostensibly framed as a crime-prevention measure, it presumes that all users are potential suspects until proven otherwise. Surveillance becomes not merely a policing tool, but a precondition for participation. For privacy-conscious users—and for populations living under regimes with histories of authoritarian overreach—this is far from neutral. It is, in effect, a political provocation cloaked in bureaucratic language.

Regulatory capture compounds these distortions. When dominant centralised exchanges, custodians, or financial conglomerates lobby for compliance measures that only they can afford, decentralisation is undermined—not through censorship, but through exclusion. Complexity becomes a gatekeeper; capital requirements a filter. The result is not a pluralistic ecosystem, but a tightly regulated oligopoly masquerading as innovation. In such a climate, the question is no longer whether crypto will be regulated, but whether regulation will preserve diversity or manufacture dependency.

The 2017 ICO boom provides a cautionary tale of the opposite extreme: absent meaningful oversight, scams flourished, accountability evaporated, and speculation overshadowed substance. Yet the pendulum swing toward strict compliance risks the reverse error: crafting an environment in which only the most capitalised, risk-averse, and institutionally aligned actors can participate. Instead of fostering an open marketplace of ideas, regulation could ossify the space into a credentialed, permissioned landscape.

Despite these challenges, there are glimmers of regulatory maturity. The EU's MiCA framework, while imperfect, seeks legal clarity without imposing ideological uniformity. Singapore, Switzerland, and the UAE have developed sandbox models that permit experimentation within defined boundaries. Even in the U.S., aggressive enforcement is beginning to give way to legislative efforts providing certainty on matters such as token classification and stablecoin issuance. These initiatives suggest a possible middle path: one that respects innovation while protecting participants and constraining systemic risk without smothering progress.

This chapter explores these tensions in depth. It begins with *The State Strikes Back*, examining how global regulatory regimes—from authoritarian crackdowns to permissive sandboxing—are shaping the geography of crypto development, both in intended and unintended ways. We then turn to *KYC, AML, and The Surveillance Dilemma*, unpacking the collision of privacy, freedom, and compliance within crypto architecture, analysing trade-offs without resorting to ideological extremes.

*The Danger of Regulatory Capture* follows, dissecting how financial incumbents—banks, exchanges, and conglomerates—leverage regulatory design to entrench advantage under the guise of consumer protection. Finally, *Creative Compliance* charts promising avenues forward: legal frameworks, technical innovations, and institutional experiments that may reconcile decentralised autonomy with public accountability.

At its heart, this discussion is about more than law. It is about power, legitimacy, and the shape of the future. As crypto evolves from insurgency to infrastructure, its survival depends not merely on scalability, but on the wisdom with which it negotiates the forces of control. The debate is no longer whether regulation is inherently good or bad—it is which regulation, by whom, and to what end. By the close of this chapter, the reader will be equipped to engage with the regulatory dilemmas that will define the coming decade of digital finance.

Crypto promised to disintermediate power. Regulation promises to tame it. What emerges from their collision may not be compromise—it may be transformation. And it is that transformation which demands our most careful, critical, and clear-eyed attention.

## "The State Strikes Back"

The idea that decentralised technologies could render governments irrelevant was always more fantasy than forecast. Yet in the early years of cryptocurrency, many adherents acted as if sovereignty could be outpaced by software. Bitcoin's emergence in 2009 was framed as a direct affront to central banking. Ethereum's smart contracts promised to automate agreements beyond the reach of courts. Peer-to-peer exchanges allowed capital to flow across borders with minimal friction. For a brief moment, it seemed possible that cryptographic tools could outmanoeuvre traditional power—*not through protest, but through protocol.* But power adapts. And as crypto crossed from obscurity into the financial mainstream, states began to respond—not merely by resisting decentralisation, but by reasserting control through a mixture of bans, regulation, co-optation, and selective legitimisation.

The state's re-engagement with monetary sovereignty is not uniform. It is multiform, pragmatic, and deeply tied to each jurisdiction's political temperament, economic strategy, and institutional maturity. In China, the response was swift and unilateral: outlawing cryptocurrency mining, banning exchanges, and launching a tightly controlled central bank digital currency (CBDC) to reinforce the supremacy of the yuan. In El Salvador, by contrast, the government went all-in, adopting Bitcoin as legal tender in a high-risk bid to attract investment and remittance flows. The contrast between these two extremes reveals the spectrum of state reactions—not as binary choices between embrace or rejection, but as calibrated efforts to reshape crypto's impact to align with national interest.

Many Western democracies have opted for a slower, more technocratic approach. The European Union has enacted the Markets in Crypto-Assets (MiCA) regulation—a sweeping legal framework that seeks to balance consumer protection, financial stability, and innovation. It is an ambitious effort to codify the rules of a still-evolving sector, and while its intentions are broadly constructive, the unintended effects may include chilling innovation among smaller developers who lack the legal and financial resources to comply. In the United States, regulatory clarity has been elusive. Agencies like the SEC and CFTC have engaged in overlapping enforcement actions, often treating tokens as securities retroactively and without a legislative mandate. This *regulation-by-lawsuit* has created an environment of uncertainty, where good-faith actors are penalised while fraudulent schemes slip through gaps in oversight.

Unintended consequences are not side effects—they are structural features of regulatory misalignment. When India imposed a harsh tax regime on crypto transactions, including a 30% flat tax on gains and a 1% tax deducted at source (TDS) on all trades, legitimate trading volumes collapsed by over 90% on domestic platforms. But the activity didn't disappear—it migrated to offshore exchanges and peer-to-peer channels, undermining the very transparency the state purported to seek. Similarly, China's mining ban in 2021 briefly destabilised Bitcoin's hash rate, but miners simply relocated to jurisdictions like Kazakhstan, Texas, and Russia—many of which offer less environmental oversight. The result was not elimination of the activity, but displacement—and with it, the loss of strategic influence over the network.

In authoritarian regimes, crypto is often perceived as both a threat to capital controls and a tool for surveillance evasion. Iran and North Korea have embraced crypto selectively as a mechanism for sanctions resistance, while simultaneously suppressing local access for ordinary citizens. Russia, too, has oscillated between banning and regulating, depending on whether the use case serves state power or undermines it. *This duality—crypto as both instrument of liberation and instrument of evasion—complicates regulatory narratives globally.* Western nations worry about illicit finance. Authoritarians worry about political dissent. Each seeks control, but their anxieties are asymmetrical.

Central Bank Digital Currencies are perhaps the clearest manifestation of the state's counteroffensive. Unlike cryptocurrencies, CBDCs are centrally issued, permissioned, and programmable. They offer efficiency, traceability, and monetary policy tools—but also raise acute civil liberties concerns. A programmable digital currency can impose spending limits, enforce negative interest rates, or revoke balances. In China, the e-CNY has already demonstrated the potential for granular surveillance. In liberal democracies, CBDCs are often justified as modern infrastructure. Yet the question remains: *will they empower citizens, or merely digitise control?*

The irony is sharp. Crypto was designed to decentralise trust. The state, in response, is re-centralising trust—this time in digital form. But even among regulators who accept crypto's inevitability, there is a tendency to conflate regulation with containment. Many officials assume that innovation can be safely domesticated through licensing regimes, know-your-customer protocols, and capital requirements. Yet these same policies often push innovation into grey markets or private channels. Telegram-based token sales, DAO-governed protocols, and zero-knowledge privacy layers are already evading conventional oversight. The more the state tries to fit decentralised technologies into centralised frameworks, the more brittle its authority may become.

This is not to suggest that regulation is inherently misguided. Some of the most devastating failures in crypto—from the collapse of FTX to the algorithmic unraveling of Terra/Luna—were preventable with baseline disclosures, audit requirements, and conflict-of-interest policies. But regulating crypto effectively requires more than applying legacy financial rules to novel systems. It demands a deep understanding of how decentralised protocols work, how their incentives scale, and how enforcement mechanisms must adapt. A regulator who cannot read a smart contract or follow a multisig transaction is ill-equipped to police a decentralised exchange.

Moreover, there is a geopolitical dimension at play. As nations craft crypto regulations, they are also shaping the future distribution of financial power. Countries that adopt clear, innovation-friendly frameworks—such as Singapore, Switzerland, or the UAE—are attracting talent and capital at scale. Conversely, jurisdictions that default to hostility risk self-marginalisation. The United States, despite its historical edge in tech and finance, is now facing an exodus of crypto founders and projects. If it continues to regulate through ambiguity, it may find itself regulating industries that no longer exist within its borders.

And then there is the cultural layer. Regulation is not just policy—it is a signal of intent. When regulators treat all crypto activity as suspect, they alienate the very communities they seek to protect. Conversely, when they engage developers, cryptographers, and decentralised communities as stakeholders rather than adversaries, they foster collaborative norms. The difference is not trivial. Trust in institutions is eroding globally. How the state chooses to regulate crypto may determine whether that trust is salvaged or further fractured.

What is needed, ultimately, is a paradigm shift—from regulation as containment to regulation as *contextual alignment.* This means recognising the diversity of crypto systems: privacy coins versus stablecoins, decentralised exchanges versus tokenised securities, DAOs versus foundations. It means building regulatory capacity that is technically fluent, procedurally transparent, and globally coordinated. And it means acknowledging that some aspects of decentralisation—such as censorship resistance or pseudonymity—are not bugs to be removed, but features to be negotiated.

The state has returned to the crypto table, but its playbook is still being written. Whether it chooses coercion, collaboration, or co-optation will shape not only the trajectory of digital finance, but the deeper question of who controls the levers of modern economic life. Crypto tested the boundaries of sovereignty. Now sovereignty is testing crypto. The outcome will not be decided in ideology alone—but in legislation, code, and the complex, evolving interaction between them.

## "KYC, AML, and The Surveillance Dilemma"

Few acronyms in the financial world evoke more friction in crypto circles than KYC (Know Your Customer) and AML (Anti-Money Laundering). On the surface, both are essential pillars of modern financial regulation—tools designed to combat terrorism financing, organised crime, and illicit flows that destabilise markets and states alike. Yet their application in the context of decentralised technologies reveals a fundamental and unresolved tension: how can we reconcile the need for public safety with the right to privacy, autonomy, and pseudonymity? It is not merely a legal debate, nor a philosophical abstraction. This is the frontline of a global clash between sovereign enforcement and personal liberty, and the consequences of how this tension is resolved will reverberate far beyond crypto.

The anti-money laundering regime that governs the global financial system is built on intermediation. Banks and financial institutions are deputised as frontline regulators, required to verify identities, monitor transactions, file suspicious activity reports, and restrict access when red flags are triggered. In traditional finance, this logic works because the structure is inherently centralised. But decentralised protocols—by design—lack these gatekeepers. A smart contract does not perform due diligence. A Bitcoin node does not ask for your passport. The very features that make these systems resilient, permissionless, and borderless are the same ones that render conventional AML compliance structurally incompatible.

Regulators have responded by extending KYC/AML obligations to centralised touchpoints within the crypto ecosystem: exchanges, stablecoin issuers, custodial wallet providers. In many cases, these firms now mirror the obligations of traditional financial institutions—collecting personal data, storing identity documents, and monitoring behaviour. But the effectiveness of this strategy is deeply questionable. First, because the truly decentralised tools—the ones that allow direct peer-to-peer transactions—exist entirely outside this perimeter. Second, because enforcing such rules at scale often requires surveillance mechanisms that conflict directly with constitutional and human rights.

Take the FATF (Financial Action Task Force) and its now-infamous "Travel Rule," which mandates that virtual asset service providers share personal information on both the sender and receiver of a crypto transaction above a certain threshold. Implementing this rule requires rearchitecting wallet infrastructure, expanding data sharing networks, and normalising surveillance as a prerequisite for participation. In effect, it criminalises privacy-by-default systems, even when used lawfully. The result is a creeping normalisation of mass surveillance—not because governments are malicious, but because the regulatory tools they rely on are blunt, dated, and ill-fitted to the technologies they seek to govern.

The deeper issue is epistemic. Regulators often assume that identity is the key to accountability. But in the crypto context, identity is not the same as behaviour. A pseudonymous address can be statistically profiled, risk-scored, and flagged for suspicious patterns without ever needing to reveal the user's name. Chainalysis, Elliptic, and other blockchain forensics firms already provide such tools to law enforcement and exchanges. *What's being tested now is whether the state will accept behavioural analytics as sufficient, or whether it will insist on real-world identity as a prerequisite for legitimacy.*

Privacy advocates are right to be alarmed. The sweeping expansion of KYC and AML obligations, when combined with machine learning, biometrics, and global data-sharing agreements, risks turning financial infrastructure into an apparatus of real-time surveillance. In many countries, financial blacklisting already functions as a form of pre-emptive punishment. Citizens can be excluded from banking, payments, or employment for reasons that are opaque, unchallengeable, and automated. Crypto was supposed to be a hedge against this form of control. If it is reabsorbed into the same frameworks without adaptation, its emancipatory potential may vanish.

Yet there are no easy answers. The volume of illicit activity that flows through cryptocurrency networks—while proportionally small relative to global finance—is not negligible. Ransomware gangs demand payment in Bitcoin. North Korean hacking groups launder millions through decentralised protocols. Fraudulent investment schemes routinely use crypto to dupe unsophisticated investors. Pretending this does not exist would be naïve. But overstating it, or using it to justify mass surveillance, is equally dangerous. The challenge is to separate genuine risks from moral panic—and to develop regulatory frameworks that are both targeted and technologically literate.

This is where the surveillance dilemma becomes most acute. In seeking to prevent harm, we risk eroding the very freedoms we claim to protect. The right to transact without pre-authorisation. The right to hold value without disclosing your identity. These are not trivial preferences. They are core components of financial agency—especially for dissidents, whistleblowers, refugees, and those living under authoritarian regimes. To demand full transparency in all contexts is to deny the legitimacy of dissent, asymmetry, and protective anonymity.

Some jurisdictions are beginning to explore more nuanced approaches. Switzerland and the Netherlands have experimented with tiered KYC thresholds, where low-volume users face lighter obligations. Hong Kong and Singapore have created regulatory sandboxes to test compliance tools without stifling innovation. Privacy-preserving analytics, such as zero-knowledge proofs, offer the promise of verification without exposure. And new models of selective disclosure—where users can prove eligibility without revealing identity—are gaining traction in both DeFi and traditional finance.

Still, the global system remains skewed toward maximal compliance. The burden of proof rests with the individual, not the state. Once collected, personal data is rarely deleted, often repurposed, and frequently breached. The very institutions tasked with protecting citizens from financial abuse often engage in data practices that are opaque, insecure, or commercially motivated. This is the regulatory paradox: the frameworks meant to ensure trust are themselves increasingly untrustworthy.

It is also worth noting the asymmetry of enforcement. KYC and AML regulations disproportionately impact individuals and small projects, while institutional actors often evade scrutiny through lobbying, jurisdictional arbitrage, or regulatory capture. Large exchanges negotiate with regulators behind closed doors. Venture-backed protocols receive informal exemptions. Meanwhile, open-source developers face threats of prosecution for merely publishing code. The balance of power is tilted—not just against privacy, but against equity.

The way forward lies not in abolishing oversight, but in reinventing it. *Accountability should not require surveillance. Compliance should not demand centralisation.* What we need is a regulatory philosophy grounded in proportionality, transparency, and technological realism. This means designing systems where anonymity and compliance can coexist. Where enforcement focuses on outcomes, not optics. And where the rights of the individual are not sacrificed on the altar of collective fear.

Ultimately, the surveillance dilemma is not a crypto problem—it is a societal one. As financial infrastructure becomes increasingly digital, the question of who gets to watch, record, and control that infrastructure becomes existential. Crypto simply accelerates this reckoning. It forces us to confront what kind of financial future we want: one governed by openness and autonomy, or one defined by monitoring and control. We cannot defer this question indefinitely. The code is being written now—and with it, the contours of our economic freedom.

## "The Danger of Regulatory Capture"

Regulation is often sold to the public as a safeguard: a framework designed to protect consumers, ensure market integrity, and prevent systemic abuse. At its best, this is exactly what regulation does. But at its worst—when shaped by those it is meant to oversee—it becomes an instrument of entrenchment, exclusion, and quiet cartelisation. Nowhere is this dynamic more perilous than in the cryptocurrency ecosystem, where the asymmetry of power between decentralised innovators and entrenched financial institutions invites a familiar but largely underexamined threat: regulatory capture.

The term itself originated in public choice theory and refers to a situation where regulatory agencies, instead of acting in the public interest, are co-opted to serve the objectives of dominant industry players. In the traditional finance world, this is not merely a theoretical risk. It is a documented reality. From banking to pharmaceuticals to telecommunications, industry incumbents have long leveraged their influence, resources, and revolving-door relationships to write—or more often, rewrite—the rules in their favour. The cryptocurrency sector, despite its ethos of disruption, is not immune to this gravitational pull. If anything, its novelty and complexity make it more vulnerable to manipulation through regulation disguised as legitimacy.

The architecture of regulatory capture is rarely overt. It often begins with a well-intentioned desire to "clarify" the legal status of a new technology. Policymakers, under pressure to respond to a fast-moving space, lean heavily on industry actors for technical education, data, and input. But when the loudest or most resourceful voices in that conversation are legacy financial institutions or centralised crypto firms, the resulting frameworks inevitably reflect their preferences: high compliance costs that deter smaller players, restrictions that favour custodial models over self-custody, and definitions of "safety" that align with existing business models.

Consider the recent wave of licensing regimes introduced across jurisdictions from the European Union's MiCA regulation to New York's BitLicense framework. Superficially, these initiatives aim to bring clarity and oversight to digital assets. In practice, they have created barriers so high that only the best-capitalised firms can afford to comply. Startups either relocate, exit, or restructure to resemble traditional financial service providers—precisely the outcome decentralisation sought to avoid. Meanwhile, incumbents gain not only regulatory blessings but also a moat against competition.

This is not simply about economics; it is about political legitimacy. When regulators publicly endorse a select group of exchanges, custodians, or stablecoin issuers, they confer an implicit seal of trustworthiness. Retail users, starved of clarity, flock to these platforms believing them to be safer. What goes unspoken is that safety is often conflated with surveillance, centralisation, and institutional backing. Smaller, more innovative, or more privacy-focused projects are left in a grey zone—functionally legal, but reputationally tainted.

The mechanisms of capture extend beyond policymaking into enforcement. Major industry players cultivate relationships with regulators, sponsor conferences, hire former officials, and pre-emptively shape narratives through white papers and lobbying campaigns. When enforcement does occur, it is often selective—targeting fringe actors while exempting major violators. The result is a kind of performative regulation: crackdowns that signal activity, without disrupting the core power structures that perpetuate risk.

Take, for example, the case of stablecoins. Tether was long viewed with suspicion for its lack of transparency, yet faced little coordinated enforcement. By contrast, algorithmic stablecoins—despite often being experimental and non-custodial—have been swiftly demonised and restricted. Why? Because they threaten the hegemony of fiat-backed coins issued by firms with close ties to banking infrastructure. *The regulatory response is not dictated by risk alone; it is mediated by political capital and institutional convenience.*

Another vivid case is the treatment of decentralised finance protocols. Platforms like Uniswap, Aave, and Compound operate through code rather than custodianship, and often lack legal entities. Yet they face increasing regulatory scrutiny, not because they are more dangerous, but because they are harder to control. Centralised exchanges, by contrast, are often permitted to function with minimal consumer protection—provided they implement KYC and AML, and maintain channels of cooperation with regulators. The result is a perverse incentive: build something truly decentralised, and you are punished for your autonomy; build something surveillance-compliant, and you are rewarded for your subservience.

This trend is not new. History offers plenty of analogues. The early internet, too, was nearly suffocated by telecom monopolies lobbying for regulatory constraints that would have favoured centralised content distribution. Open-source software was dismissed for years as a security threat, until incumbents realised they could monetise it. The lesson is clear: *incumbents rarely fight innovation directly; they capture the levers of rule-making to shape it in their image.*

The danger here is not that all regulation is bad—far from it. Rather, it is that regulation, when misused, becomes a tool to crush the very decentralisation it claims to legitimise. This is not a hypothetical concern. It is already unfolding in real time. Financial Action Task Force (FATF) guidelines now encourage nation-states to impose obligations that only centralised firms can feasibly meet. The requirement to collect and share personal data on crypto users favours custodians over self-custody, payment processors over peer-to-peer systems, and monitoring over autonomy. None of this has stopped crime. But it has made it harder for grassroots, privacy-respecting projects to survive.

The irony is profound. In a world supposedly celebrating financial innovation, the actual architecture being constructed closely resembles the old system—only with new logos. The core values of permissionlessness, censorship-resistance, and user ownership are being quietly traded for regulatory convenience. *What began as a rebellion against gatekeepers now risks becoming a new regime of intermediated compliance.*

So how should the crypto community respond? Not by rejecting all regulation, but by demanding better regulation—rules that are technologically literate, proportionate, and structurally resistant to capture. That means supporting frameworks that lower entry barriers, protect individual rights, and ensure accountability without mandating centralisation. It means amplifying the voices of open-source developers, civil liberties advocates, and technologists—not just venture capitalists and fintech lobbyists. It means building coalitions that can hold both regulators and incumbents to account.

Ultimately, the threat of regulatory capture is not confined to the crypto industry. It is a systemic vulnerability of any democracy where power is concentrated and oversight is weak. But in crypto, the stakes are uniquely high. This is not merely about who wins market share—it is about whether the architecture of the future will be open or closed, pluralistic or monopolised, free or quietly coerced. The battle for the soul of crypto is not just technical. It is political. And its outcome will determine whether we build systems that serve the public—or systems that pretend to, while serving only themselves.

## Creative Compliance: Finding the Middle Path

The most dangerous idea in regulation is not that we regulate too much or too little—it's that we believe the only options are extremes. In the discourse around cryptocurrency policy, we are often trapped between binary opposites: total control or total anarchy, permissioned systems or ungovernable protocols, state surveillance or unchecked fraud. But as the industry matures and governments begin to understand the technology's nuances, a more sophisticated model is quietly emerging. It is not universally implemented nor fully coherent, but it represents something crucial: an attempt to reconcile the core tension between innovation and oversight, between individual liberty and collective security. This model is what we might call *creative compliance.*

Creative compliance is not regulatory evasion, nor is it blind obedience to frameworks designed for a previous century. It is the act of designing legal, technical, and organisational systems that *adapt intelligently to the intent of regulation*, without compromising the transformative qualities that make decentralised technologies meaningful. It is the strategic application of transparency without surveillance, accountability without coercion, and risk mitigation without fossilising progress.

To understand why such a model is both necessary and possible, we must begin with the failures of existing approaches. The dominant model of financial regulation today is built around a few assumptions: that institutions have physical headquarters, that they serve identifiable customers, that they process transactions through clear intermediaries, and that rules can be enforced through licences and penalties. These assumptions do not hold in the world of decentralised finance (DeFi), permissionless protocols, or pseudonymous communities operating across borders. Smart contracts do not sign legal declarations. DAOs do not file tax forms. Wallet addresses do not fit neatly into Know Your Customer (KYC) boxes. And yet, insisting that they must—or that all crypto must behave like banks—invites either failure of enforcement or the death of innovation.

Consider the case of the Financial Action Task Force's Travel Rule, which requires that personal information be collected and transmitted during digital asset transactions above a certain threshold. For centralised exchanges, this is difficult but feasible. For self-hosted wallets or automated smart contracts, it is technically incoherent. No human is present to verify identity. No counterparty exists to receive the data. To apply the rule blindly would mean criminalising open-source code or banning foundational crypto practices. But to ignore the risks entirely—money laundering, terrorist financing, fraud—would be equally irresponsible.

The emerging solution is not to abandon regulation, but to reformulate it. Jurisdictions like Switzerland, Singapore, and even parts of the European Union are exploring regulatory sandboxes—frameworks that allow crypto projects to operate within defined parameters while regulators observe and learn. These sandboxes offer time-limited licences, reduced reporting burdens, and collaborative feedback loops. They treat developers not as adversaries but as partners. *Such models are valuable not just because they are tolerant, but because they are adaptive.*

Another frontier of creative compliance lies in the field of decentralised identity. Projects like Polygon ID, Worldcoin's proof-of-personhood (however controversial), and the broader ecosystem of zero-knowledge proofs aim to provide attestations about users—citizenship, age, uniqueness, or criminal risk—*without revealing their personal data.* This satisfies the spirit of anti-money laundering (AML) laws—ensuring that bad actors can be excluded—without violating the principle of privacy that crypto communities rightly defend. The use of cryptographic techniques such as zk-SNARKs makes it possible to demonstrate compliance *without disclosure.* It is an inversion of the surveillance paradigm: verification without visibility.

Still, there is no such thing as neutral architecture. Every design decision—what gets stored on-chain, who holds admin keys, how governance is structured—has legal and political consequences. Creative compliance, therefore, must not be reduced to technical fixes alone. It requires a cultural shift: from adversarial posturing to mutual literacy. Developers must understand that regulatory frameworks are often born of real harms, not just bureaucratic whim. Regulators must recognise that technical constraints are not excuses, but hard realities of how decentralised systems function. *Compliance is not a checkbox; it is a dialogue.*

Nowhere is this more evident than in the rise of regulatory DAOs—organisations that attempt to self-regulate in anticipation of external oversight. For instance, the MakerDAO ecosystem has debated internal mechanisms for risk disclosure, audit, and creditworthiness assessment, long before regulators have stepped in. Other projects are experimenting with built-in kill switches, community-driven sanctions, or smart contract parameters that adapt to geopolitical circumstances. These are imperfect and often controversial, but they point toward a future where *regulation is encoded not imposed.* The protocol becomes a policy tool—not just a product.

That said, creative compliance cannot be allowed to become mere rebranding. Some institutions use the language of innovation to cloak old centralised habits. A crypto bank that collects user data, freezes accounts arbitrarily, and lobbies for restrictive laws that benefit only itself is not practicing creative compliance—it is practicing rent-seeking under the flag of progress. The litmus test for true creativity in compliance is whether the solution *preserves decentralisation* while mitigating risk—not whether it makes regulators comfortable at the cost of public empowerment.

Indeed, the challenge is not only institutional but philosophical. What does it mean to protect users? Is it to limit their options, or to give them tools to make informed choices? Should financial freedom be curtailed because some people misuse it? These are not rhetorical questions. They shape how we design law, technology, and markets. *To protect without infantilising, to regulate without suppressing—this is the paradox we must solve.*

Progress is underway. In the United Kingdom, the Financial Conduct Authority (FCA) has shifted from a posture of blanket suspicion to one of conditional approval—working with innovators to build safe experimentation environments. In the United States, although federal agencies remain fragmented, states like Wyoming and initiatives like the Crypto Council for Innovation have laid groundwork for rules that respect autonomy. And in emerging markets—where crypto adoption is often highest due to real systemic failures—local governments are showing a willingness to develop novel hybrid frameworks, not just import Western templates.

Still, this is a moving target. Regulatory regimes that work today may falter tomorrow as technology evolves. Tools like decentralised exchanges, privacy coins, and algorithmic governance stretch the limits of existing categories. What is a custodian when no entity holds the funds? What is a broker when trades occur via peer-to-peer relayers? What is jurisdiction when code runs globally? These are not esoteric legal puzzles—they are live operational questions, with direct implications for how billions will interact with finance in the coming decades.

Thus, creative compliance must remain iterative. It must be open to revision. It must embrace the experimental spirit of the technology it seeks to govern. But it must also be grounded in principle: *protect the user, honour transparency, ensure accountability, and never allow regulation to become a tool for exclusion.* Done well, compliance can become an ally to innovation—not its antagonist.

This is not a compromise. It is a maturation. Crypto, in its rebellious adolescence, often saw regulation as a threat. But adulthood demands nuance. The path forward is not maximalism, nor submission—it is design. And like all good design, it must work for those who use it, not just those who write it.

# Chapter 8
# Crypto and the New Geopolitics

Power is rarely fixed; it courses through the structures we construct—legal frameworks, capital markets, and technological infrastructures—and when those channels are disrupted, influence shifts accordingly. Cryptocurrency has moved beyond the realm of experimental finance. What began as a cypherpunk critique of central banking has now become a matter for treasury departments, national security councils, and global monetary institutions alike. Discussing the future of geopolitics today inevitably involves digital assets and the seismic ripples they have set in motion.

Cryptocurrency does more than challenge the existing financial order; it rewrites it. It offers alternative mechanisms of monetary coordination, stretches the reach of fiscal oversight, and recasts the relationship between citizens and the state. In this chapter, we explore how technologies such as stablecoins, Bitcoin, and central bank digital currencies (CBDCs) have themselves become geopolitical actors. They are far from neutral tools; embedded within them are strategies of dominance, evasion, and influence.

Stablecoins exemplify this phenomenon. Superficially simple—tokens pegged to fiat, usually the US dollar—they conceal a profound geopolitical weight. USDC, Tether, and others act as dollar proxies outside traditional banking rails, crossing borders and circumventing the jurisdictional constraints that govern conventional finance. In nations facing sanctions, capital controls, or banking crises, these tokens extend the reach of the dollar while remaining beyond the direct command of the Federal Reserve. The paradox is clear: the U.S. benefits from the dollar's digital spread yet cedes granular control. Stablecoin issuers are not central banks; their reserves are opaque, governance is private, and operations politically neutral. The dollar globalises, but oversight fragments.

Bitcoin presents a different strategic challenge. Unlike stablecoins, it exists independent of state currency. Increasingly, nations view it not merely as speculative, but as a potential strategic reserve. El Salvador's adoption in 2021 was initially seen as eccentric, yet it has prompted a wider question: could borderless, algorithmically finite assets serve as reserve instruments? For countries facing high inflation, dollar dependency, or sanctions, Bitcoin offers advantages beyond gold: instantaneous transfer, censorship resistance, and programmable liquidity. Iran and North Korea have reportedly mined Bitcoin to evade sanctions; Russia has explored it for cross-border settlements under restrictions; even China, despite banning retail trading, studies blockchain's impact on capital flows. In each case, Bitcoin is leveraged pragmatically, valued for being beyond unilateral control—a new form of power in a world where finance itself is weaponised.

States respond with CBDCs: digital fiat issued directly by central banks. Unlike decentralised cryptocurrencies, these are programmable, traceable, and tightly aligned with policy objectives. China's digital yuan illustrates the potential—real-time surveillance, expiration on stimulus, usage restrictions. Unlike Bitcoin, it embodies centralised precision rather than algorithmic autonomy. Western experiments—Europe's digital euro and the U.S.'s Project Hamilton—signal caution, balancing technological innovation against privacy and institutional relevance. The message is clear: if the rails of value transfer become dominated by stablecoins or DeFi, central banks risk losing practical authority. CBDCs are less about innovation than preservation of institutional influence.

The result is a new contest over monetary architecture. Control over money now has multiple contenders: governments, corporations, protocols, and individual users. Sovereignty is no longer tied strictly to geography; it hinges on custody, consensus, and code. Multinational stablecoin issuers operate globally, maintain enormous reserves, and influence fragile economies without democratic accountability. DeFi protocols facilitate liquidity and credit, often dominated by pseudonymous whales. Power diffuses, but not necessarily equitably. Individuals, meanwhile, can now custody assets, transact globally, and participate without intermediaries—a profound shift in agency. Yet with empowerment comes responsibility. Self-custody entails self-accountability; there are no bailouts, reversals, or intermediaries to mitigate loss.

This raises a fundamental question: is decentralisation inherently liberating, or merely a redistribution of responsibility to those least prepared? States argue for stability and consumer protection; crypto advocates argue that institutional trust has eroded too far. The answer, as ever, is somewhere in between, yet the tension is shaping geopolitical alignments.

The EU, U.S., and China offer contrasting playbooks. The EU encourages innovation within strict regulatory perimeters; the U.S. operates a fragmented, multi-agency landscape; China enforces full-spectrum control with rapid technological deployment. International institutions like the IMF and World Bank scramble to provide guidance, fearing a fragmented global financial system. Divergent national approaches may lead to a splintering of money itself—across legal, ideological, and technical boundaries.

This chapter unpacks these dynamics. It examines stablecoins as instruments of soft power, Bitcoin as a potential reserve for excluded nations, CBDCs as both technological innovation and instrument of surveillance, and the philosophical struggle for monetary sovereignty in a world where personal, corporate, and political lines blur.

Cryptocurrency does more than disrupt finance; it redraws the map of global influence. Understanding this terrain requires more than technical literacy. It demands geopolitical awareness, ethical reflection, and the humility to recognise that old categories no longer suffice. The battleground is not only physical but digital, economic, and ideological—and the instruments of influence are ledgers as much as missiles.

## Weaponizing Stablecoins

It begins not with a government directive or a military mobilisation, but with a line of code. A smart contract, deployed on a public blockchain, creates a token backed one-to-one with U.S. dollars held in a regulated bank account. This is a stablecoin—ostensibly mundane, yet quietly transformative. At first glance, it appears to be nothing more than a programmable dollar. But under scrutiny, it reveals itself as a geopolitical instrument, capable of bypassing capital controls, destabilising monetary policy, and extending American financial influence into places Washington cannot directly reach. In this way, *the most powerful weapon in the twenty-first century may not be a missile or a trade embargo, but a stablecoin issued by a private company.*

Stablecoins like USDC and Tether are more than digital facsimiles of fiat currency. They are borderless, frictionless, and programmable alternatives to the traditional banking system—capable of moving billions in seconds, with minimal fees, and often with little regulatory oversight. In fragile economies where local currencies are unstable or access to U.S. dollars is tightly controlled, stablecoins provide a lifeline. In authoritarian regimes, they offer citizens a covert escape from inflationary collapse. In crypto markets, they serve as the liquidity backbone, enabling trading, lending, and arbitrage without ever touching a traditional bank.

But this very utility is what makes them so politically charged. Stablecoins *extend the reach of the dollar without requiring the permission of the U.S. government.* They reinforce dollar hegemony in the digital realm, often at the expense of weaker national currencies. In countries like Argentina, Nigeria, or Lebanon—where inflation has corroded savings and access to dollars is scarce—citizens increasingly turn to stablecoins to preserve value, remit funds, or conduct commerce. These digital dollars flow outside the control of central banks, undermining their ability to conduct monetary policy or regulate capital flows. *The dollar spreads—but the state fades.*

This phenomenon has profound consequences. Consider Venezuela, where economic mismanagement and international sanctions have led to one of the most severe cases of hyperinflation in modern history. For years, Venezuelans have turned to the black market to acquire U.S. dollars. But stablecoins like USDT and DAI now offer a faster, safer, and more accessible alternative. With a smartphone and a crypto wallet, Venezuelans can move money in and out of the country without relying on banks, remittance firms, or government intermediaries. In this sense, stablecoins become not just financial tools, but *vehicles of resistance* against authoritarian monetary regimes.

Yet the same mechanics that empower the oppressed can also serve malign actors. Stablecoins have been used in ransomware payments, darknet transactions, and regulatory arbitrage schemes. They enable capital flight on an unprecedented scale. In jurisdictions with strict currency controls—such as China, India, or Russia—stablecoins allow for the rapid, borderless movement of wealth that evades official scrutiny. *The very quality that makes stablecoins efficient also makes them difficult to contain.* When capital moves at the speed of code, regulators struggle to catch up.

It is tempting to think of stablecoins as purely technological artefacts—neutral tools that simply reflect how people choose to use them. But this view misses the political stakes. Stablecoin issuers make decisions that affect billions of dollars in capital. They choose who can mint and redeem tokens, which addresses to blacklist, and what transparency standards to maintain. These choices have real-world implications. When Centre, the consortium behind USDC, froze $100,000 worth of tokens at the behest of law enforcement, it demonstrated that even decentralised systems have chokepoints. *The power to freeze is the power to govern.*

More troubling is the fact that many stablecoin issuers operate in a legal grey zone. Tether, which has repeatedly been scrutinised for the opacity of its reserves and its affiliations with offshore exchanges, continues to facilitate billions in daily volume. Despite regulatory warnings, it remains widely used across Asia, the Middle East, and Latin America—often in jurisdictions where access to traditional dollars is constrained. This creates a perverse dynamic: the demand for reliable digital dollars grows precisely where trust in institutions is weakest, and *private actors rush to fill the void without necessarily bearing public accountability.*

The geopolitical implications extend further. Stablecoins effectively allow U.S.-based entities to project monetary infrastructure into foreign economies. But unlike traditional banking networks, this infrastructure is not deployed by the U.S. Treasury or the Federal Reserve. It is deployed by start-ups, consortiums, and decentralised communities. Washington's soft power is thus extended *indirectly*, through code and contracts rather than treaties or diplomacy. While this may serve strategic interests—such as countering Chinese monetary expansion—it also creates feedback loops that are harder to manage. What happens when a stablecoin becomes *too big to ban* in a country where U.S. foreign policy is under strain?

China's response to this challenge has been unambiguous. It has banned virtually all public cryptocurrency activity, accelerated the development of its digital yuan, and explicitly positioned its CBDC as a counterweight to dollar-based stablecoins. The People's Bank of China recognises that monetary sovereignty in the digital age requires *not only regulating private innovation but building public alternatives.* Other countries are taking note. The European Central Bank, the Reserve Bank of India, and the Central Bank of Nigeria are each developing their own digital currencies, in part to defend against the encroachment of foreign stablecoins.

This sets the stage for a new kind of monetary competition—one where states, corporations, and decentralised communities vie for influence over the infrastructure of digital value. In this contest, stablecoins are not simply instruments of finance. They are instruments of strategy. They shape how capital moves, how sanctions are enforced, how currencies are trusted, and how financial identities are formed. The nation-state is no longer the sole issuer of economic legitimacy. That legitimacy is now *shared, contested, and renegotiated through code.*

Yet the full weaponisation of stablecoins is not inevitable. It depends on how they are designed, governed, and regulated. A well-structured stablecoin can promote financial inclusion, preserve user privacy, and complement state monetary policy. A poorly designed one can enable crime, fuel instability, and weaken democratic accountability. The difference lies not in the technology itself, but in the *values embedded within its architecture.* Are reserves independently audited? Is governance transparent? Can users access recourse mechanisms? These questions are not technical—they are political.

Some forward-thinking policymakers and technologists are beginning to explore hybrid models. One proposal is to create "regulated stablecoins" backed by high-quality liquid assets, issued by licensed entities, and subject to real-time audit requirements. These stablecoins would be interoperable with CBDCs, integrated into existing payment systems, and designed to preserve both user autonomy and regulatory oversight. Another proposal is for decentralised autonomous organisations (DAOs) to issue algorithmic stablecoins that are fully collateralised and governed by transparent rules. Both approaches seek to avoid the binary of chaos versus control. *The challenge is not whether to regulate, but how to regulate without smothering innovation.*

Ultimately, the question is not whether stablecoins are good or bad. It is whether we understand their political gravity. Like the internet before them, they are reshaping foundational institutions at a pace that outstrips public debate. They affect who can participate in the global economy, how financial sovereignty is asserted, and what forms of accountability are possible in an increasingly digitised world. If monetary policy was once the exclusive domain of central banks, it is now also the domain of developers, entrepreneurs, and protocol designers.

To grasp the stakes, we must move beyond the surface narrative of disruption. Stablecoins are not just technical tools or market products. They are *new instruments of power.* And power, once encoded, tends to follow the path of least resistance—and the path of greatest consequence.

## Bitcoin as Digital Gold

When central banks buy gold, they are not merely purchasing a commodity—they are making a strategic statement. Gold is slow, heavy, and offers no yield, yet it remains embedded in the architecture of state power and monetary resilience. For centuries, gold has been the sovereign hedge: a neutral store of value outside the politics of fiat, unprintable and uncorrelated. Today, a new contender is emerging to fulfil that same role—Bitcoin. Where gold is physical, inert, and ancient, Bitcoin is digital, decentralised, and programmable. Yet both promise the same conceptual foundation: *an asset beyond the reach of any single government.* As geopolitical tensions sharpen and monetary orthodoxy frays, the question is no longer whether Bitcoin is relevant to global finance. It is whether Bitcoin is beginning to matter to governments themselves.

In El Salvador, this question has already been answered with radical clarity. When President Nayib Bukele declared Bitcoin legal tender in 2021 and allocated state resources to accumulate it as part of national reserves, the move was widely dismissed as performative populism. But beneath the headlines and volcanic PR stunts lies a more consequential shift: a nation-state actively experimenting with monetary sovereignty by *bypassing traditional financial rails and anchoring value in a decentralised network*. While the scale is small, the precedent is not. El Salvador's bet, though controversial, represents the earliest live case of a sovereign integrating Bitcoin not just as policy rhetoric, but as economic infrastructure.

To understand the deeper stakes, one must ask why gold has held its privileged status in sovereign balance sheets. Gold operates as a reserve of last resort because it is scarce, universally recognised, and—critically—independent of political systems. In times of war, sanctions, or inflation, gold offers insulation. Bitcoin, for all its volatility, offers a digital equivalent of this logic. It is finite in supply, globally transferable, and resistant to seizure when properly secured. *Its value proposition is not just economic but strategic.* For states with strained relationships to Western financial institutions—or who expect to be cut off from them—Bitcoin provides a parallel channel for liquidity, settlement, and long-term store of wealth.

Iran offers a particularly instructive case. Facing crushing sanctions and limited access to SWIFT, Iran has explored Bitcoin mining not only as an economic activity but as a tool for *circumventing dollar-dominated infrastructure*. By harnessing domestic energy to mine Bitcoin, the country effectively converts a stranded asset—natural gas—into borderless digital capital. That capital can then be used to pay for imports or fund covert activities without touching the traditional banking system. The scale remains limited, but the concept is clear: Bitcoin is not just a speculative asset; it is a sovereign tool. Whether embraced publicly or employed discreetly, it enters the calculus of asymmetric financial strategy.

This emergent use case is forcing a quiet recalibration among policymakers in Washington, Brussels, and Beijing. As the global financial order fractures under pressure from multipolar rivalry and debt-driven economic models, Bitcoin introduces a wildcard. It is not issued by a central bank, cannot be inflated, and cannot be sanctioned in the traditional sense. A Bitcoin transaction, once confirmed, is irreversible and censorship-resistant. For adversarial states, this makes Bitcoin attractive. For incumbent powers, it is a liability. The very attributes that make Bitcoin "hard money" in the Austrian economic sense also make it a vehicle for sanctions evasion, wealth obfuscation, and geopolitical asymmetry.

Yet sovereign adoption of Bitcoin is not limited to autocracies or sanctioned pariahs. In democracies experiencing institutional mistrust or inflationary stress, Bitcoin's allure grows. Consider Turkey, where monetary policy has been bent to political will, interest rates have plummeted in the face of inflation, and the lira has seen prolonged devaluation. Turkish citizens have flocked to crypto not merely for profit, but as a protective hedge. The state, meanwhile, has experimented with regulatory containment while quietly acknowledging that it cannot stamp out the tide. In such environments, one can imagine future scenarios where governments—especially those with high dollar exposure—add small Bitcoin allocations to diversify risk. Not as a full reserve shift, but as a *hedge against systemic fragility*.

This introduces complex questions for monetary policy. Unlike traditional reserve assets, Bitcoin has no central issuer, no lender of last resort, and no diplomatic interface. It cannot be coordinated through the IMF or the Bank for International Settlements. It operates independently of realpolitik. This independence is a feature for some, a bug for others. If Bitcoin were to constitute even a minor portion of global reserves, it would challenge the cartel-like dynamics of fiat reserve currencies. The petrodollar system, the eurodollar market, and the machinery of debt diplomacy all assume centralised settlement layers and politically entangled currencies. Bitcoin breaks those assumptions.

Still, the volatility of Bitcoin remains a major impediment to mainstream reserve adoption. Gold fluctuates, but rarely in double-digit percentage terms over short periods. Bitcoin is far more volatile, in part because its liquidity base remains shallow compared to major currencies and commodities. No central bank wishes to explain a 20% drawdown in its reserve assets to its legislature. And no finance minister wants to stake political capital on a technology that still suffers from regulatory ambiguity and technical opacity. Yet over time, *as Bitcoin's market cap deepens and its infrastructure matures*, these objections may carry less weight.

Moreover, the mechanics of sovereign custody introduce new layers of complexity. How does a state secure its Bitcoin? Through multisignature wallets held by the central bank? Via a cold-storage protocol with geographic distribution? If a regime changes, who holds the keys? These are not academic questions—they are matters of national security. Unlike gold, which can be stored in physical vaults and audited through inventory, Bitcoin requires operational security at the software level. Human error, cyberattacks, or internal sabotage could jeopardise holdings worth billions. This raises critical questions around *institutional competence*, not just technical capacity.

Despite these hurdles, institutional exploration is growing. The Central African Republic, following El Salvador's lead, has passed legislation embracing Bitcoin. While its execution is nascent, the symbolic impact is significant: *nation-states are no longer mere observers in the crypto economy—they are participants*. Meanwhile, private banks and hedge funds are increasingly building custody and exchange infrastructure tailored for sovereign clients, anticipating a future in which Bitcoin features—however modestly—in the sovereign portfolio landscape.

Importantly, Bitcoin's entry into the realm of sovereign finance also redefines what monetary neutrality means in a geopolitical context. If a nation accumulates Bitcoin and its price appreciates due to global adoption, that nation benefits without exerting monetary influence. It cannot print more coins, but it can enjoy the fruits of early adoption. This creates a rare condition in international finance: an *asset whose benefits are determined by code and consensus, not by diplomacy or military force*. It levels, ever so slightly, the power asymmetries between small states and global superpowers.

But this levelling effect is not guaranteed. If Bitcoin becomes overly concentrated in a few sovereign hands—or if large holders coordinate to manipulate markets—it risks replicating the monopolistic structures it claims to undermine. Transparency, therefore, becomes essential. Sovereign Bitcoin holdings should be disclosed, verifiable on-chain, and subject to independent oversight. Without such measures, the promise of decentralisation could devolve into a new form of digital oligarchy.

Finally, the narrative of Bitcoin as "digital gold" is not just an analogy; it is an evolving thesis. It began with retail investors seeking an inflation hedge, matured into institutional adoption during global macro instability, and is now cautiously entering the realm of geopolitics. Each step reinforces Bitcoin's credibility as a non-sovereign monetary asset. But it also raises the stakes: *as Bitcoin becomes systemically relevant, it will invite systemic pushback*. From capital controls to mining bans to diplomatic tensions, the path from speculative asset to sovereign tool will not be linear or frictionless.

Still, it is underway. And once a technology begins to shape the strategic calculations of states, it is no longer merely economic—it is political. Bitcoin is now on the world stage, not as a passing fad, but as a permanent variable in the calculus of twenty-first-century power. The only question left is how that power will be used—and by whom.

## The Central Bank Digital Currency (CBDC) Response

Central banks have long held a monopoly over money. But the emergence of cryptocurrencies challenged not just the medium of money, but its very architecture. Bitcoin, Ethereum, and their progeny introduced programmable, permissionless finance—networks where trust is placed in cryptographic consensus rather than state authority. For central bankers, this development was not merely novel—it was existential. The result has been swift and coordinated: an international push to develop Central Bank Digital Currencies (CBDCs), designed not to emulate the open ethos of decentralised crypto, but to reassert state control through digital precision. Where crypto dreams of liberation, CBDCs promise surveillance in high resolution.

At first glance, a CBDC appears as a simple upgrade to state money—a digitised version of the currency already used in everyday life, backed by the full faith of a sovereign government. But this framing is misleading. A CBDC is not simply an electronic dollar or euro. It is programmable money. It can be issued directly to individuals, spent with conditions attached, or even revoked after issuance. Its ledger can be centralised, monitored in real time, and adjusted at will. Unlike cash, which is anonymous and bearer-held, or even commercial bank deposits, which are intermediated by private institutions, CBDCs shift the centre of gravity back to the state. *They are not digital cash—they are digital control.*

Nowhere is this tension clearer than in China's Digital Currency Electronic Payment (DCEP) system, more commonly referred to as the digital yuan. Launched in pilot programmes across major cities and now entering broader deployment, the digital yuan is not built on a blockchain per se, but borrows its logic of verifiability and traceability. Transactions can be tracked with unprecedented granularity. The People's Bank of China can issue money directly to citizens, monitor how it is spent, and even design "expiry dates" for stimulus distributions to force consumption. In the Chinese model, monetary policy becomes behavioural policy. Economic stimulus turns into social engineering.

This template has not gone unnoticed. Across Europe, Asia, and the Americas, central banks have initiated CBDC research, prototypes, and pilot deployments. The European Central Bank's "digital euro" project explicitly cites the desire to maintain "monetary sovereignty" in a world where foreign digital currencies—including dollar-backed stablecoins and cryptocurrencies—could displace national units of account. In the United States, the Federal Reserve has taken a slower, more cautious approach, citing privacy concerns and the potential disintermediation of the commercial banking sector. Yet even without a formal digital dollar, the debate is no longer if, but *when* and *how*.

Supporters of CBDCs argue that these instruments offer clear benefits. They can streamline payments, reduce settlement risk, improve financial inclusion, and ensure central banks remain relevant in an increasingly digital economy. By bypassing intermediaries, CBDCs can also reduce transaction fees and speed up monetary transfers. Governments could target stimulus more precisely, distribute welfare benefits instantly, and combat illicit activity with improved audit trails. These are not trivial improvements. But they come at a cost: *the erosion of financial privacy and the rise of programmable oversight.*

The shift from bearer cash to account-based CBDCs introduces an unprecedented data layer into monetary life. Every transaction could, in principle, be logged, analysed, and stored by the issuing authority. While current banking systems already collect data, CBDCs could centralise this information within the monetary authority itself. The result is a toolset for social control. Consider a scenario where politically disfavoured purchases—say, donations to a protest movement—are flagged and frozen. Or where access to CBDC wallets is made contingent upon vaccine records, carbon footprints, or loyalty to party platforms. Such use cases are no longer speculative fiction; they are entirely feasible within the programmable structure of a CBDC.

This raises critical questions about architecture and governance. Should CBDCs be token-based or account-based? Will they be issued directly by central banks or through a tiered model involving commercial institutions? Will anonymity be preserved in any form, or will identification be mandatory? These design choices are not merely technical—they are constitutional. They determine the contours of economic freedom in the digital age. *To code a CBDC is to legislate in software.*

A particularly contentious issue is whether CBDCs will disintermediate commercial banks. If citizens can hold digital currency accounts directly with the central bank, why deposit funds with private banks at all? This "narrow banking" model would render banks obsolete as custodians of capital, upending their traditional role in credit creation. To avoid this scenario, many proposals favour a hybrid system where CBDCs are distributed through licensed intermediaries who still play a role in financial services. But the direction is clear: *CBDCs recalibrate the relationship between citizen, bank, and state.*

Contrasting views have emerged within the crypto-native community. Some see CBDCs as a vindication of blockchain's underlying innovations, finally embraced by the legacy system. Others view them as a betrayal—a perversion of crypto's decentralised ideals used to create a panopticon of financial surveillance. Both perspectives hold elements of truth. The very architecture of a CBDC often borrows from the language of crypto—distributed ledgers, digital wallets, smart contracts—yet the control structures invert the founding logic of decentralisation. *The state does not abdicate power with CBDCs; it refines it.*

There are also geopolitical dimensions. A CBDC issued by a major power like China or the EU could, in theory, be used for cross-border trade in ways that challenge the dominance of the US dollar. If a critical mass of countries begins accepting the digital yuan for trade settlement, it could fragment the current SWIFT-based global financial order. While the dollar's position is deeply entrenched, CBDCs introduce a new vector of competition—not through brute force, but through *infrastructure choice.* Trade partners may not need to buy dollars if they can transact via bilateral CBDC arrangements.

This has not gone unnoticed by US policymakers. Some see the lack of a digital dollar as a strategic vulnerability, ceding first-mover advantage to rivals. Others warn that an American CBDC, if designed without robust privacy protections, could accelerate domestic political backlash. The United States faces a unique paradox: the need to preserve dollar hegemony globally, while protecting civil liberties at home. *CBDCs sit at the intersection of monetary dominance and constitutional constraint.*

Yet amid all the geopolitical jockeying, one must not overlook the deeper philosophical challenge. At stake is not merely who controls money, but *what money becomes.* In the analogue era, money was passive—an instrument of exchange. In the CBDC era, money becomes active, embedded with rules, conditions, and behavioural nudges. It is no longer neutral. It is shaped by algorithms, monitored in real time, and embedded with policy preferences. This transformation redefines the citizen's relationship to the state. It elevates the central bank from an arbiter of liquidity to a programmer of economic life.

That is why the design of CBDCs must be treated not as a technical upgrade, but as a democratic imperative. The question is not simply whether CBDCs are efficient, but whether they are just. Who audits the code? Who sets the rules for programmability? Can dissenters opt out? These are not questions to be outsourced to technocrats. They belong in parliaments, courts, and public discourse. The architecture of digital money is fast becoming the architecture of power. And if that power is concentrated without consent, it risks becoming unaccountable.

Already, cracks in the consensus are emerging. Civil liberties groups warn of a slippery slope toward financial authoritarianism. Cryptographers argue for zero-knowledge proofs and privacy-preserving protocols within CBDC systems. Some economists propose dual-track models where small transactions remain anonymous, while large ones are traceable. These are not fringe ideas—they are necessary safeguards in a future where every transaction could be logged, analysed, and weaponised.

The future of CBDCs is not yet written. They could reinforce democracy, if built with transparency, privacy, and open access. Or they could accelerate state overreach, embedding surveillance and control in the most intimate layer of economic life. *The technology is neutral, but the intentions behind it are not.* That is why public scrutiny matters. CBDCs are not just a tool of monetary innovation—they are a test of civic maturity.

As the world's monetary systems digitise, the key question will not be how fast central banks can build CBDCs. It will be whether they build systems that *enhance freedom or erode it.* That choice, more than any technical feature, will define the legacy of the CBDC era.

## The Battle for Monetary Sovereignty

For most of modern history, the question of who controls money was easily answered: the state. Through central banks, fiscal authorities, and legal tender laws, nation-states monopolised the issuance and regulation of currency. Monetary sovereignty—defined as the exclusive right to issue and manage a national currency—was considered not only a technical instrument of macroeconomic management, but a pillar of political autonomy. Yet that foundation is now under pressure. Not from other states, as in previous geopolitical contests, but from a newly emergent triad: decentralised technologies, transnational corporations, and individuals demanding agency. At the heart of this triad sits crypto. Not just as a technical phenomenon, but as a *political rupture*—an architecture that removes the need for permission and, in doing so, redraws the boundaries of monetary power.

The idea that a protocol maintained by voluntary consensus could function as a rival to sovereign currency would have seemed absurd even a decade ago. But the rise of Bitcoin, Ethereum, and other blockchain-based assets has forced governments to reckon with a novel and disquieting reality: *monetary systems can now be built outside of state control, and still command value.* This challenges not only the monopoly of issuance, but also the presumption that legitimacy flows downward from state to citizen. In the crypto paradigm, legitimacy is emergent, decentralised, and rooted in code and community, not sovereign decree.

To understand the magnitude of this challenge, consider the case of El Salvador. In 2021, the country declared Bitcoin legal tender alongside the US dollar—a radical departure from the norm. This wasn't just a policy experiment in financial inclusion; it was a symbolic act of defiance. By adopting a stateless currency, El Salvador signalled its willingness to bypass the international financial system and the conditionalities often imposed by institutions like the IMF. Whether or not the initiative succeeds economically, the geopolitical message was unmistakable: *monetary sovereignty can be redefined from the bottom up.*

But if small nations are experimenting at the margins, it is the world's largest tech firms that present a more systemic challenge to traditional sovereignty. Facebook's ill-fated Libra project (later rebranded Diem) was a turning point. Its ambition was clear: to launch a global stablecoin backed by a basket of fiat currencies, integrated directly into the platforms used by billions. Although ultimately thwarted by regulatory pressure, Libra revealed what is possible when monetary infrastructure is embedded within global networks. *A currency doesn't need borders if it lives inside your phone.* The backlash it provoked was not only about consumer protection—it was about power. Policymakers across the globe understood that if private actors control payment rails and unit-of-account systems, then states risk becoming second-tier players in their own economies.

This fear has accelerated the development of Central Bank Digital Currencies (CBDCs), as discussed elsewhere in this volume. But CBDCs are as much a defensive manoeuvre as they are an innovation. They attempt to recapture the terrain that crypto has opened—digital bearer instruments, instant settlements, programmable features—without ceding control. Yet their very existence confirms the core premise: that *the architecture of money is now contestable.* Once designed exclusively by states, it is now co-authored by code, capital, and consensus.

This contest has major implications for individuals. Crypto, at its best, allows users to hold their own funds, transact without intermediaries, and escape the gatekeeping of banks and payment processors. It enables financial self-sovereignty in a way that no state-issued system ever could. But that empowerment comes with trade-offs. The absence of intermediaries means users shoulder the burden of security. The lack of central authority means lost keys are irretrievable. The irreversibility of transactions removes avenues for redress. *Sovereignty, in the crypto context, is not just a right—it's a responsibility.* Many are ill-prepared to wield it.

This raises a difficult question: should monetary sovereignty be distributed equally, or should it be mediated through institutions that cushion against individual failure? States argue that financial systems require oversight to prevent exploitation, fraud, and systemic collapse. Crypto advocates argue that the very institutions meant to protect often end up excluding, censoring, or surveilling. The tension is not easily resolved. It is a clash of visions—between paternalism and empowerment, between central command and distributed coordination.

And then there is the corporate layer. Companies like PayPal, Square, and Visa increasingly mediate access to both fiat and crypto systems.

They determine what is acceptable, who can participate, and under what terms. Their decisions are opaque, their incentives driven by profit, and their influence on monetary flows significant. In many ways, *corporate intermediaries have become de facto monetary governors*, especially in regions where state capacity is weak. This blurs the lines of accountability. Who sets the rules when money is issued by code, transferred through platforms, and stored in private custodianships? Who governs the governors?

Nowhere is this fragmentation more evident than in sanction regimes. Traditional sanctions rely on choke points—banks, SWIFT networks, correspondent accounts—to block access. Crypto, by contrast, operates on neutral, borderless rails. In 2022, reports surfaced of Russian oligarchs allegedly moving wealth through Bitcoin and privacy coins to evade sanctions. While the scale of these transactions remains debated, the theoretical possibility is undeniable. Similarly, regimes under heavy international sanctions, like Iran and North Korea, have explored crypto mining and ransomware as shadow revenue streams. This introduces a paradox: *the same property that makes crypto resilient to censorship also makes it attractive to those evading lawful restrictions.*

States have responded with increasing scrutiny. The US Treasury's Office of Foreign Assets Control (OFAC) has sanctioned smart contracts and mixer protocols like Tornado Cash, marking a new chapter in the enforcement of law in cyberspace. But these moves expose a conceptual fault line. Can code itself be sanctioned? Is a decentralised protocol a legal entity, a tool, or a speech act? The battle for monetary sovereignty now bleeds into the realm of jurisprudence. What constitutes control in a world of decentralised finance? And who bears liability when that control is absent?

These tensions are not merely legal—they are structural. As capital flows shift from traditional rails to decentralised networks, the effectiveness of monetary policy itself comes into question. If a significant portion of wealth is held in crypto assets beyond the control of central banks, then interest rate adjustments and open market operations lose potency. Crypto introduces *monetary leakage*: assets that behave like money but do not respond to policy levers.

This undermines the core function of monetary sovereignty—macroeconomic stewardship.

It also invites strategic recalibration. Countries facing inflation or currency debasement—such as Turkey, Argentina, and Nigeria—have seen surges in crypto adoption. For their citizens, Bitcoin and stablecoins are not speculative assets but tools for survival. This grassroots adoption bypasses domestic monetary policy entirely. It also renders capital controls porous. When economic sovereignty fails at the national level, crypto becomes a form of *personal sovereignty*. The consequences are profound: states lose grip not only over currency issuance, but over the behaviour of their economic agents.

So where does this leave us? The battle for monetary sovereignty is not a linear tug-of-war. It is a complex, multi-polar contest involving nation-states, tech giants, decentralised protocols, and individuals asserting control over their economic identities. No single actor holds the full deck. States can regulate, but not un-invent. Corporations can build infrastructure, but not legislate legitimacy. Protocols can enforce rules, but not guarantee justice. The result is a fragmented monetary order—one that is still evolving, still unstable, and still profoundly political.

What emerges from this contest may not be a binary outcome—sovereignty won or lost—but a new equilibrium. One in which *monetary pluralism* becomes the norm. State currencies will coexist with stablecoins. CBDCs will compete with Bitcoin. Individuals will navigate between custodial platforms and self-sovereign wallets. Control will be layered, contested, and dynamic. The future of money, in other words, will not be monolithic. It will be modular, programmable, and geopolitically fraught.

The essential task, then, is not to declare victory for one model or another, but to understand the stakes. Monetary sovereignty is no longer a matter of borders and printing presses. It is a question of access, agency, and architecture. And in that contest, every design choice—every wallet protocol, every regulatory framework, every line of code—is an act of political authorship. The struggle for control over money is, and always has been, a struggle over power.

Crypto did not start this struggle. But it made it visible—and irreversible.

# Chapter 9
# Cultural Tribes of the Crypto Universe

Cryptocurrency is not merely a technical invention—it is a social current, a contested philosophy, and increasingly, a cultural battleground. To describe it only in terms of codebases, consensus mechanisms, and financial primitives is to miss its animating spirit. The crypto world is stitched together as much by tribes, myths, and rival ideologies as by protocols and wallets. From heated arguments on Twitter to the austere prose of GitHub commits, from chaotic Discord forums to hushed investment retreats, what emerges is a dense cultural tapestry: adversarial, fragmented, yet deeply revealing of the forces shaping its evolution.

The distributed structure of the technology has allowed mutually incompatible interpretations to thrive side by side. Bitcoin maximalists occupy one pole of the spectrum, treating their fixed-supply currency not simply as superior, but as singular—every other project, in their telling, is a distraction, or worse, a deception. On another pole sit Ethereum advocates and multi-chain enthusiasts, animated by dreams of digital states, decentralised economies, and programmable trust. Scattered around these poles swarm traders, yield chasers, and memecoin speculators, whose interest lies not in philosophy but in volatility and virality. And orbiting them all are the critics—some caustic, others careful—arguing that crypto risks dressing up age-old problems in glittering, digital garb.

To understand crypto properly, you must reckon with these factions. They are not background noise; they are the soil in which innovations take root, the atmosphere in which markets move, the scaffolding for narratives that later harden into reality. Ideology in this realm is structural. It decides what gets built, what gains traction, and how communities distribute trust or absorb risk. Like political parties or religious sects, crypto tribes define themselves not only by what they stand for, but also by what they reject. The result is a restless, fractious landscape that resists neat categories but illuminates the struggle over meaning and power.

Among these factions, Bitcoin maximalists are the clearest in creed. Their conviction is simple to state, but uncompromising: Bitcoin is money's final form, the only project that matters. To them, the protocol's refusal to change—its stubborn resistance to tinkering—is not a weakness but a virtue, proof of incorruptibility. Bitcoin is presented not as software to be endlessly patched, but as monetary bedrock: stable, scarce, and incorruptible. Maximalists scorn Ethereum's upgrades and DeFi's experiments as unserious and dangerously reckless. In their worldview, money must inspire trust, not novelty. For them, Bitcoin is more than digital gold; it is a covenant against inflation, state overreach, and arbitrary power.

By contrast, Ethereum's universe revels in dynamism. Complexity is embraced as a sign of possibility, not peril. Smart contracts, DAOs, decentralised finance, and NFTs—these are not appendages but the essence of Ethereum's identity. Its culture is experimental, open-ended, and restless. Developers treat the blockchain less as a ledger and more as an operating system for new economies. Its shift to proof-of-stake, experiments with scaling, and modular architecture reveal a faith in adaptability. Yet the Ethereum camp is rife with contradictions: it aspires to transform global finance while courting regulators and corporations; it extols decentralisation while crafting narratives palatable to ESG committees. This dual posture—radical and institutional at once—defines both its attraction and its fragility.

Beyond these ideological poles lies a less doctrinal group: the speculators. They approach crypto as a casino with better marketing. Their creed is neither scarcity nor decentralisation, but opportunity. If belief can be monetised, even briefly, they are there first. Dismissing them would be naïve. Speculators are often the earliest liquidity providers, the first to stress-test new protocols, and the quickest to flee when winds shift. They supply the lifeblood of markets—liquidity, volatility—yet their aims often diverge entirely from those of the builders. For them, decentralised networks are not tools of emancipation but instruments of leverage.

Then there are the critics. Some are academics and policy thinkers, others disillusioned insiders. Their questions cut sharply: does decentralisation really decentralise power, or does it simply reassign it to coders, auditors, and token holders? Are systems marketed as "trustless" merely relocating trust? Do speculative tokens advance financial inclusion, or do they entrench new barriers beneath a utopian gloss? Such critiques are often met with derision by crypto loyalists, who dismiss them as fearmongers or Luddites. Yet serious criticism is less an act of sabotage than of diagnosis. If crypto is to claim the mantle of re-engineering trust, it must withstand scrutiny that goes beyond cheerleading.

What makes this cultural topography so intriguing is the proximity of its factions. They inhabit the same conferences, interact on the same protocols, even exchange liquidity through the same contracts—yet their assumptions about what all this *means* could not be further apart. The DeFi platform seen by one group as a step toward sovereignty may be, for another, a quick speculative punt, and for regulators, a new systemic risk. An NFT collection can be heralded as a breakthrough in digital art, derided as a speculative mania, and flagged as a money-laundering tool—all at once. Shared tools do not imply shared values.

Culture in crypto is not only reflected in debate—it is embedded in code. Bitcoin's 21 million cap is not merely a monetary parameter; it is a cultural artefact declaring that scarcity is sacred. Ethereum's emphasis on composability is likewise a cultural stance, privileging openness and modularity. Protocols that dangle aggressive yields are sending a signal too: this is a playground for gamblers. The loop runs both ways—values shape design, and design shapes behaviour. To understand crypto's future, you must read its culture as carefully as its white papers.

As this ecosystem matures, its tribal lines may blur, fracture, or deepen. Some maximalists might mellow, some builders might turn cynical, and some critics might become reformers. But the divisions will not vanish; they are constitutive of the field. If anything, they will intensify as crypto moves further into the fabric of finance, governance, and society. What began as an eccentric experiment has become a contested domain of power and imagination.

This is not a chapter that seeks resolution. It offers, instead, a mirror: a way of seeing the crypto phenomenon not only as a technical shift but as a human drama unfolding in real time. To make sense of it, one must account for the tribes, their beliefs, their antagonisms. For in their disputes lie the deeper story—not simply of what crypto *is*, but of what it might yet become.

## The Maximalists and True Believers

The most powerful ideologies are not the ones that demand belief—they are the ones that make disbelief feel irrational. This is the intellectual foundation upon which crypto maximalism rests. Within the volatile, often contradictory world of cryptocurrency, a particular kind of conviction has emerged that transcends typical technological enthusiasm. For some, it is not enough that Bitcoin or Ethereum are useful or innovative—they must be *right*, not only technically, but morally. They must represent the correct view of how money should work, how systems should govern, and how people should live. To understand this tribe of maximalists and true believers is not merely to explore a demographic—it is to enter a worldview fortified by logic, history, and a distinctive kind of faith.

Bitcoin maximalism, the oldest and perhaps most intellectually coherent of these belief systems, centres on a singular, provocative claim: *Bitcoin is the only cryptocurrency that matters.* Everything else—whether it's Ethereum, Solana, or the latest DeFi coin—is viewed as either redundant or deceptive. Maximalists don't just believe in Bitcoin's technological superiority; they assert its moral primacy. They view it as a protocol designed not only to resist inflation or censorship, but to correct the failures of fiat currencies, central banking, and the political distortions that underpin global finance. For them, the appeal of Bitcoin lies not in its novelty but in its finality. A fixed supply. Predictable issuance. Radical transparency. No CEO. No upgrades by committee. No redefinition of purpose. It is monetary policy enshrined in code—immutable, apolitical, incorruptible.

This conviction is not baseless. Bitcoin emerged in the shadow of the 2008 financial crisis, a moment that laid bare the fragility of the traditional monetary system. Its pseudonymous creator, Satoshi Nakamoto, embedded into the genesis block a message referencing a bank bailout—"The Times 03/Jan/2009 Chancellor on brink of second bailout for banks." It was a statement of intent, and many have taken it as a declaration of independence from the legacy system. For maximalists, Bitcoin is not an investment; it is a principled opt-out. *Owning Bitcoin is not just a financial decision—it's a declaration of dissent.*

But what elevates Bitcoin maximalism from advocacy to orthodoxy is its relationship to change. To Bitcoiners, the refusal to alter the protocol—to add features, expand supply, or tweak consensus mechanisms—is a feature, not a flaw. Stability in a chaotic world becomes not just strategic but sacred. As such, proposals for increased programmability, integration with other blockchains, or governance experimentation are met with deep scepticism. Bitcoin's simplicity, its lack of bells and whistles, is held as evidence of its purity. It doesn't need to do everything; it needs to do one thing well—be money. And if others want to build, they can build elsewhere.

By contrast, Ethereum loyalists—the second most organised contingent of true believers—embrace an entirely different ethos. If Bitcoin is ideological minimalism, Ethereum is philosophical pluralism. Vitalik Buterin's original white paper in 2013 laid out a vision not for digital gold, but for a global, decentralised computer—a platform where applications could run without central servers, intermediaries, or gatekeepers. From this stemmed a worldview in which *code is not only law, but also governance, identity, finance, and coordination.* Ethereum is not just a currency—it is a sandbox for reimagining institutions.

The Ethereum community is characterised by a fervent belief in the power of decentralised infrastructure to reshape society. Smart contracts, DAOs, layer-two scaling solutions, zero-knowledge proofs—these are not just technical innovations but philosophical commitments. They are attempts to reduce reliance on trust, to encode fairness, and to allow coordination among strangers without the traditional apparatus of the state or corporation. Ethereum maximalists—though they often resist that label—believe this architecture can host everything from voting systems and supply chains to universal basic income and censorship-resistant social media.

But unlike Bitcoin maximalists, Ethereum's tribe welcomes evolution. It embraces a culture of open-ended development, community governance, and ideological debate. The migration from proof-of-work to proof-of-stake was not just a technical milestone but a declaration that *Ethereum is a living organism, not a finished product.* That flexibility, however, also makes it vulnerable to internal conflict. The DAO hack of 2016 and the ensuing hard fork gave birth to Ethereum Classic, splitting the community over whether code truly is law, or whether humans should intervene when things go wrong. This tension remains unresolved and points to a central paradox: how does one preserve decentralisation while still exercising judgement?

These two cultures—Bitcoin and Ethereum—are often in dialogue, but more frequently in debate. Their respective forums, podcasts, and conferences reveal differing assumptions not only about the future of crypto, but about human nature. Bitcoiners tend to see trust as inherently dangerous, prone to abuse, and best minimised through rigid systems. Ethereum loyalists, while also wary of centralisation, are more likely to view trust as a resource—something that can be mediated, incentivised, and made resilient through better tools. This divide runs deeper than code; it reflects differing visions of how civilisation itself should be governed.

Yet, despite these differences, both groups share a remarkable similarity in tone and temperament. Their discourse is frequently framed in terms of moral clarity and existential stakes. Bad actors are not merely wrong—they are dangerous. Projects that deviate from the "correct" path are labelled as scams, distractions, or regressions. This moral intensity can be exhausting to outsiders, but it is precisely what gives these movements their coherence and momentum. *True belief may narrow perspective, but it also strengthens resolve.*

Critics often deride these tribes as cults—cloistered, inflexible, resistant to critique. And indeed, there are moments when the discourse veers into zealotry. Meme warfare, purity tests, and dismissive jargon can create an exclusionary culture. But this critique, while not unfounded, misses the sociological function of belief in technological movements. Early internet pioneers, free software advocates, and cypherpunks all relied on similar forms of internal coherence and moral urgency. When a technology is young, misunderstood, and under attack, its defenders must believe not only that it will work—but that it *must* work. Without such belief, the effort required to build decentralised systems in a centralised world would likely collapse under its own contradictions.

There is also a more generous reading: that these maximalists are not dogmatists, but stewards. Their rigidity is not a rejection of innovation but a defence against dilution. They fear that compromise—whether with regulators, venture capital, or convenience—will render crypto indistinguishable from the very systems it sought to replace. And in an industry where hype often outpaces integrity, there is something admirable about the refusal to bend to fashion. *Conviction may be unfashionable, but it is not without value.*

To be sure, the maximalists are not the majority. Most crypto users are pragmatists—interested in utility, gains, or novelty. But the influence of the maximalists far exceeds their numbers. They write the essays, host the podcasts, set the terms of debate. They act as cultural custodians, even if others find their style abrasive. And in a world where attention is fragmented and values are increasingly fluid, *clear convictions—even controversial ones—carry disproportionate weight.*

As the crypto ecosystem matures, these belief systems will be tested. New technologies, new crises, and new actors will challenge the assumptions of even the most ardent maximalists. Bitcoin may be forced to reckon with energy debates and regulatory resistance. Ethereum may confront the limitations of governance by code. But whatever the outcome, these true believers will have played an indispensable role in shaping the ethos, architecture, and imagination of crypto's early era.

Understanding them is not optional. It is essential. Because behind every protocol, white paper, and token price is a worldview. And if we are to take crypto seriously—as a social, political, and economic force—then we must also take seriously those who believe in it most.

## The Speculators and Opportunists

Every new technological frontier attracts its prophets—and its profiteers. While some participants in the cryptocurrency ecosystem are motivated by philosophical commitments to decentralisation or economic reform, an equally significant contingent is fuelled by a very different impulse: the pursuit of profit, often at dizzying speed and scale. These are the speculators and opportunists, a loosely affiliated tribe whose defining characteristic is not loyalty to any protocol or vision, but a relentless sensitivity to market signals, hype cycles, and cultural moments. To understand this group is not to dismiss them as shallow or unserious; it is to confront one of the most powerful driving forces behind crypto's meteoric rise, chaotic volatility, and persistent public fascination.

Speculation is not new. Nor is it unique to crypto. From the tulip mania of the 17th century to the dot-com boom of the late 1990s, financial history is littered with frenzies in which prices decoupled from fundamentals and fortunes were made or lost in days. What distinguishes the crypto speculative class is the sheer speed, scale, and *interactivity* of their domain. Thanks to decentralised exchanges, meme-driven social platforms, and around-the-clock global trading, today's speculator operates in a digital casino with infinite tables, no dress code, and few rules. Every tweet is a tip. Every chart is a confession. Every meme, a weapon in the fight for liquidity.

The entry points into this world vary. Some arrive as retail traders, lured by tales of overnight riches. Others come through online subcultures—Reddit, Discord, Telegram—where information, hype, and tribalism swirl together in volatile mixtures. Then there are the influencers and content creators who monetise attention as much as investment insight. For these figures, crypto is not merely an asset class—it's a lifestyle brand, one where wealth, clout, and credibility are collapsed into a single performance metric: engagement. *To win in this arena, one must not only be early, but loud.*

Nowhere has this dynamic been more visible than in the meme coin phenomenon. Dogecoin, originally created as a satire of crypto's excesses, evolved into a multibillion-dollar asset propelled largely by irony, community sentiment, and celebrity endorsement—most infamously by Elon Musk. It had no cap, no clear purpose, and no roadmap, but it had a culture. This culture, self-aware yet strangely earnest, revealed a generational shift in how financial assets are perceived. For many younger investors, Dogecoin wasn't a joke—it was a protest against the perceived elitism of Wall Street, a way to mock the gatekeepers while participating in the game.

The same logic applies to projects like Shiba Inu, PepeCoin, or countless other ephemeral tokens that erupt in value and disappear just as quickly. These assets are not judged by cash flow projections or use case viability, but by *narrative velocity*. Can they capture attention, go viral, create FOMO? If so, they are valuable—at least temporarily. This blending of speculation and entertainment has given rise to the term "financial theatre," where market movements are not just economic events but collective spectacles. Traders aren't just investors; they are participants in a kind of gamified drama, complete with heroes, villains, and recurring plot twists.

But while the meme culture and speculative ethos are often derided as unserious or destabilising, they perform important functions within the broader crypto ecosystem. First, they provide liquidity. Speculators chase volatility, and volatility generates trading volume, which in turn funds infrastructure, incentivises development, and attracts new users. Second, they test boundaries. Projects that might be dismissed by traditional venture capital or ignored by academic circles can receive grassroots attention and funding from speculative communities. This democratises access to early-stage capital, albeit in unpredictable and often irrational ways.

Yet the speculative dynamic is not without cost. Market manias lead to misallocations. Bad actors exploit hype to launch pump-and-dump schemes, draining wealth from latecomers. Influencers front-run their followers. Rug pulls—where developers abandon projects after raising capital—have become an all-too-common hazard. These behaviours corrode trust, fuel regulatory scrutiny, and tarnish the legitimacy of legitimate innovation. More subtly, the dominance of short-term incentives can displace long-term thinking. Projects may optimise for token price rather than protocol resilience. Developers may prioritise user growth over governance design. In a speculative market, *optics often eclipse architecture*.

There's also a psychological toll. The 24/7, high-volatility nature of crypto trading encourages compulsive behaviour. Retail investors report symptoms of addiction, burnout, and anxiety. The fear of missing out—amplified by constant notifications, screenshots of gains, and social validation—creates a pressure cooker environment where rational decision-making is easily overridden by emotional impulse. Even experienced traders, aware of the risks, find themselves caught in cycles of overconfidence, loss chasing, and regret.

And yet, the speculators persist. Many are self-taught, shaped by experience rather than formal education. They develop instincts, rituals, and heuristics—technical indicators, sentiment tracking, liquidity analysis—that make them agile, if not always accurate. They are students of momentum, volatility, and crowd psychology. While institutional players analyse fundamentals, speculators read *vibes*. This intuitive, culture-aware approach can be surprisingly effective in a market where perception drives value as much as utility.

There's a deeper sociological story here, too. For many, crypto speculation is not just a financial strategy—it's a form of participation in an economy that has otherwise excluded them. In countries with limited job prospects, high inflation, or capital controls, trading tokens may offer more opportunity than traditional employment. In communities disillusioned with the financial establishment, meme coins become vehicles of resistance, however flawed. *Speculation is often a symptom of exclusion, not excess.*

Indeed, the decentralised nature of crypto allows participation without permission. There are no investor minimums, no accreditation requirements, no banking intermediaries. This openness enables innovation—but also exploitation. The speculator operates in a liminal space: somewhere between liberation and manipulation, agency and addiction. Their actions are often dismissed as noise, but they are part of the signal. They show us what excites, what spreads, what compels belief—or at least attention.

Regulators and technologists alike struggle with this class. Attempts to impose investor protections or limit access are often interpreted as paternalistic, or worse, as attempts to preserve existing power structures. Yet the absence of guardrails creates systemic fragility. During major crashes—such as the implosion of Terra/Luna in 2022 or the collapse of FTX—retail speculators bore the brunt of the damage. These events prompted soul-searching across the industry. Can decentralised markets offer both freedom and fairness? Is it possible to embrace speculation while mitigating its excesses?

Some believe the solution lies in better tools: improved risk management protocols, decentralised insurance, on-chain reputation systems. Others advocate for financial literacy—arming participants with the knowledge to navigate markets more intelligently. Still others argue for cultural reform: shifting the narrative away from "get rich quick" toward "build something lasting." But culture, like markets, resists central planning. The speculators will remain. They are part of crypto's DNA—its id, its energy, its edge.

To dismiss them is to misunderstand the movement. Crypto, unlike traditional finance, is not a monolith. It is a messy, pluralistic, and sometimes contradictory space where idealists and opportunists collide. The speculators may not write the white papers or maintain the protocols, but they amplify what resonates. They surface what's emotionally compelling, what feels new, what promises escape or transformation. They are accelerants—sometimes reckless, sometimes revelatory.

Understanding this group is not just a matter of market analysis. It is a study in human behaviour, cultural adaptation, and technological disruption. The line between innovation and speculation is not always clear, but it is precisely in that ambiguity that new paradigms emerge. The speculators and opportunists are not merely reacting to the crypto revolution—they are shaping it, often in ways that surprise even its architects.

## The Builders and Idealists

Crypto has no shortage of noise: speculative manias, social media theatrics, high-profile collapses, and ideological flame wars. But beneath the frenzy lies a quieter, more consequential stratum of the ecosystem—one composed not of traders or influencers, but of people who build. Developers, cryptographers, protocol designers, social scientists, legal theorists, and activists—this is the cohort that treats blockchain technology not as a slot machine or ideological totem, but as a *toolbox* for reimagining foundational systems. They are motivated not by hype, but by *possibility*. And while their voices are often drowned out by louder market participants, their work constitutes the intellectual and infrastructural core of the crypto movement.

It is tempting to assume that blockchain's early evangelists were all libertarian iconoclasts seeking to bypass government control. In reality, many of the most influential builders come from backgrounds in systems engineering, game theory, cryptography, or economics, driven less by ideology than by curiosity. For them, the appeal of decentralised technology lies in its design constraints and coordination challenges—how to create trust without a central authority, how to design economic incentives that align individual interest with collective outcomes, how to build resilience into systems that must operate in adversarial environments. These are not abstract puzzles; they are engineering imperatives, and the stakes are real.

Consider Ethereum's origin story. While Bitcoin offered a proof of concept for decentralised value transfer, Ethereum's creators—led by Vitalik Buterin—saw a broader opportunity: a general-purpose computational platform governed by smart contracts. This was not simply a technological extension but a philosophical shift. It reframed the blockchain from a monetary network into a new substrate for organisational experimentation. Decentralised finance (DeFi), decentralised autonomous organisations (DAOs), and non-fungible tokens (NFTs)—each emerged from this programmable layer, allowing new structures for economic and cultural value to take shape without traditional intermediaries.

These structures are not just codebases; they are social systems. Every protocol is a miniature polity with its own rules, incentives, and governance models. Builders must therefore think like constitutional designers. Should decision-making power be based on token ownership, reputation, or participation? How can systems remain secure without being ossified? What forms of recourse or redress are available when things go wrong? These are not technical questions alone—they require insight into human behaviour, organisational dynamics, and the sociology of trust.

This is where the idealists emerge. Some are privacy maximalists designing zero-knowledge proof systems that allow computation without exposing data. Others are decentralisation purists building peer-to-peer protocols resistant to censorship or corporate capture. Still others focus on economic justice, exploring how blockchain-based universal basic income, co-operative ownership models, or remittance platforms can address global inequities. These are not idle experiments—they are serious proposals that test the edges of political economy using live infrastructure.

One can look to projects like Gitcoin, which experiments with quadratic funding to support public goods through community-driven allocation mechanisms. Or to Protocol Labs, which advances decentralised storage through Filecoin and IPFS while investing in long-horizon R&D across governance and cryptography. Or to RadicalxChange, a movement of technologists and theorists proposing mechanisms like data dignity, plural voting, and self-assessed taxation—often operationalised through blockchain prototypes. These initiatives ask not only what decentralisation can achieve, but what it *should* achieve.

The contrast with the speculative wing of crypto could not be starker. Builders are often underpaid, under-recognised, and overwhelmed by the need to coordinate across fragmented, fast-moving landscapes. Unlike venture-backed startups with centralised leadership, open-source crypto projects rely on distributed contributors, ambiguous intellectual property norms, and rough consensus. Progress is slow, incentives can misalign, and forks are common. Yet there is an authenticity to this mode of development that distinguishes it from the performative churn of token launches or the centralised theatrics of Web2 platforms.

That authenticity is often born of constraint. Many of the most impactful crypto builders operate from the Global South, where inflation, currency controls, or weak institutions have made decentralised infrastructure not a luxury, but a necessity. Projects like Celo, focused on mobile-first financial access, or Grassroot Economics, which uses blockchain to run community currencies in Kenya, demonstrate that crypto's idealism is not merely theoretical or Western. It is being tested, lived, and iterated in environments where the failures of the legacy system are not abstract policy concerns, but daily survival issues.

Still, idealism is not the same as naïveté. Builders are increasingly aware of the dangers posed by regulatory hostility, protocol capture, or ideological rigidity. Many have watched as powerful actors—venture capitalists, exchanges, governance whales—have replicated old hierarchies under new names. The promise of decentralisation can quickly become performative if control remains concentrated. Recognising this, builders are experimenting with novel governance models that seek to hard-code fairness and transparency into the system itself. From conviction voting to futarchy, from retroactive funding to identity-layer protocols, the aim is to design rules where legitimacy is endogenous—not imposed from above, but emergent from participation.

Yet these experiments carry deep philosophical tensions. Should protocols enshrine neutrality, or encode values? Can decentralised systems maintain coherence at scale without reintroducing centralisation? What should happen when community goals conflict with market incentives? Builders face these dilemmas not as abstract theorists, but as participants shaping institutions in real time. Their answers are provisional, debated, sometimes contradictory—but they reflect a commitment to deliberation rather than dogma. *In the best cases, crypto's builders act not as disruptors, but as constitutional reformers in digital clothing.*

What unites these disparate actors—despite differing geographies, disciplines, or technical stacks—is a belief that systems can be designed better. Not perfect, but better. More transparent, more inclusive, more accountable. This belief is not utopian; it is pragmatic. It is grounded in hard engineering, careful trade-offs, and open experimentation. And it is animated by the conviction that *architecture matters*. How we build determines what we can sustain.

In many ways, the builders and idealists offer crypto's strongest long-term claim to relevance. Markets fluctuate. Narratives shift. Technologies decay. But institutional design—when done well—endures. It adapts. It scales. If crypto is to move beyond its adolescence, it will do so not through another bull run or hype cycle, but through the maturation of its infrastructure and the evolution of its governance. That work is already underway, often unnoticed, frequently thankless. But it is the work that matters.

To study these builders is to study the future—not as a prediction, but as a series of design decisions unfolding in real time. Their tools are code and community. Their medium is incentive. Their canvas is protocol. And while they may not dominate headlines or markets, they shape the conditions under which both evolve. They are, in the deepest sense, the authors of what crypto might still become.

## The Skeptics and Ethical Critics

If cryptocurrency evangelism is often couched in the language of revolution—disintermediation, sovereignty, freedom—its critics serve as the necessary counterweight: interrogating not only the claims made by blockchain advocates, but the very philosophical premises underpinning the industry's self-image. These are not uninformed naysayers or knee-jerk reactionaries. The most compelling sceptics of the crypto universe are deeply knowledgeable, methodically rigorous, and ethically anchored. They do not reject technological innovation outright. Rather, they ask a harder, more uncomfortable question: *Does this technology meaningfully solve real problems—or merely redistribute power and risk under the guise of liberation?*

At the core of the ethical critique lies a suspicion about *means versus ends*. Crypto purports to decentralise power, democratise finance, and protect privacy. Yet many of its most visible outcomes—extreme wealth concentration, energy-intensive mining operations, predatory token schemes, and a parallel financial casino—seem to conflict with those ideals. For critics like software engineer Stephen Diehl, a prominent voice in this space, the industry is less a paradigm shift than a repackaging of speculative capitalism. He argues that crypto does not eliminate intermediaries so much as replace them with *less accountable ones*. The myth of trustlessness, in this view, obscures how human power remains embedded in protocol design, governance models, and access to capital.

The energy debate is a prime flashpoint. Bitcoin's proof-of-work consensus mechanism, while securing the network, has also drawn widespread scrutiny for its ecological footprint. Critics question whether a decentralised monetary system should come at the cost of unsustainable resource consumption—particularly when, as they point out, the system's utility is itself debated. Proponents cite renewable migration and Layer 2 scaling solutions, but the broader question remains: *What externalities are we willing to tolerate in the name of technological purity?* Environmentalists argue that crypto has become a case study in how ideological fixation on decentralisation can blind builders to systemic consequences. A digital currency that requires massive energy inputs to function begins to resemble less a leap forward and more a regression into externalised harm.

Ethical criticism extends beyond the environment into questions of equity and access. Despite rhetoric about banking the unbanked, many critics point out that crypto participation often presupposes digital literacy, speculative risk tolerance, and capital—factors disproportionately available in the Global North. In theory, anyone can participate in DeFi or own Bitcoin. In practice, meaningful engagement requires navigating volatile markets, complex interfaces, and frequent scams. *Financial empowerment without protection can quickly turn into financial exploitation.* Airdrops, initial coin offerings (ICOs), and meme coins have repeatedly proven susceptible to pump-and-dump dynamics that enrich insiders and leave retail participants burned.

For legal scholars and regulators, the decentralised nature of crypto presents a jurisdictional paradox. If no one controls the protocol, who is liable when things go wrong? This diffusion of accountability is not seen as a virtue but a design flaw—one that obfuscates recourse and undermines user protection. From the lens of consumer safety, crypto's architecture appears *structurally indifferent* to harm. Hacks, rug pulls, and exploitations are often met with shrugs and memes, a cultural signal that participation comes with caveat emptor baked in. Critics argue that such fatalism reflects not maturity, but ethical abdication.

Then there are the philosophical sceptics, who challenge the very *premise* of crypto as a tool for liberation. They note how quickly decentralised protocols have been co-opted by speculative finance, how rapidly idealistic communities give way to whales, bots, and corporate interests. They question whether decentralisation, as commonly pursued, *actually produces better outcomes*—or simply makes them harder to regulate. Rather than a flat, democratic field, crypto ecosystems often replicate power asymmetries under the banner of openness. Token-based governance systems risk becoming plutocratic, where votes are allocated by wealth rather than by deliberation, expertise, or community trust.

Even crypto's supposed resilience to censorship is contested. Ethereum's transition to proof-of-stake and its compliance with sanctions via centralised validators has raised alarms among privacy advocates. Blockchain forensic tools increasingly allow governments and corporations to track flows across public ledgers—raising the uncomfortable possibility that crypto could *enhance* surveillance rather than resist it. Critics ask: If censorship-resistance is a core value, why are decentralised platforms increasingly beholden to regulatory and capital pressures? This is not a call for recklessness but a reminder that *design choices have ideological consequences*, and decentralisation is not a binary state but a spectrum shaped by trade-offs.

Ethical critics also dissect the cultural dynamics of crypto. They observe how narratives of liberation often coexist with toxic masculinity, exclusionary jargon, and performative libertarianism. The culture valorises risk and scorns caution, often marginalising those who raise legitimate concerns. Female technologists, underrepresented communities, and less technically literate participants frequently encounter barriers to entry—not due to formal exclusion, but because of *ambient hostility* and opaque gatekeeping. The irony, critics note, is that a movement ostensibly rooted in openness often thrives on tribalism and derision.

Notably, many of the most incisive critics *are not outside the crypto space*, but within it. They are disillusioned developers, civic technologists, data ethicists, and economists who once believed in crypto's promise but became disenchanted with its trajectory. Their criticisms are not calls for prohibition, but *for coherence, humility, and accountability*. They push the community to confront its blind spots, to build with intention rather than impulse, and to interrogate its assumptions with the same rigour it applies to its code.

The tension between builders and sceptics is not a sign of failure, but a necessary dialectic. Healthy systems require internal dissent to evolve. But the crypto ecosystem has often been hostile to critique, viewing it as betrayal rather than engagement. This defensiveness stems from a perceived siege mentality—an industry long vilified by governments and banks is understandably wary of external attack. Yet without internal critique, the movement risks becoming *ideologically brittle*, unable to recognise when its tools are causing harm or when its rhetoric has outrun its reality.

To dismiss critics as anti-innovation is to miss the point. Their role is not to stop progress but to *sharpen its edge*. By exposing contradictions, unintended consequences, and blind spots, they compel the ecosystem to do better. To be worth building, a system must be able to withstand scrutiny. The more radical the promise, the more rigorous the examination must be.

If crypto is truly to mature—beyond bubbles, beyond maximalism—it must engage with its sceptics not as enemies but as interlocutors. *It is in the space between conviction and criticism that wisdom emerges*. Crypto's promise is not guaranteed. It must be earned, refined, and sometimes reimagined. The ethical critics, whether celebrated or ignored, are the necessary conscience of the movement—reminding it that freedom without responsibility is not liberation, but evasion.

# Chapter 10
# Crypto and the Self: Identity, Privacy, and Autonomy

Cryptocurrency did not emerge solely as a technological innovation; it began as a philosophical assertion. Long before DeFi protocols commanded billions in liquidity or NFT marketplaces dominated headlines, the earliest Bitcoin forums buzzed with a far more elemental concern: resistance to institutional oversight, bureaucratic intrusion, and the enforced conformity of centralised systems. At its heart, the argument was personal and uncompromising: mastery over one's money is inseparable from mastery over oneself. Yet as blockchain networks have expanded—growing more intricate, more interconnected—the contradictions inherent in that premise have multiplied. This chapter probes the uneasy, often disquieting intersections between crypto and human agency, digital identity, and autonomy.

Cryptographic systems promise liberation, yet exact a price. They offer sovereignty, but frequently at the cost of usability. They aspire to shield users from surveillance while at times replicating—or amplifying—it. The vision is of self-directed individuals, but the reality is that humans are fragile, inconsistent, and entwined in complex social fabrics. At its most ambitious, crypto is not merely reinventing finance; it is attempting to redesign the self. But the self imagined in code is far from straightforward.

Consider the tension between pseudonymity and anonymity. Though often conflated in popular discussions, these are distinct in function and philosophy. Bitcoin is pseudonymous: addresses are not formally linked to legal identities, yet every transaction is permanently recorded on a public ledger. A paradox arises: participants are "nameless," yet entirely visible in action. Off-chain data, combined with analytics tools, can re-identify users with remarkable precision. This is not a flaw; it is intentional. The blockchain engenders a new form of digital subjecthood: anonymous by label, transparent by behaviour.

The implications for privacy are profound. Traditional finance is regulated by law; blockchain is regulated by code. In conventional systems, privacy violations can be challenged legally. On-chain, privacy is contingent on protocol design. Users must shield themselves from both malicious actors and the transparency baked into the system itself. Technologies such as zero-knowledge proofs and mixers attempt to mitigate exposure, yet adoption remains limited. The consequence is a central contradiction: privacy and usability are often mutually exclusive, with users navigating trade-offs they scarcely understand.

Self-Sovereign Identity (SSI) seeks to address this tension, attempting to return digital identity control to individuals. Unlike centralised identifiers—emails, government-issued IDs—SSI positions users as custodians of their own credentials, verified cryptographically rather than through intermediaries. It is not merely a technical shift but a philosophical one: the individual becomes their own issuer, curator, and gatekeeper.

Yet SSI is far from a panacea. Questions abound: Which credentials carry weight? How can uniqueness be demonstrated without disclosing identity? Can such systems scale without replicating the very gatekeeping they aim to circumvent? Crucially, SSI presumes a user capable of managing keys, permissions, backups, and revocations. Those unable—or unwilling—to shoulder this burden are excluded. Autonomy, in this sense, risks becoming a privilege of the technically adept.

This intersects with the broader dynamics of surveillance capitalism. Blockchain enthusiasts often cast crypto as a corrective to the data-harvesting practices of tech giants, yet public ledgers and smart contracts generate unprecedented visibility. Meanwhile, AI models increasingly analyse blockchain data, extending predictive surveillance. Far from dismantling oversight, some implementations of crypto merely displace it: the state retreats, the network steps in.

Platforms claiming to enable sovereignty complicate matters further. DAOs, NFT-based communities, and Web3 identity systems promise control while retaining authority over interface, defaults, and data flows. Users may hold the keys, but the architecture channels behaviour and choices. This is governance by design: subtle, structural, and persistent.

The psychological stakes are equally acute. Self-sovereign finance assumes rational, disciplined actors—individuals who will secure seed phrases, track market risks, and resist phishing. Yet humans err: they forget passwords, click malicious links, misjudge risk. The ideal of disintermediation quickly becomes an obligation to perpetual vigilance. Traditional systems allow recourse and reversal; crypto offers little. A single error can be irrevocable. Paradoxically, greater autonomy imposes stricter demands on fallibility.

The mantra "not your keys, not your coins" embodies this duality. It is a call to empowerment, and simultaneously a warning of isolation. Self-custody entails total responsibility, absent safety nets. Ethical questions arise: does a system demanding perfection from its users truly empower, or merely expose them to inevitable failure?

Beneath these technical concerns lies a philosophical tension between freedom and responsibility. Crypto discourse often celebrates liberty, yet neglects the obligations it entails. True autonomy extends beyond code execution; it requires social trust, psychological support, and imaginative institutions. Identity is relational, not just credentialed. Privacy is not merely opacity; it is selective disclosure. Autonomy is agency exercised in connection with others, not isolation.

By exploring pseudonymity, decentralised identity, surveillance implications, and the emotional labour of self-custody, this chapter seeks to illuminate what is genuinely at stake in crypto's redesign of the self. These are not abstract dilemmas—they shape trust, personhood, and the negotiation of power in a digital era.

If crypto aspires to remake the foundations of human coordination, it must confront the human it presumes. Not a wallet, not a node, but a fallible, embodied, context-bound individual. Systems reflect assumptions; the question is moral as much as technical: what kind of person does crypto envision, and is that the person we wish to become?

**Pseudonymity vs. Anonymity:**

The word *anonymous* is often carelessly used in conversations about cryptocurrency. Yet the blockchain is not, and has never been, truly anonymous. It is *pseudonymous*—a distinction that is not merely technical but foundational to understanding what privacy means in the architecture of blockchain systems. In an age where identity is both commodified and weaponised, and where data invisibility is increasingly rare, this distinction cuts to the heart of one of crypto's most fraught philosophical battlegrounds. Blockchain systems did not set out to eliminate identity, but to *redefine* its terms. Whether they have succeeded—or can—remains a matter of urgent debate.

Pseudonymity refers to the use of identifiers that are not directly tied to legal names or real-world personas. On a blockchain like Bitcoin or Ethereum, participants transact through alphanumeric wallet addresses rather than government-issued IDs. These addresses serve as stand-ins—persistent, consistent, and publicly viewable. A pseudonymous identity can build history, reputation, and trust. It can receive payment, execute contracts, even act as a delegate in a decentralised autonomous organisation. But it cannot, by default, be easily traced to a specific individual without auxiliary data.

Anonymity, by contrast, means *no enduring identifier at all.* A truly anonymous system severs the link between action and actor entirely. Tor, Monero, and other privacy-enhancing technologies aim to preserve such unlinkability. The problem—and the power—of pseudonymity lies in its halfway state. It offers a veneer of detachment without full invisibility. It allows users to mask their legal identity, yet leaves a breadcrumb trail of transactions, interactions, and patterns—all stored immutably and accessible to anyone with a blockchain explorer and some analytical ingenuity.

The implications of this design are profound. On the surface, pseudonymity grants a kind of freedom. It allows activists to fundraise without fear of reprisals. It enables dissidents to escape censored financial systems. It lets citizens in collapsing economies move assets beyond the reach of predatory governments. But that same design permits invasive financial surveillance, with tools more forensic than anything in traditional banking. Unlike the fragmented, permissioned databases of legacy finance, blockchain ledgers are global, timestamped, and permanent. Once a wallet is tied to a person—via a careless exchange withdrawal, an IP leak, or social media brag—the entire history becomes legible. *The pseudonym ceases to protect; it becomes a proxy of exposure.*

Blockchain analytics firms like Chainalysis and Elliptic have industrialised this process. Working with law enforcement and regulators, they de-anonymise wallets, cluster addresses by ownership, and create probabilistic models of illicit behaviour. These capabilities are not hypothetical—they are already central to investigations in money laundering, sanctions evasion, and cybercrime. While such efforts arguably advance public safety, they also challenge the early crypto ethos that privacy is a right, not a privilege. *What began as a libertarian tool of financial autonomy is increasingly a data-rich honeypot for surveillance regimes.*

The contradiction here is not an accident. It is embedded in the architecture. Most public blockchains are designed to be trustless, meaning participants do not need to know or trust one another—or any central authority—to verify state. This trustlessness is secured through transparency. Every transaction is verified by every node. This is the innovation, but also the trade-off. The same openness that enables decentralised consensus makes privacy technically difficult. *Privacy is not the default; it is something that must be added, often awkwardly and with limitations, to systems never designed for opacity.*

Efforts to reclaim privacy in blockchain systems have taken multiple forms. Privacy coins such as Monero and Zcash offer more robust anonymity guarantees, using ring signatures and zero-knowledge proofs to obfuscate transaction data. Layer-2 solutions and mixers like Tornado Cash aim to break linkability by shuffling transactions. However, these tools come with regulatory and reputational risks. In 2022, the U.S. Treasury sanctioned Tornado Cash, arguing it facilitated North Korean money laundering. The move was controversial—not just for targeting a tool rather than a user, but for *criminalising privacy-preserving infrastructure itself.* Developers were arrested. Code was removed from GitHub. The precedent was chilling: *in the eyes of some governments, privacy itself had become suspect.*

This raises ethical and strategic questions. Is it legitimate for privacy tools to be criminalised because they can be misused? Should the ability to transact discreetly be reserved only for state-approved actors? Or should privacy be treated as a digital civil liberty—no less essential than encryption, free speech, or the presumption of innocence?

The deeper problem is that most blockchain users do not understand the limits of the systems they use. Wallet addresses feel anonymous, but are not. Interactions on DeFi platforms are tied to wallets; NFTs link to user profiles; DAOs publish votes. The ecosystem nudges users to identify, stake, and build reputational capital. As a result, *crypto culture often invites overexposure without adequately communicating risk.* This isn't just a UX failure. It's a structural one.

The dilemma becomes more acute as crypto moves into the mainstream. Governments increasingly require Know Your Customer (KYC) and Anti-Money Laundering (AML) compliance. Exchanges, wallet providers, and even some decentralised platforms are being pressured to collect and report user data. This leads to a bifurcated ecosystem: on one side, pseudonymous protocols running at the edge of legality; on the other, compliant onramps surveilled by state authorities. The middle ground is narrowing. *The more crypto integrates with the legacy system, the more it inherits its surveillance logic.*

Yet pseudonymity still matters. It creates space for experimentation. It allows for multiple identities—separating personal finance from creative expression, professional presence from political dissent. It resists the collapsing of all digital life into a single profile optimised for advertisers. In an online world increasingly defined by biometric tracking, behavioural analytics, and algorithmic enforcement, *pseudonymity offers one of the last lines of defence for contextual identity.*

There are lessons to be learned from how pseudonymity functions in other systems. In academic publishing, peer reviewers are pseudonymous to protect honest critique. In online forums, long-standing pseudonyms earn respect through contribution. In whistleblowing platforms, anonymity is essential to truth-telling. The challenge for blockchain developers is to design systems where pseudonymity enables accountability without surrendering privacy—*where identity can be verified without being revealed.*

Solutions are emerging. Projects like Nym, Aztec, and zkSync are experimenting with privacy-preserving proofs. New credential systems use cryptography to confirm facts ("is over 18," "is not on sanctions list") without revealing full identity. These advances hold promise, but they also demand careful stewardship. Privacy is not just a feature to be toggled; it is a *norm to be defended.* It requires collective discipline, political will, and informed users.

This is why privacy remains a battleground. It is not just about technology; it is about power. About who gets to see, who gets to hide, and who gets to decide. Pseudonymity, properly understood, is a middle path—imperfect, fragile, and contingent. It is not the endpoint, but a compromise in an evolving struggle over identity, transparency, and freedom in digital space. As regulators close in, analytics tools proliferate, and cultural norms shift, the core question persists: *Can we build systems that are both open and respectful of the individual? Or will transparency become the new tyranny, masked as trust?*

The answers will not be found solely in code. They will require choices—legal, ethical, and social—about how we define identity in the digital age. Pseudonymity is not a relic of crypto's anarchist past. It may be one of the most important battlegrounds for its future.

## Self-Sovereign Identity:

Control over one's identity has long been a function of bureaucracy and centralisation. Governments issue passports. Banks verify customers. Tech platforms assign usernames and demand credentials. These institutions serve as gatekeepers of legitimacy—deciding who is seen, heard, hired, or allowed to transact. But in a digital world where identity is fragmented across hundreds of services, each demanding its own logins, verifications, and metadata trails, this centralised model is cracking under its own weight. What emerges in its place is not merely a new authentication tool, but a new philosophy: *Self-Sovereign Identity* (SSI)—a concept that proposes individuals should own and manage their own digital identities without relying on a central authority.

At its core, self-sovereign identity flips the prevailing architecture of trust. Rather than depending on a provider to hold and vouch for your identity, it enables you to control the credentials that define who you are. Through the use of cryptography, decentralised networks, and verifiable claims, individuals can store proofs of identity (like citizenship, education, or age) in a digital wallet—issuing them to others when needed, selectively and privately. These claims are cryptographically signed by trusted issuers—such as universities, banks, or governments—and validated on a public ledger. But crucially, the ledger does not store the sensitive information itself. It only verifies that the claim is authentic and untampered with. *This separation of control from custody marks a conceptual shift as radical as the move from banks to Bitcoin.*

The appeal of SSI is not theoretical. It speaks to real, urgent failures in today's digital identity systems. In many parts of the world, people lack formal identification entirely—barred from banking, voting, or accessing services. Refugees, undocumented workers, and stateless individuals are functionally invisible. Meanwhile, those who do have formal IDs are often forced to over-disclose—handing copies of passports, driver's licences, and social security numbers to every service provider, creating vast honeypots of personal data vulnerable to leaks, theft, and misuse. The 2017 Equifax breach in the United States exposed the data of 147 million individuals. India's Aadhaar system, one of the world's largest biometric ID databases, has faced repeated legal and ethical challenges. These systems are not just centralised—they are brittle, leaky, and coercively extractive.

SSI frameworks attempt to resolve these failures by aligning identity with agency. Instead of maintaining dozens of siloed identities across institutions, individuals can anchor their credentials in a single, portable, and cryptographically secure identity wallet. For example, a user could receive a digitally signed certificate from their university proving they hold a degree. When applying for a job, they could present this certificate directly to an employer, without going through a central clearinghouse. The employer verifies the signature via the issuing institution's public key on the blockchain. The transaction requires no middleman, no third-party data broker, and no unnecessary data disclosure. *Only the minimum needed proof is shared, under the user's control.*

This model is gaining traction in diverse contexts. The European Union's eIDAS framework has accelerated research into cross-border digital identities using verifiable credentials. Estonia's digital residency programme includes elements of SSI. Projects like Sovrin, uPort, and Microsoft's ION (built on the Bitcoin blockchain) are actively exploring decentralised identifiers (DIDs) and verifiable credentials that can be used in everything from healthcare to travel. In the developing world, NGOs and governments are investigating SSI as a way to provide digital ID to unbanked populations—linking credentials not to a central database, but to individuals directly.

But with this promise comes complexity. SSI is not a monolithic standard. It is a shifting landscape of protocols, schemas, and philosophical disagreements. For instance, how decentralised should the ledger be? What level of trust should be placed in issuers versus verifiers? Should governments participate in these ecosystems, or should they be kept deliberately independent? These questions are not trivial. The risk of "pseudo-SSI" systems—those that claim user control but hardcode central dependencies—could undermine the very autonomy SSI purports to guarantee.

There are also fundamental trade-offs to navigate. SSI puts users in control, but with control comes responsibility. If a user loses their digital identity wallet, or is coerced into sharing credentials under duress, there is no recovery hotline. This mirrors the problem of private key management in cryptocurrency—an elegant system in theory, but fragile in practice. *What happens to the elderly, the disabled, the less tech-savvy? Can a system truly be self-sovereign if it is not also inclusive and humane?*

Moreover, SSI intersects uncomfortably with state power. While many proponents see it as a tool for freedom from authoritarian oversight, others fear it could be co-opted to build *more* efficient surveillance systems. A government-issued SSI credential could tically be used to track behaviour across services, correlate ses, or implement social credit schemes. The tools of autonomy can be repurposed for control. China's blockchain-based service network (BSN), for example, explores digital identity within a state framework that is anything but self-sovereign. The architecture may be decentralised; the governance is not.

A similar tension exists with corporate actors. Big tech companies increasingly express interest in identity solutions that promise both interoperability and user trust. But will corporations that have built empires on data extraction willingly relinquish control? If Google or Meta issue SSI credentials, do they become arbiters of truth? Can decentralised ID survive a world where network effects push users toward branded platforms and proprietary wallets? *The danger is that self-sovereignty becomes a rhetorical shield for digital feudalism—where the castle changes shape but the serfdom remains.*

Despite these dangers, the philosophical foundation of SSI is difficult to dismiss. In a digital world characterised by fragmentation, overexposure, and loss of control, the idea that one can selectively and privately disclose truth is profoundly attractive. It reframes identity not as a fixed profile but as a set of dynamic assertions. It acknowledges that identity is context-dependent—that who we are in a medical setting differs from who we are as voters, as consumers, as citizens. SSI gives language to this plurality without forcing convergence. *It allows for trust without total transparency.*

There is also cultural significance in how identity is performed through SSI. In many systems, identity is a top-down assignment: name, date of birth, ethnicity, occupation. But self-sovereign identity makes space for bottom-up expression. It lets individuals construct, curate, and project identity across boundaries, offering proofs without surrendering personhood. This matters in marginalised communities, activist networks, and online subcultures. It supports reputational capital without doxxing. It empowers people to verify facts about themselves while maintaining narrative control. *It makes privacy not a wall, but a filter—one that the user configures, not the institution.*

Still, the road ahead is not linear. SSI must navigate a world of legal grey zones, platform monopolies, and cultural inertia. It must be interoperable across jurisdictions, resilient to coercion, and accessible to the digitally excluded. It must prioritise usability without sacrificing sovereignty. It must avoid being co-opted by the very actors it was meant to displace. Most of all, it must be understood not just as a technological protocol, but as a *normative claim* about what identity ought to be in a networked society.

The success of self-sovereign identity will not be measured by how many blockchains it runs on, or how many wallets are downloaded. It will be judged by whether it genuinely shifts power—from credentialing empires to individual actors; from opaque institutions to transparent protocols; from compulsory disclosure to voluntary trust. It asks not only whether we can be seen online, but whether we can choose *how* and *when* to be seen. And that is not just a technical question—it is a deeply human one.

## "The Surveillance Capitalism Dilemma":

Surveillance capitalism was not born from blockchain—it was perfected in the data centres of Silicon Valley. It emerged quietly, under the banner of convenience, wrapped in the language of personalisation and free access. But its mechanism is simple and ruthless: extract behavioural data, analyse it at scale, predict future actions, and monetise that predictive power. Tech platforms became surveillance empires not because they had to, but because the economic logic of data extraction was too profitable to ignore. What began as targeted ads evolved into behavioural nudging, social manipulation, and algorithmic control. The more data you give, the less autonomy you have. Now, as blockchain and AI enter this already-compromised ecosystem, a paradox arises—*can decentralised technologies genuinely resist surveillance capitalism, or are they being subsumed by it?*

Blockchain was supposed to be a counter-force. With its roots in cryptographic transparency and peer-to-peer architecture, it promised freedom from centralised control and opaque data brokerage. Bitcoin did not ask who you were; it simply validated that you controlled a key. Ethereum allowed anyone to execute contracts without intermediaries. But beneath these ideals lies an inconvenient truth: public blockchains are transparent by design. Every transaction, every contract, every movement of value is etched immutably into a ledger visible to all. While that transparency ensures auditability and trustlessness, it also creates an unprecedented behavioural record—a map of every financial choice, every interaction, every pseudonymous wallet, available for analysis forever. *In resisting centralised surveillance, blockchain introduced a new, decentralised kind.*

Enter AI. The convergence of blockchain with machine learning supercharges the dilemma. Large language models, predictive engines, and behavioural analytics can now sift through blockchain data with ease—correlating wallet addresses, transaction patterns, token movements, and smart contract activity. Combined with off-chain data—IP addresses, browser fingerprints, Know Your Customer records—AI doesn't just see pseudonyms. It re-identifies them. It models their intentions. It forecasts their next move. *An open ledger is a goldmine to an adversarial AI.*

Take Chainalysis and similar blockchain analytics firms. Originally framed as tools for law enforcement and compliance, they now serve as institutional gatekeepers—enabling exchanges, banks, and governments to trace flows of crypto assets and assign probabilistic identity scores to wallets. They bring order to the chaos of decentralised systems by reconstructing identities from behavioural patterns. The tools are powerful, precise, and profitable. But they also raise profound ethical questions. If blockchain was meant to eliminate trust-based intermediaries, why are we outsourcing its interpretation to opaque analytics firms? If pseudonymity was meant to protect privacy, why are we algorithmically undermining it?

Even privacy-focused cryptocurrencies like Monero or Zcash are not immune. While they implement advanced cryptographic techniques such as ring signatures and zk-SNARKs to obfuscate transactions, they remain under scrutiny by regulators and surveillance firms who view such systems as threats. Exchanges have delisted privacy coins under pressure. Developers have faced legal harassment. And ironically, using a privacy coin can itself be a red flag—drawing attention simply because one has chosen not to be observed. *In a world of total visibility, opacity itself becomes suspicious.*

The dilemma is sharpened when blockchain intersects with decentralised identity. As explored earlier, self-sovereign identity

(SSI) systems aim to give individuals control over their credentials. But what happens when these credentials are used across hundreds of services, recorded immutably on ledgers, and correlated through AI? If not carefully designed, SSI can become the infrastructure for permanent behavioural records—enabling perfect compliance, but also perfect surveillance. The very tools meant to liberate identity can entrench it. The same verifiable claims that free a refugee from bureaucracy can also tether a dissident to their digital trail.

This is the core irony of blockchain surveillance: it often arises not from malevolent design, but from noble intent. Transparency, accountability, compliance—these are legitimate goals. But when combined with the economic incentives of surveillance capitalism, they drift. Platforms and protocols begin to prioritise traceability over privacy, data liquidity over user control, institutional trust over individual sovereignty. Blockchains are open by default, but open data is not neutral. *Who interprets it? Who profits from it? Who decides what is visible, and why?*

Consider decentralised finance (DeFi). The explosion of DeFi protocols has created a sprawling ecosystem of lending, trading, staking, and speculation. But DeFi also produces highly granular data—liquidations, yield farming behaviours, liquidity provision, wallet interactivity—all of which can be analysed, scored, and monetised. Firms now offer credit scoring based on wallet behaviour. Others build AI-based bots that front-run trades based on public mempool data. Some projects rank users based on "reputation" scores that mimic credit bureaus. *What began as freedom from banks is slowly reconstructing financial surveillance—without the consumer protections that once accompanied it.*

And yet, the answer is not to reject blockchain, but to interrogate its design. Surveillance capitalism thrives in systems that lack friction—where data flows unimpeded, identities are loosely guarded, and accountability is outsourced. Resisting it requires intentional architecture. It demands zero-knowledge proofs, selective disclosure, decentralised encryption, and local-first design. Projects like Tornado Cash (before its sanctioning), Aztec Network, and Nym explore how anonymity can be reclaimed without sacrificing functionality. But these are not silver bullets—they come with trade-offs in scalability, usability, and regulatory friction. The battle is not technological alone. It is political, economic, and cultural.

One cannot ignore the role of regulation. Compliance regimes such as FATF's Travel Rule or the EU's Markets in Crypto-Assets (MiCA) framework increasingly require visibility into crypto transactions. Exchanges must collect and report data. Validators and nodes may be deputised. Smart contracts may be required to implement compliance logic. These rules are framed as protections against money laundering and terrorism financing. But they also shape how protocols evolve—biasing them towards transparency, custodial design, and institutional alignment. Privacy becomes a liability. Pseudonymity becomes untenable. The burden of proof shifts to the individual, who must now explain why they want to be left alone.

This dilemma extends beyond crypto. It reflects a broader crisis in the digital economy. Surveillance capitalism is not just a business model; it is an epistemology—a way of knowing people through data. Blockchain, for all its radical potential, has not yet escaped this logic. Its transparency, once revolutionary, is being co-opted into predictability. Its immutability, once empowering, is now permanent exposure. Its decentralisation, once liberating, is often too abstract to defend the vulnerable.

Yet there is still room to push back. Thoughtful protocol design, strong encryption, community governance, and ethical development practices can re-centre human dignity in blockchain infrastructure. Privacy need not mean secrecy. It can mean choice. It can mean being able to transact without being profiled, to explore without being scored, to exist online without being reduced to a dataset. *True privacy is not the absence of observation—it is the presence of agency.*

Ultimately, the surveillance capitalism dilemma is not just a tension between blockchain and big tech. It is a question of values. Do we build systems that assume people are to be watched, or systems that trust them to choose? Do we privilege prediction over autonomy? Do we accept compliance at the cost of freedom? These are not technical questions. They are civic ones. And as blockchain matures, its builders and users will need to decide whether it becomes an instrument of liberation—or just another mirror of the world it sought to disrupt.

## "Autonomy and the Fragility of Self-Custody":

The rallying cry of the cryptocurrency movement—*"Not your keys, not your coins"*—sounds deceptively simple. It asserts that true ownership requires self-custody: the act of holding your own private keys and managing your own assets without reliance on banks, exchanges, or intermediaries. On its surface, it's a noble ideal. In practice, it is one of the most psychologically demanding revolutions in modern finance. It shifts responsibility from institutions to individuals—removing the safety nets, the redundancies, the forgiveness of human error that traditional finance builds in by design. *It's not just a technical change. It's an existential one.*

Self-custody asks users not merely to act like their own banks, but to internalise the habits, discipline, and paranoia of institutional security teams. It demands digital literacy, threat awareness, backup systems, and above all, a tolerance for irrevocability. Lose your private keys, and your assets are unrecoverable. Sign a malicious smart contract, and your funds can vanish. Share a seed phrase in a moment of inattention, and your identity may be compromised. There is no customer support. No password reset. *Just consequence.*

This level of autonomy can be exhilarating—but it can also be deeply isolating. In traditional systems, the distribution of risk is socialised. A bank absorbs fraudulent charges. A family member can call support to help settle an estate. In decentralised finance, self-custody means the burden falls squarely on the individual. This creates a psychological tension: *the freedom to operate without permission is inseparable from the responsibility to accept all consequences, even catastrophic ones.*

For some, this is empowering. They find in crypto a philosophical home—where personal sovereignty is paramount, and external dependency is a form of soft tyranny. They embrace cold storage, air-gapped devices, and multi-signature schemes. But even within this community, the cognitive overhead is significant. Managing assets securely requires constant vigilance, a mastery of evolving attack vectors, and an acceptance that one's own mistakes are irreversible. It is the financial equivalent of living without a smoke detector—safe only as long as you are perfectly alert, every day, for life.

The anxiety is not hypothetical. Real-world losses from self-custody failures are widespread and often devastating. Users have misplaced hardware wallets, lost access after death with no inheritance plan, or fallen prey to phishing sites that perfectly mimic trusted interfaces. The blockchain does not discriminate. It executes. And for many, the permanence of its memory becomes a psychological weight. *There is no undo button. Only reflection after the fact.*

This fragility becomes more apparent when examined through the lens of behavioural economics. Human beings are notoriously poor at handling abstract, irreversible risks. We procrastinate, we overestimate our abilities, and we are susceptible to manipulation. These tendencies are magnified in high-stakes environments like cryptocurrency. Cognitive biases—overconfidence, recency, optimism—make users prone to errors that are unforgiving in a self-custody regime. In this light, the decentralised ideal clashes with human nature. *We are fallible. Blockchains are not.*

To mitigate this tension, various technical innovations have emerged—multi-signature wallets, social recovery mechanisms, threshold cryptography, time-locked contracts. These tools introduce shared responsibility or conditional access into the custody equation. They offer a middle path: maintaining control while reducing single points of failure. But these systems are complex, unevenly adopted, and require trust in code, platforms, or communities that themselves may not be fully understood. The user still bears the psychological weight of choosing the right tools, configuring them correctly, and managing them over time.

Then there is the social dimension. Self-custody, by its nature, decouples individuals from institutions—but it can also decouple them from communities. In a world where people increasingly rely on collective services for convenience and support, managing one's entire financial life in solitude is not just difficult; it can be alienating.

The crypto world tends to valorise the lone sovereign individual, but ignores the emotional and social costs of that isolation. When something goes wrong, there may be no one to call, no recourse, no human hand to hold. *The dream of absolute control can quietly become a nightmare of absolute loneliness.*

This contradiction raises difficult philosophical questions. What is autonomy without support? What does it mean to be free if the systems enabling that freedom are so brittle, so unforgiving, that only the most disciplined can truly exercise it? Crypto's promise is not just technological—it is moral. It says individuals should be empowered, trusted, respected as agents of their own economic destinies. But if the tools to realise that promise are out of reach for the average person—or so psychologically taxing that most avoid them—then the movement risks becoming exclusive, even elitist. *Freedom without accessibility is just a different kind of gatekeeping.*

The industry's response has been mixed. On one end of the spectrum are custodial exchanges, centralised wallets, and platforms that abstract away all responsibility—trading autonomy for convenience. These solutions are attractive to newcomers and offer user-friendly interfaces, insurance policies, and customer support. But they reintroduce central points of failure. Hacks, account freezes, regulatory overreach, and censorship remain threats. On the other end are maximalist purists who insist on full sovereignty, even if it limits adoption. Both camps misunderstand the real challenge: *not custody as a technical function, but as a psychological experience.*

There is growing interest in hybrid models—smart contract wallets with recovery logic, decentralised custody services with legal oversight, or peer-to-peer recovery frameworks. These approaches accept the messiness of human life. They acknowledge that true autonomy does not mean isolation, but supported independence. They suggest that the future of self-custody will not be one-size-fits-all, but modular, adaptable, and context-sensitive. Autonomy, after all, should include the ability to choose your level of responsibility, not be forced into a binary of full control or full delegation.

Ultimately, the fragility of self-custody lies not in its cryptography, but in its anthropology. It assumes a user who is rational, disciplined, consistent, and resilient. But people are emotional, distracted, social, and sometimes vulnerable. The systems we build must honour those realities. We cannot wish them away with ideology or protocol design. *To truly empower individuals, we must meet them where they are—not where we hope they will be.*

The future of decentralised finance depends on resolving this tension. If autonomy is to become more than an aspiration, it must be sustainable. It must be designed for lives that are unpredictable, for users who are diverse, for moments that are messy. That does not mean abandoning the principles of sovereignty or personal control. It means humanising them—embedding empathy into design, building forgiveness into infrastructure, and recognising that responsibility is not just a technical choice but a moral one. *To hold your own keys is to hold your own future. But even the strongest hands get tired. The question is whether we will build systems that support them—or systems that silently punish them when they fail.*

# Chapter 11
# The Philosophies Beneath the Protocols:

It is easy to speak of cryptocurrency purely in technical terms: distributed consensus, cryptographic proofs, decentralised networks. These are the languages of engineers and investors alike. Yet beneath this veneer of protocols and ledgers lies a subtler terrain—philosophy. Crypto is never merely a collection of tools; it is a worldview encoded in software, a moral argument folded into computational logic, a political stance enacted through code. To understand it fully, one must look not only at what it does, but at what it presumes about the world.

Every blockchain, every smart contract, every wallet carries an implicit proposition. Bitcoin wagers that monetary policy should be insulated from human discretion. Ethereum bets that contractual obligations can and should be enforced by machines rather than institutions. DAOs suggest that governance can be algorithmically distributed. Even a simple wallet embodies the claim that the individual—rather than the state or a bank—is the proper custodian of value. These are not mere technical affordances; they are philosophical statements. Crypto, at its essence, is a rebellion against centralisation—not simply of authority, but of interpretation itself. It is a decentralised struggle over narratives as much as a software revolution.

In its earliest incarnation, the movement drew heavily on libertarian and anarcho-capitalist thought. Privacy as resistance, encryption as civil disobedience, money as speech: these were not abstract ideals, but practical design imperatives. Bitcoin's genesis block famously embedded the Times headline: "Chancellor on brink of second bailout for banks." A protest rendered in protocol. Developers were steeped in the cypherpunk ethos and the intellectual legacy of thinkers such as Hayek, Rothbard, and Friedman. For them, crypto was more than financial innovation—it was digital defiance, a secession from fiat regimes and the gaze of centralised authorities.

Yet the libertarian narrative is only one thread. Crypto has evolved into a plurality of visions, sometimes competing, sometimes coexisting. Some see it as a social experiment as much as a financial one: blockchains as laboratories for new forms of cooperation. DAOs propose governance without executives, quadratic voting attempts to weight influence by conviction, and mutual credit systems seek to reconceive debt as a communal resource. These projects are less about libertarian self-interest and more about techno-communitarianism: exploring solidarity and coordination at scale through programmable incentives.

Such experiments raise profound questions: can software replicate social trust? Can incentive structures substitute for leadership? Can code distribute power without creating new hierarchies? These are ontological challenges, not merely technical ones, forcing a reconsideration of what society is and whether algorithms can shoulder moral complexity.

Crypto also carries its mythology. The lone genius founder, the immaculate white paper, the unstoppable protocol: Bitcoin has Satoshi, Ethereum has its canonical pre-sale. These narratives often assume the tenor of prophecy, suggesting inevitability and convergence. But myth can obscure as much as it illuminates, flattening nuance, silencing critique, sacralising code. When inevitability dominates, excess is rationalised, exploitation justified, and accountability sidelined. "It's just the protocol" becomes both shield and excuse.

These myths have tangible consequences for risk perception. Crypto evangelists speak of "trustless" systems, yet trust never vanishes; it migrates—from institutions to developers, from courts to validators, from regulators to cryptographic assumptions. Unlike banks or legal systems, protocols cannot apologise, evolve ethics, or assume responsibility. They are tools, not moral agents. To treat them otherwise is naïve and hazardous.

Perhaps most strikingly, crypto functions as a mirror for human nature. Strip away ideology and one finds psychological truths: tensions between freedom and security, autonomy and solidarity, fairness and ambition. It enables generosity and greed, experimentation and exploitation, cooperation and conflict. The system exposes behaviour when levers of power are new, possibilities abundant, and constraints minimal. It reveals not only what can be built, but what people choose to build when oversight is sparse.

Consider the juxtaposition: the NFT artist creating digital culture alongside the pump-and-dump schemer extracting profit in seconds; grassroots DAOs funding disaster relief alongside protocols hacked for millions. Crypto is neither inherently utopian nor dystopian. It is a complex ecosystem of incentives—and incentives, ultimately, are reflections of human values. The blockchain records actions faithfully, but it does not moralise. That task remains ours.

This chapter traces these philosophical foundations and fault lines. It examines how libertarian impulses informed early architecture, how cooperative experiments are being tested at the margins of code and culture, and how mythologies of inevitability distort accountability. It interrogates not only what crypto seeks to become, but what it reveals about those who build and use it. These are not abstract concerns; they bear directly on governance, policy, community design, and technological development. Philosophy, in this context, is not an academic luxury—it is essential to navigating systems that increasingly shape economic, social, and political life.

The aim is not to provide definitive answers, but to cultivate better questions: questions that challenge simplistic narratives, uncover embedded moral assumptions, and sharpen awareness of the consequences of design choices. Beneath the layers of code, consensus, and tokenomics lie people. And it is their choices—often subtle, often profound—that will determine not only the trajectory of blockchain networks, but the future of freedom, fairness, and responsibility itself.

## Crypto as Libertarian Rebellion:

It is no coincidence that Bitcoin's genesis block contains a headline—not from a tech journal or a blockchain manifesto, but from *The Times* of London: *"Chancellor on brink of second bailout for banks."* This was not a throwaway detail. It was a deliberate act of subversion. A timestamped protest against the fiscal policies of central banks and the moral hazard of government bailouts. More than software, more than finance, Bitcoin was born as ideology. It emerged not from Silicon Valley but from a global subculture deeply sceptical of the state's role in monetary affairs. To understand early crypto is to trace the architecture of rebellion—one that fused libertarian politics, cypherpunk encryption, and anarcho-capitalist theory into a programmable critique of institutional power.

The ideological roots of crypto lie in the libertarian imagination. Long before Satoshi Nakamoto wrote the Bitcoin white paper, there was Friedrich Hayek arguing for the denationalisation of money, Milton Friedman proposing computer-based currencies, and David Chaum experimenting with digital cash. But what distinguished crypto's first true believers was not just economic theory—it was distrust. Distrust of governments to manage currency responsibly. Distrust of central banks to resist inflationary pressure. Distrust of financial intermediaries to operate without coercion or surveillance. The early architects of the crypto movement viewed the traditional financial system not as a flawed but reformable apparatus, but as a fundamentally illegitimate monopoly on money creation.

This deep scepticism of the state positioned crypto not as a tool of policy innovation, but as a tool of *exit*. If you cannot reform the system, build outside it. This was the cypherpunk ethos, articulated in manifestos circulated across early internet forums in the 1990s and 2000s. "Privacy is necessary for an open society," wrote Eric Hughes in his foundational Cypherpunk Manifesto. But privacy was never just about data—it was about sovereignty. The ability to communicate, transact, and coordinate without the permission of gatekeepers. Crypto was their technological lever. Decentralised networks. Strong encryption. Public-key cryptography. These were the weapons of digital dissent.

Anarcho-capitalism—a more radical offshoot of libertarian thought—went even further. Here, the goal was not merely to remove the state from money, but from law, governance, and even the provision of security. Bitcoin was embraced as a blueprint for stateless order. In this framework, consensus algorithms substituted for parliaments. Code replaced policy. Market incentives, not democratic processes, ensured stability. The sovereign individual, not the social contract, became the core political unit. It was a profound reimagining of governance: not by rules, but by protocols; not by courts, but by consensus.

This ideological DNA can be seen in how early crypto networks were architected. Bitcoin's hard cap of 21 million coins was a rebuke to inflationary monetary policy—*a deflationary design encoded in mathematics rather than debated in committee rooms*. Ethereum's programmable smart contracts offered a vision of law without lawyers, regulation without regulators. These were not value-neutral tools; they were expressions of belief. Belief in spontaneous order. Belief in markets as mechanisms of truth. Belief that systemic trust could be replaced by cryptographic certainty.

Yet, for all its rhetorical clarity, libertarian crypto ideology was not without internal contradictions. Chief among them: *Who builds the trustless system, and who maintains it?* Bitcoin claims to operate without intermediaries, but the ecosystem depends on miners, developers, and core maintainers. These actors wield disproportionate influence, even if not codified as formal authority. The same is true for

Ethereum, whose development is guided by technical councils and working groups. These roles are often informally centralised, yet ideologically disavowed. The tension between decentralisation as aspiration and centralisation as operational reality has never fully resolved.

Moreover, libertarianism's emphasis on autonomy and non-intervention faltered when confronted with real-world complexity. Self-custody of assets, while philosophically pure, exposed users to significant risk. Hacks, lost keys, and exploitations of smart contract bugs—these highlighted the fragility of radical responsibility. With no recourse to legal protection or institutional redress, users bore full liability. The question emerged: *How much freedom is too much freedom when error becomes irreversible?* The uncompromising purity of early crypto often left no room for nuance.

Another paradox: crypto's libertarian roots animated some of the most speculative and extractive behaviours in its later evolution. Token pumps, leverage-based gambling, and zero-sum memecoins often masqueraded under the banner of "financial freedom." But these practices mirrored the very predatory logic that libertarians claimed to resist—opaque systems, insider advantage, and asymmetric information. The protocol may be open, but outcomes were often unequal. Here, ideology was not merely stretched; it was sometimes weaponised.

Critics also point to a larger concern: that by refusing to engage with public institutions, crypto's libertarian fringe may inadvertently cede terrain to authoritarian actors. If democratic states cannot integrate or regulate decentralised systems, others will. Surveillance regimes, rogue states, and oligarchic entities have proven adept at co-opting blockchain infrastructure for their own ends—be it censorship-resistant propaganda, sanctions evasion, or opaque fundraising. Libertarian withdrawal may clear the path for *new* forms of coercive power, not less.

Despite these tensions, the libertarian influence on crypto remains foundational. It shaped the ethos of Bitcoin maximalism. It fuelled the early explosion of ICOs and self-organised DAOs. It continues to animate debates over privacy, censorship resistance, and regulatory overreach. Most crucially, it shifted the Overton window of what is imaginable in finance. Before Bitcoin, the notion of state-independent money was utopian at best, seditious at worst. After Bitcoin, it became a live proposition—one that central banks, financial regulators, and geopolitical strategists could no longer ignore.

The question now is not whether libertarianism shaped crypto—it unquestionably did. The question is whether that framework remains adequate for the challenges ahead. Decentralised systems are no longer theoretical or marginal. They are being tested at scale, in financial markets, political movements, and conflict zones. They intersect with energy consumption, climate policy, digital identity, and cross-border capital flows. They do not merely operate *outside* institutions—they increasingly shape how institutions must respond.

For crypto to mature, it must grapple with the philosophical legacy it has inherited. That includes honouring its libertarian insights—on censorship resistance, autonomy, and open-source innovation—while acknowledging their limits in a world that is both interconnected and adversarial. The next phase of crypto ideology may not be about rebellion, but about *integration without surrender*. The ability to remain sovereign without being solipsistic. The courage to participate in public discourse, not just code around it.

And so the arc bends, not towards inevitability, but towards complexity. Crypto's libertarian rebellion was a necessary rupture. It challenged monopoly power, reignited debate on the nature of money, and proved that decentralised coordination at scale was not only possible, but perhaps preferable in certain domains. But if it is to realise its deeper potential—not just as a hedge against tyranny but as a substrate for more equitable systems—it must evolve beyond its founding myths. Freedom, after all, is only meaningful if it enables more than just escape. It must enable responsibility, reciprocity, and ethical imagination. Crypto's next rebellion may not be against the state, but against its own dogmas.

## Crypto as Social Experiment:

Crypto's most revolutionary promise was never financial speculation—it was social coordination. In its more imaginative incarnations, the technology has served as a staging ground for rethinking how humans cooperate at scale: how they govern, allocate resources, resolve disputes, and build shared futures without depending on traditional hierarchies. Far from merely creating new types of money, the crypto universe is home to experiments in collective intelligence, democratic tooling, and economic mutualism that reach far beyond the ledger. In this sense, crypto does not just *support* alternative social models—it *embodies* them in code, offering a programmable substrate for reinventing the machinery of collaboration itself.

The question is not whether these experiments will work perfectly—few ever do in early stages—but whether they push us to reconsider the institutional defaults we take for granted. Representative democracy, for example, is widely accepted as the best scalable method for large-group decision-making, yet it is riddled with voter apathy, lobbying distortion, and winner-takes-all stagnation.

Traditional corporate governance structures centralise power in opaque boards and C-suites, where shareholder primacy trumps stakeholder inclusion. Public goods—from climate protection to open-source infrastructure—suffer from coordination failures that neither markets nor states have adequately resolved. Into this landscape steps a new breed of crypto-enabled experimentation: *mechanisms that try to solve coordination problems not by mandate, but by design.*

Take decentralised autonomous organisations (DAOs). At their most basic, DAOs are smart-contract governed communities that make decisions via token-based voting. But at their most radical, they are attempts to rewrite the grammar of institutions themselves. Unlike traditional entities, DAOs operate without central leadership, instead coordinating through pre-agreed rules encoded on the blockchain. Members propose, deliberate, and vote—often with treasuries holding real assets, from stablecoins to governance tokens. While many DAOs resemble early-stage cooperatives or investment clubs, others function as grants bodies, protocol stewards, or even algorithmic city-states.

DAOs represent a move away from personality-driven leadership and towards rules-based trust. But this shift comes with trade-offs. The same transparency that ensures auditability can also lead to performative signalling and decision paralysis. Token-weighted voting, while simple, risks plutocracy—where the wealthy dominate decisions regardless of merit. Many DAOs have struggled with voter engagement, suffering from chronic under-participation and unclear accountability. Yet, rather than dismiss the entire concept, these failures should be seen as iterative. Traditional democracies took centuries to develop basic checks and balances; DAOs are barely a decade old and already fielding innovations such as *conviction voting*, *reputation-weighted governance*, and *delegated councils*. They are not perfected systems—they are open-source blueprints, being battle-tested in public.

If DAOs rethink governance, quadratic voting reimagines fairness. Developed by economist Glen Weyl and adopted by a growing number of blockchain-based platforms, quadratic voting allows individuals to express preference strength, not just binary choices. Rather than casting one vote per person per issue, participants are given a fixed budget of voting credits and can allocate multiple votes to signal intensity. The cost of each additional vote increases quadratically, discouraging vote hoarding while amplifying minority passions. For example, if someone deeply cares about a single policy while being ambivalent about others, they can spend more credits to reflect that depth—something first-past-the-post systems cannot capture.

Quadratic voting has already found pilot applications in grant distribution, such as Gitcoin's funding rounds for open-source software. Here, matched contributions from a common pool are determined not just by the amount donated, but by the number of unique contributors—ensuring that broad-based support is weighted more than concentrated wealth. The result is not only more democratic, but more *informationally rich*: projects that command real community interest tend to rise in visibility and sustainability. Of course, challenges remain. Quadratic voting assumes identity verification and sybil resistance, both unsolved problems in decentralised systems. But these are design frontiers, not terminal flaws.

Another ambitious frontier is mutual credit systems—non-monetary exchange networks in which credit is created at the point of transaction rather than issued top-down by banks. In mutual credit, participants do not require pre-existing capital; they extend value to one another on the basis of trust and reputational reciprocity. Historically used in local exchange trading systems (LETS) and timebanks, mutual credit models have been revived on blockchain infrastructure to overcome the limitations of scale and trust. Projects like Holochain and Credit Commons propose distributed ledgers where communities issue credit internally and settle balances across federated networks. These systems seek to decouple money from scarcity and inflation, redefining liquidity as a social relationship rather than a commodity.

At its heart, mutual credit challenges the scarcity paradigm embedded in fiat systems. Whereas traditional currencies rely on artificial scarcity to preserve value—through central bank controls, interest rates, and legal tender laws—mutual credit treats value as emergent from social contribution. In this worldview, economies are not driven by extractive accumulation, but by cooperative surplus exchange. It is a radical inversion of mainstream financial logic, and one made technically feasible by decentralised record-keeping and cryptographic assurance. Yet, such models still face hurdles of network effect, cultural adoption, and interoperability. They do not scale easily in a world accustomed to price signals and private capital. But they persist—small, experimental, and deeply instructive.

Critics rightly point out that these models often remain idealistic, underfunded, or co-opted. Some DAOs devolve into personality cults or oligarchies. Some quadratic voting experiments are manipulated by bots or whales. Mutual credit systems may fail to attract critical mass. Yet, the criticism that these systems are imperfect misses the point. *The real question is whether our existing institutions are adequate for the complexities of 21st-century coordination—and whether crypto offers not a replacement, but a new toolkit.* A laboratory of mechanisms, from which both decentralised and centralised systems might borrow.

There are deeper philosophical tensions here. Can social trust be reduced to code? Can governance be fully automated without compromising deliberation, empathy, and context? The best crypto social experiments acknowledge these tensions and design around them. They do not pretend that smart contracts can eliminate human politics, but rather seek to channel its energy more productively. Where traditional institutions hide behind bureaucracy and inertia, crypto systems reveal their assumptions in plain sight—public, editable, forkable. Governance becomes a living protocol, not a static constitution.

Indeed, one of the greatest contributions of the crypto social imagination is not any particular mechanism, but *the meta-idea that institutions themselves can be versioned.* Forking is not just for code; it is for governance structures, economic arrangements, and collective rules. This opens a pluralist vista—one in which communities can experiment with many micro-political forms, learn from their outcomes, and iterate. Just as open-source software thrived through decentralised contributions and modularity, so too might open-source institutions.

Of course, the fact that something can be forked does not mean it will succeed. The replication of institutional form requires more than code—it requires norms, narratives, and long-term stewardship. Many DAOs have faltered not because of technical failures, but because they lacked the cultural infrastructure to weather conflict or cultivate shared purpose. Coordination is not just a technical problem—it is an emotional and psychological one. Incentives may align, but without trust, patience, and vision, they rarely endure.

Crypto as a social experiment, then, is best understood not as a utopian escape from politics, but as a pragmatic rehearsal of new political forms. It is neither purely libertarian nor technocratic. It is a protean field of experiments—some naive, some profound—about how humans can coordinate without coercion, govern without hierarchy, and exchange value without exclusion. Its success will not be measured only in market capitalisation or transaction throughput, but in its contribution to the broader repertoire of institutional design.

In this light, the question becomes: how do we learn from these experiments, even when they fail? What do DAOs teach us about participation? What does quadratic voting teach us about preference intensity? What does mutual credit teach us about relational economies? These are not only technical inquiries—they are moral and philosophical ones. They force us to ask: what kinds of systems are worth building? And who gets to decide?

Crypto may never fully replace existing institutions, but it is already reshaping the horizon of what is thinkable. As long as the experiments continue—with humility, rigour, and imagination—they will remain among the most important laboratories for the future of cooperation.

## Crypto as Technological Mythology:

Technologies rarely rise on function alone. They require stories—compelling, simplified, and repeated until believed. Cryptocurrency, perhaps more than any digital innovation since the internet, has been built not just on code but on myth. These myths aren't accidental;

they are cultural scaffolding. They carry ideological payloads, recruit believers, suppress dissent, and justify extreme bets. *Crypto is not merely a technology—it is a mythology in motion, built on narratives of inevitability, emancipation, and salvation.* But myth, when left unexamined, can obscure risk, silence complexity, and immunise a movement against self-correction.

The most persistent myth in crypto is that of *inevitability.* According to this narrative, the arc of financial history bends inexorably toward decentralisation. Central banks, fiat currencies, and legacy institutions are relics awaiting disruption. In this frame, crypto is not an option—it is a destiny. The rhetoric echoes a kind of digital manifest destiny: "you can't stop an idea whose time has come." This framing serves a purpose—it rallies confidence, attracts capital, and sustains belief through volatility. But it also short-circuits critical inquiry. *When something is treated as inevitable, asking whether it is desirable becomes irrelevant.* The techno-determinist position conflates possibility with necessity, marginalising debate about what kind of systems we actually want to build and live under.

The narrative of inevitability is often paired with one of *techno-salvation*—the belief that crypto will solve foundational societal problems through engineering alone. Inflation, censorship, inequality, corruption: all are assumed to yield to cryptographic elegance. Bitcoin becomes the antidote to irresponsible central banking; Ethereum, a substrate for economic democracy; smart contracts, a replacement for corrupt bureaucracies. This is not mere optimism—it is the elevation of code to cure. The assumption is that because a problem is technical in part, it must be solvable in full by technical means. This belief aligns closely with Silicon Valley's historical posture: that social problems are design flaws awaiting disruptive solutions. But not all trust failures can be resolved through trustlessness. Not all corruption is the result of insufficient transparency. *Engineering can create infrastructure—but legitimacy, accountability, and justice are emergent social phenomena that resist full automation.*

This mythology has a psychology. It appeals not only to the mind, but to the identity of the believer. In the same way that political ideologies or religious convictions offer frameworks for understanding the world, crypto mythologies give adherents a coherent narrative of resistance, superiority, and transformation. They offer moral clarity in a chaotic age: the state is the enemy, fiat is fraud, the protocol is truth. Doubt is interpreted as betrayal, and critique is pathologised as ignorance or fear. This explains the tribal ferocity with which some defend even broken projects. Their allegiance is not only to the utility of the technology, but to its symbolic role as a vehicle of personal and collective transcendence.

The problem is not that narratives exist—they always will—but that they can become so monolithic that they stifle necessary nuance. Take the veneration of decentralisation. While often a worthy goal, decentralisation is not inherently good. It introduces trade-offs: slower governance, weaker user protections, fragmented UX, and coordination gridlock. Yet in much of the crypto discourse, decentralisation is positioned as an unqualified virtue. The deeper question—*decentralisation of what, for whom, and to what end?*—is rarely explored in detail. Similarly, the idolisation of immutability ignores legitimate needs for adaptability, redress, and error correction. Systems that cannot evolve may avoid tampering, but they also ossify in the face of complexity.

Another myth worth interrogating is that of meritocratic utopia. Crypto is often presented as a level playing field where talent, vision, and code determine success. The permissionless nature of blockchain networks fuels this story: anyone can build, transact, participate. But in practice, early access, capital concentration, social signalling, and insider knowledge all shape outcomes. Whales dominate governance. Early investors extract rent from protocols they no longer contribute to. "Community" often serves as a euphemism for founder-controlled networks with opaque decision-making. *The myth of the open meritocracy can obscure structural inequalities and reproduce them in decentralised form.*

Even more insidious is the myth of apolitical neutrality. Many projects claim to be "just tools," mere infrastructure awaiting use. This stance is seductive because it sidesteps moral responsibility. If a protocol is neutral, then its designers are not accountable for how it is used. But this is a profound evasion. Every technological architecture embeds values—what it optimises for, what it excludes, what it makes easy or hard. The decision to prioritise anonymity over auditability, speed over verification, openness over safety—these are not technical trade-offs alone. They are ethical positions, whether acknowledged or not. *To deny this is to abdicate the very responsibilities that decentralised systems claim to improve upon.*

The mythology also flattens history. Bitcoin did not emerge from a vacuum, but from a lineage of libertarian, cypherpunk, and post-crisis dissatisfaction with financial institutions. Ethereum was born not just from technological curiosity, but from a desire to experiment with institutional design and digital law. DAOs, NFTs, DeFi, and beyond are not inevitabilities—they are choices among many possible futures. Myth compresses this history into a single arc of "progress," often brushing over the failures, dead ends, and ideological contradictions that complicate the picture. It romanticises early developers as prophetic visionaries and overlooks the messy, contested, and sometimes self-interested realities of project governance and funding.

Importantly, technological mythologies are not unique to crypto. The internet, artificial intelligence, and biotech have all spawned their own cults of inevitability. But crypto is especially susceptible because its tools are simultaneously financial and ideological. They affect power directly. The stakes are not limited to technological adoption—they implicate questions of sovereignty, identity, and control. That is why critical thinking within crypto is so essential—and so often unwelcome. *When mythology reigns unchecked, self-regulation becomes self-congratulation.*

This is not an argument against crypto's promise, but against its complacency. A mature movement does not fear critique—it demands it. Honest inquiry strengthens resilience. A culture that can entertain doubt, welcome dissent, and adapt with humility is far more likely to survive than one that silences introspection in favour of unfalsifiable slogans. The true strength of decentralised systems lies not in their narratives, but in their capacity to absorb complexity without collapsing into dogma.

That requires new habits of thought. Projects must learn to articulate not only what they do, but *why they matter*, *to whom*, and *at what cost.*

Communities must build norms that reward transparency over theatrics, governance over charisma, and reflection over hype. Protocols must stop pretending they are above politics and begin grappling with the realities of power, inequality, and unintended consequence. *The mythology must give way to a more grounded ethic: one that treats crypto not as a messianic deliverance, but as a contested terrain of opportunity and risk.*

What we need is not less imagination—but more responsible storytelling. The future is not written in code alone. It is shaped by who tells the story, how it is told, and who has the power to question it. Crypto has always been about rewriting the rules. But perhaps the most important rule to rewrite now is the one that insists it will all work out because it must. It won't. It will only work out if we build with eyes open, mythologies interrogated, and reality as the standard—not the slogan.

## Crypto as Mirror for Human Nature:

There is a peculiar honesty to decentralised systems: they do not mask human nature—they amplify it. Cryptocurrencies and blockchain networks, for all their technological novelty, are not departures from the human condition but rather intensified reflections of it. When you remove intermediaries, automate enforcement, and decentralise control, what remains is not neutrality—it is raw exposure. *Crypto is not just code; it is a behavioural experiment conducted in real time on a global scale, illuminating the best and worst of who we are.*

The early idealism surrounding crypto often spoke in utopian registers: financial inclusion, trustless cooperation, censorship resistance. These aspirations were not unfounded. Blockchain technology offers mechanisms that can empower the unbanked, dismantle monopolies, and reduce dependence on corrupt institutions. But alongside these ambitions, crypto has also nurtured greed, deception, tribalism, and chaos. The same networks that enable radical transparency also allow for wash trading, rug pulls, and Ponzi schemes. The same tools that promise autonomy can isolate users and expose them to irreversible loss. What crypto reveals, more than anything, is that *technology cannot transcend human nature—it simply reconfigures its expression.*

Consider the psychology of markets. Crypto's volatility isn't just a technical feature—it is a crucible for fear and euphoria. Price action becomes a mirror for collective emotion, with greed driving irrational rallies and panic fuelling sudden crashes. Memecoins rise on hype and insider games. NFTs sell not just as digital art but as status tokens and speculative chips. At the heart of many of these phenomena is *the deeply human craving for status, certainty, and community.* Traders form digital tribes, complete with their own vernaculars, mascots, and rituals. Maximalists defend their protocol of choice not unlike fans defending a sports team—or, more troublingly, like partisans defending ideology. Rational discourse gives way to belief enforcement. Reason yields to religion.

At the same time, crypto has surfaced extraordinary examples of altruism, experimentation, and civic imagination. During the early stages of the Ukraine war, crypto donations poured in faster than fiat transfers, supporting everything from medical aid to drone technology. When centralised fundraising channels failed in crisis regions, decentralised autonomous organisations (DAOs) stepped in to coordinate relief. In moments like these, *crypto exhibits what may be its most redeeming quality: the capacity to coordinate goodwill across borders at speed and scale.* The protocol is agnostic—its use is human.

This duality is not accidental—it is structural. Open networks invite open participation. There is no identity verification required to deploy a smart contract, launch a token, or spin up a DAO. This openness is empowering but also vulnerable to manipulation. Scammers thrive not despite decentralisation, but because of it. Without central authority or enforcement, the integrity of the system depends on user vigilance, peer reputation, and hard-coded safeguards. Yet these are blunt instruments against manipulation, and as history shows, *humans often prove eager to believe what benefits them financially.* Fraud flourishes in the fog between technical literacy and economic desperation.

Ethically, crypto does not escape old dilemmas—it intensifies them. Anonymity protects dissidents in authoritarian regimes, but it also shields money launderers and dark web markets. Immutability prevents state censorship but also locks in bugs, exploits, and controversial histories. Permissionless systems resist exclusion but enable exploitation. The value-neutral architecture of blockchains means that every ethical choice is ultimately deferred to users and developers. *Crypto does not dictate outcomes—it decentralises moral responsibility*. This redistribution can be empowering, but also destabilising. It places ethical agency in the hands of those who may or may not be prepared to wield it.

Even the most basic function of crypto—holding one's own assets—asks psychological questions few are trained to answer. Self-custody represents the pinnacle of financial autonomy, but it also comes with burdens: the fear of losing seed phrases, the paralysis of decision-making without recourse, the anxiety of navigating scams and bugs without protection. For many, these pressures create a paradox: *the more freedom one gains, the more isolated and uncertain one may feel*. This is not merely a technical support issue—it is a psychological and sociological challenge. Autonomy is not just about removing intermediaries; it is about preparing individuals for responsibility in systems designed without safety nets.

Community governance, another pillar of the decentralised dream, offers a further glimpse into collective human behaviour. DAOs, in theory, promise democratic coordination. In practice, many are plagued by apathy, groupthink, plutocracy, and poor information hygiene. Participation rates are low. Power often consolidates in the hands of large token holders. Proposals become battlegrounds for influence rather than sites of deliberation. The promise of collective intelligence is frequently undercut by cognitive overload and rational disengagement. *Direct democracy without deliberative infrastructure often becomes the theatre of token-weighted performativity*.

Yet these failures are not reasons to dismiss crypto. They are signals. They suggest that any system, no matter how elegant its architecture, must grapple with the limits and contradictions of its users. Crypto has exposed how easy it is to design mechanisms that work in theory but fail under real social pressures. It has shown how abstract incentives can distort behaviour in ways that no white paper predicted. It reminds us that *trustless systems still require trust—in the code, the community, the intent.* And that trust, like any human resource, is both scarce and fragile.

Perhaps most revealing is how crypto surfaces tensions between individual agency and collective responsibility. On one hand, it promises liberation from institutions: you are your own bank, your own custodian, your own governor. On the other, it asks for new forms of cooperation, shared infrastructure, and mutual accountability. These dual demands are deeply human—they mirror the broader political tension between autonomy and solidarity. Crypto does not resolve this tension. It replays it on-chain, in new forms, every day.

The way forward is not to sanitise or suppress these reflections, but to embrace them as diagnostic. Crypto is a tool, but it is also a test. It asks: what do we do when no one is watching? How do we build when consensus is slow and trust is thin? What does it mean to own value, to govern networks, to build institutions in public? These are not engineering questions. They are human ones. *Crypto is not a mirror of perfection—it is a mirror of potential.* What we see in it depends on where we look, and how honestly we're willing to see ourselves.

Ultimately, crypto is not an escape from human nature—it is a confrontation with it. The question is not whether the technology works. It is whether we are willing to wrestle with what it reveals about us—and whether we have the courage to build systems that make us not just richer, but wiser.

# Conclusion
# Living with Radical Uncertainty:

There is no final curtain in a system that refuses stillness. Cryptocurrency is not a completed puzzle, nor a perfected protocol. It exists as a living, shifting landscape of risk and opportunity—equal parts innovation and vulnerability. As it seeps into finance, governance, law, identity, and ethics, one reality grows unavoidable: code alone cannot rescue us from the human condition. Algorithms enforce rules, but they cannot embed wisdom. Blockchains can foster trustless environments, yet they cannot substitute for judgment, moral discernment, or the capacity to navigate complexity.

What excites is what unsettles. Crypto offers tools for sovereignty, yet demands the vigilance that sovereignty entails. It displaces central authority, but leaves behind a void that must be managed. It accelerates coordination, but magnifies fragility. Beneath it all lies an enduring question that code cannot answer: how should we relate to power—ours, others', and the systems we collectively construct? This is the question that shapes the stakes of the crypto era, far more than any white paper or price chart.

We inhabit a moment of institutional fragility. Confidence in banks, governments, and platforms is eroding. Crypto does not arrive as a fully formed alternative; it arrives as a provocation. It does not promise flawless systems, only a chance to reconsider participation in structures that may be simultaneously more open and more perilous. Decentralisation offers agency, not safety. That trade-off is radical, and not everyone will—or should—embrace it.

The appeal of cryptographic certainty is easy to understand. In a world rife with opacity and manipulation, the idea that mathematics can supplant fallible institutions is alluring. Smart contracts replace bureaucrats; immutable ledgers expose fraud; tokenised incentives correct the failures of fiat. Yet clarity in code does not translate to clarity in consequence. Flash loan exploits obey the rules; so do DAO breaches and MEV front-running. Precision is not justice. Execution is not ethics.

Technological optimism has its limits. The assumption that good code guarantees good outcomes ignores the messiness of human life. Social norms must be interpreted, ethical trade-offs debated, and moral responsibility negotiated. The fantasy of automated fairness neglects that fairness is contextual, contested, and evolving. Crypto, at its most reflective, wrestles with this reality; at its most dogmatic, it clings to the illusion that incentives alone can engineer virtue.

A more candid perspective recognises crypto as substrate, not solution. It does not resolve politics; it illuminates them. It does not abolish inequality; it reshapes its mechanics. It does not prevent abuse; it shifts its vectors. Decentralisation offers design latitude, not moral advantage. How this latitude is used—whether to entrench extraction or foster cooperation—is a collective decision still being written.

To engage seriously is to accept radical uncertainty. There are no blueprints, no fixed definitions, no universally agreed objectives. Bitcoin maximalists, Ethereum innovators, DAO architects, privacy advocates, meme traders, and regulatory sceptics coexist, yet speak different languages of value. Each reflects a distinct approach to power: some seek to evade it, others to reshape it, others to gamify it. Crypto does not resolve these tensions; it contains them.

Self-awareness becomes paramount. Participants—developers, policymakers, investors, observers—must confront their own priorities. What do they seek from systems of money, identity, and exchange? Which risks are acceptable in pursuit of autonomy? Which compromises are tolerable between efficiency and inclusion, privacy and compliance, experimentation and safety? These are not technical questions; they are philosophical, and unavoidable.

Closure is seductive but illusory. No platform, consensus mechanism, or legal framework can stabilise the chaos. Crypto advances by iteration, not destination: every exploit triggers forks, every scandal prompts governance reform, every collapse tests resilience anew. Movement occurs through conflict as much as consensus, and within that dynamism lies both promise and peril.

The lesson is attentiveness, not dogma. The future of crypto will not be dictated solely by manifestos or regulation. It will emerge from countless small decisions: wallet design, community voting, narrative framing, and the distribution of responsibility. Crypto is not a revolution behind us; it is an experiment still unfolding.

Living with crypto means living with ambiguity. Decentralisation empowers yet isolates. Openness fosters innovation yet invites exploitation. Trustless systems depend, paradoxically, on trust. This ambiguity is not a flaw—it is the terrain itself. Navigating it demands critical thought, ethical imagination, and, above all, humility.

Code alone is insufficient. Protocols cannot arbitrate morality. Systems reflect the care and judgment of those who design them. And the designers—humans—remain brilliant, fallible, and unfinished. That is not a reason for despair, but for engagement: eyes open, values clear, responsibility embraced. Not as passive passengers of inevitability, but as stewards of possibility.

## "The Code Can't Save You":

It is tempting to believe that if we can only write the right code, we can eliminate failure, corruption, or deceit. This is the central myth of the crypto age: that trust can be fully abstracted into mathematics, that human imperfection can be engineered out through elegant protocols, and that systemic risk is simply a coordination problem waiting to be solved by better logic. But this vision, however well-intentioned, misjudges the deeper realities of human complexity. *The promise of cryptographic trust is powerful—but it is not redemptive.* The code can optimise processes, but it cannot absolve responsibility. It can execute a function flawlessly, but it cannot determine whether the function should have been executed in the first place.

The dream of replacing fallible humans with incorruptible code is not new. In fact, it reflects a long-standing aspiration within techno-utopian thinking: that we might finally bypass the ambiguities of politics, ethics, and emotion with systems that are precise, impartial, and self-governing. In crypto, this dream finds its purest expression in the smart contract—a piece of software that performs exactly as programmed, without the need for courts, intermediaries, or appeals. But even the most sophisticated smart contract cannot resolve questions of fairness, harm, or justice. *Code is not conscience. It is process without perspective.*

Consider The DAO, Ethereum's early decentralised venture fund, which famously collapsed in 2016 after a hacker exploited a vulnerability not in the Ethereum network itself, but in the smart contract code that governed The DAO's treasury. The attacker didn't break the rules—they followed them. The logic of the contract permitted the exploit, even if the spirit of the project did not. This distinction—between what is allowed and what is acceptable—cannot be resolved by better syntax. It is a question of judgement, not computation.

And yet, many within the crypto community continue to treat the codebase as sacred text—immutable, authoritative, immune to interpretation. This software fundamentalism creates a dangerous form of tunnel vision. By insisting that "code is law," the movement risks conflating enforceability with legitimacy. But not all laws are just, and not all contracts are ethical. If a smart contract allows a predatory transaction, it may be technically valid and socially destructive. *Execution does not equal wisdom.*

There is also the matter of social context. Cryptographic systems operate within human networks, and those networks are rife with asymmetries—of information, access, and power. A decentralised exchange may function flawlessly on a technical level, but if it's dominated by insiders using MEV bots to front-run trades, the experience becomes extractive for ordinary users. The code does what it's supposed to. *The system still fails the people it was meant to serve.*

Moreover, the belief in technological neutrality is a convenient fiction. Every design decision embeds assumptions about behaviour, values, and priorities. Do we optimise for speed or censorship resistance? For privacy or compliance? For individual sovereignty or collective governance? These trade-offs are not mere engineering choices—they are philosophical commitments. Pretending otherwise allows builders to avoid the moral weight of their architectures. But *design is never neutral. It is always political.*

Even cryptographic primitives themselves are not immune to misuse. Zero-knowledge proofs, for instance, are a powerful tool for privacy-preserving computation. But they can also be leveraged to conceal financial flows from regulators, launder funds, or facilitate fraud. The same can be said for decentralised autonomous organisations (DAOs), which can coordinate global collaboration—or serve as shell entities to offload liability and accountability. Technology doesn't dictate outcomes. *It enables a range of outcomes—some liberatory, some exploitative.*

There is a deeper irony here. The same systems built to eliminate trust often end up requiring it in more subtle forms. We trust the maintainers of open-source code not to insert backdoors. We trust oracle providers to relay accurate information. We trust developers not to rug-pull their communities. We trust validators to act in good faith. Trust doesn't disappear—it just migrates. The question is whether that trust is visible, distributed, and accountable—or hidden behind layers of abstraction.

The fallacy of code as salvation is particularly dangerous because it conceals these dependencies. It suggests that once a system is cryptographically secure, its users are safe. But history shows otherwise. Users routinely lose access to their funds due to misplaced keys, phishing scams, protocol bugs, or governance failures. Entire ecosystems have been wiped out by seemingly minor oversights—Terra-Luna's collapse being one of the most dramatic examples. None of these events were prevented by code. All were amplified by the belief that the system itself was self-correcting.

This belief also underestimates the role of narrative. In crypto, stories are as powerful as protocols. Bitcoin's origin story, for instance, frames it as a response to state overreach and financial repression. Ethereum's narrative celebrates programmability and collective coordination. These stories shape how communities interpret events, justify behaviour, and enforce norms. But stories can also be manipulated. The myth of "number go up" has driven countless retail investors into speculative frenzies, often orchestrated by insiders. The tale of decentralisation can mask centralised power structures hidden behind multisig wallets and foundation boards. *Narrative without scrutiny is propaganda.*

To navigate this terrain honestly, we must reject the binary thinking that pits decentralisation against centralisation as good versus evil. Both models contain risks. Centralised systems can be abusive, opaque, and exclusionary. Decentralised systems can be chaotic, unaccountable, and captured by early movers. The goal is not to replace one flawed model with another, but to ask better questions: Who benefits? Who decides? Who takes responsibility when things go wrong?

This brings us to the hardest truth of all: no system—whether built on paper or protocol—can insulate us from moral complexity. Trustlessness is not a moral escape hatch. It is a shift in how power is distributed, and it still demands vigilance, empathy, and reflection. When something breaks, we must still decide what to do. When harm is done, we must still reckon with its causes. When progress is made, we must still ask who was left behind. *There is no software patch for ethics.*

Ultimately, the greatest risk is not technical failure—it is ethical abdication. If we come to believe that the code will handle everything, we stop asking the hard questions. We assume that what works is what's right. That what's permissionless is what's fair. That what's decentralised is what's democratic. These are dangerous illusions. Crypto's real promise lies not in eliminating human flaws, but in confronting them more transparently. Systems can be improved. Incentives can be aligned. But *none of it matters without people willing to take responsibility for what they build.*

The future will not be written in Solidity alone. It will be shaped by values, debate, and design. And the question facing every participant in the crypto ecosystem is not whether the code will run—but *whether we are prepared to live with what the code enables*. Responsibility does not vanish because systems are decentralised. If anything, it multiplies. The architecture of trust has changed. The burden of stewardship has not.

## "Choosing Your Relationship to Power":

There was a time when most people never questioned where power resided. It sat inside institutions—governments, banks, religious bodies, universities—and those institutions, whether trusted or resented, formed the stable scaffolding of public life. Today, that scaffolding is visibly fraying. The modern individual stands exposed in a paradoxical space: empowered by technology yet encumbered by its opacity; more autonomous in theory, but increasingly accountable for choices once managed by distant gatekeepers. Crypto, in this context, is not just a financial tool. It is an invitation—perhaps even a demand—for each participant to *reassess their personal relationship to power.*

This reassessment is not a technical matter. It is philosophical, psychological, and profoundly political. What does it mean to be sovereign in a world where digital systems mediate our money, our identity, and our information flows? How much responsibility are we truly willing to accept in exchange for freedom? And when trust shifts from institutions to protocols, what new vulnerabilities emerge—social, ethical, and personal?

One of crypto's most disruptive contributions is its redefinition of where control lives. In traditional finance, custody and authority are outsourced: your bank safeguards your assets, your government regulates the system, and your legal apparatus offers recourse if something goes wrong. In decentralised finance (DeFi), that scaffolding is replaced by smart contracts, public keys, and immutable code. But here's the friction: the moment control returns to the user, *so too does the burden.* Misplace a seed phrase, and your funds are gone. Misread a protocol, and your transaction is irreversible. There are no help desks in sovereignty. *Autonomy without comprehension is perilous.*

Yet many are attracted to precisely this responsibility. For them, the ability to transact without permission, store value without surveillance, and participate in systems without gatekeeping is worth the trade-offs. This is not naïve idealism—it is a response to decades of creeping mistrust. The 2008 financial crisis, mass data breaches, central bank interventions, and the weaponisation of economic systems have all shown how centralised structures can collapse or conspire. Crypto offers an alternative narrative: if you can't trust the system, become the system. *Power, once abstract and distant, is now programmable and personal.*

Still, there is a romanticism here that warrants interrogation. While decentralised technologies promise disintermediation, they also create new centres of power—developers, miners, validators, influencers, and whales—who wield significant control under the banner of neutrality. Choosing autonomy in this landscape doesn't mean rejecting all power; it means becoming vigilant about where it hides. *You can exit the bank, but you may have entered a Discord server governed by a pseudonymous founder with admin keys and opaque motives.*

The practical implication is this: users must learn to navigate power not as a fixed structure, but as a moving landscape. Every action in the crypto ecosystem—buying tokens, delegating stake, voting in DAOs, or running nodes—carries implications. Are you reinforcing centralisation by following convenience? Are you relying on reputational trust while claiming technical trustlessness? Are you contributing to systems you understand, or blindly participating in gamified markets engineered for engagement, not enlightenment? These are not incidental questions. They are *ethical coordinates in a decentralised map.*

Education, then, becomes political. In a world where financial tools are increasingly self-directed, literacy is no longer optional—it is the new gatekeeper. Knowing how private keys work, understanding gas fees, recognising wallet permissions, and evaluating tokenomics are not just technical skills; they are exercises in power-awareness. Every user must become their own auditor, their own risk officer, their own trustee. This may sound empowering, but it is also exhausting. *Responsibility at scale is not frictionless—it is fatiguing, even isolating.*

This fatigue gives rise to a temptation: the delegation of power under the illusion of empowerment. Many platforms offer "user-friendly" abstractions that reintroduce custodianship behind a sleek interface. Many communities claim to be decentralised while deferring all decision-making to charismatic founders or core dev teams. The paradox is that *decentralised systems often regress toward centralised behaviours*—because centralisation is cognitively easier. Choosing autonomy requires vigilance not once, but continuously.

It also demands clarity about your own values. Do you value privacy enough to accept usability compromises? Do you value sovereignty enough to accept legal grey zones or regulatory risks? Do you value community enough to participate in slow, messy governance processes instead of passive consumption? These are deeply personal calculations. Crypto does not impose answers. It merely sharpens the questions and forces them into your wallet, your browser, and your digital identity.

And what of trust? If crypto decentralises systems by removing the need to trust institutions, does it eliminate trust altogether? Not quite. It reconfigures it. You may not need to trust a bank, but you do trust the math behind cryptographic algorithms. You trust open-source contributors. You trust the GitHub repo hasn't been hijacked. You trust economic incentives will align network participants. These forms of trust are implicit, structural, and invisible—yet profoundly influential. *The absence of a nameplate does not imply the absence of trust—it only displaces it.*

This displacement has a psychological cost. Humans are social, relational beings. We are conditioned to build trust through cues—tone, eye contact, history, shared culture. Code has none of these. It offers logic, not empathy. In the cryptosphere, betrayal is often legal, sanctioned by the code itself. Rug pulls are not breaches of contract—they are fulfilments of it. That inversion leaves users in a strange position: *more responsible for their own protection, and more exposed to sophisticated manipulation.*

So what does it mean to choose your relationship to power in this context? It means knowing what kind of systems you want to inhabit—not just technically, but philosophically. Are you willing to participate in structures where failure is personal, but success is communal? Where transparency replaces accountability, and performance replaces intent? Where resistance to authority comes bundled with exposure to chaos? Crypto is not a panacea. It is *a mirror held up to your preferences about freedom, risk, and control.*

And like all mirrors, it can be confronting. Some users will conclude that complete autonomy is worth the price of complexity. Others will seek hybrid models, where some responsibilities are outsourced to trusted third parties. Still others will retreat entirely, finding the demands of crypto citizenship too high. All of these are rational responses. The point is not to prescribe a path, but to *equip individuals to make conscious, informed choices about how they relate to power.*

This choice extends beyond finance. It touches identity, data ownership, communication channels, governance models, and the very infrastructure of the internet. The decentralised stack is still being built—but its shape will be determined by who shows up, and what they value. If users abdicate their role as shapers, they will become subjects once again—this time, not to bankers or governments, but to algorithms and anonymous multisig councils.

Choosing your relationship to power, then, is not a one-time declaration. It is an ongoing negotiation. A commitment to literacy, to ethical reflection, and to participation. Power is not eliminated by protocols—it is re-routed, reconfigured, and re-contested. Crypto gives you tools. It does not give you meaning. That part is still, and always, up to you.

## The Ongoing Experiment:

Crypto is often described in the past tense—as if it were already a resolved category. Investors speak of market cycles and narrative arcs, regulators issue sweeping classifications, and developers pitch new projects as "the future" as though the future had already been settled. But this framing is misleading. The most honest way to think about crypto is not as a product or a movement, nor even as a technology. It is, at its core, *an experiment still very much in progress.* It is a shifting field of social, political, and technical engineering whose ultimate outcomes remain profoundly undecided. And like all live experiments, it demands a posture of critical engagement rather than belief, vigilance over celebration, and a willingness to interrogate not just what we're building—but *why we're building it.*

This fundamental indeterminacy is not a flaw. It is the defining feature. In contrast to traditional finance, where regulatory precedent and institutional inertia enforce stability (or stagnation), crypto exists on an unsteady frontier where assumptions are contested, norms are emergent, and legitimacy is fluid. Every year, new protocols propose to rewrite how we think about money, governance, identity, ownership, or cooperation. Some are brilliant. Many are naive. A few are dangerous. *The signal-to-noise ratio is low—but the stakes are increasingly high.*

Take decentralised governance. It was once the poster child of blockchain idealism: a way to ensure that protocols remained open, equitable, and responsive to user communities. Yet in practice, many Decentralised Autonomous Organisations (DAOs) have struggled with voter apathy, governance capture, opaque decision-making, and coordination failures. Token-weighted voting systems—meant to democratise control—often concentrate it. Community treasuries, initially envisioned as engines of collective benefit, are frequently raided or mismanaged. These outcomes do not invalidate the premise of decentralised governance. They *illuminate the fragility of coordination under decentralisation*, and remind us that software alone does not confer wisdom or fairness.

Then there is the issue of financial inclusion. Crypto has promised to bank the unbanked, reduce remittance costs, and bypass legacy systems that have excluded billions. And indeed, some real progress has been made—particularly in countries with unstable currencies, poor access to banking infrastructure, or high levels of financial censorship. But these gains coexist with predatory dynamics: yield farming schemes that implode without warning, token economies designed to pump and dump, and platforms that offload complexity onto users without adequate education or risk disclosures. *Inclusion is meaningless if it simply introduces people to new forms of volatility or exploitation.*

Technological experimentation, in this context, does not automatically equate to progress. Crypto's pace of innovation is relentless—zero-knowledge proofs, restaking protocols, rollups, NFT-based governance, composable DeFi, modular chains—but its capacity for institutional memory is limited. Projects are often abandoned within months; critical design lessons are forgotten, repeated, or ignored. Unlike scientific disciplines where peer review and reproducibility serve as guardrails, crypto often moves by hype and narrative. This makes it exhilarating. It also makes it deeply unstable. *Velocity without reflection risks entrenching the very problems crypto set out to solve.*

The idea that crypto is a permanent experiment also exposes a deeper discomfort: there is no guarantee it will "work" in any singular or final sense. The technology might scale, but the social contract may fail. The governance models may mature, but participation may wither. The code may be secure, but the incentives may be misaligned. Even the most elegantly decentralised system can succumb to human dynamics—greed, tribalism, short-termism, factionalism. *Code can encode logic; it cannot encode ethics.* The belief that cryptographic trust can transcend moral ambiguity is seductive—but mistaken.

That doesn't mean the experiment should be abandoned. On the contrary, it means we should treat it with the same rigour and humility we apply to other complex systems—scientific research, public policy, constitutional design. The question is not whether crypto is "good" or "bad." The question is *what values, risks, and trade-offs it surfaces—and how we choose to engage with them as informed participants rather than passive consumers.* Just as democracy requires a literate citizenry, decentralisation requires a literate user base. Technical knowledge, political awareness, and ethical sensitivity are no longer optional—they are essential survival skills.

It also means acknowledging the boundaries of technological solutionism. Not all problems are best solved by code. Many require trust, empathy, cultural change, or legal mechanisms. Crypto excels at eliminating intermediaries, automating agreements, and enforcing transparency. But it struggles to address ambiguity, intent, or restorative justice. It cannot replace diplomacy, resolve value conflicts, or substitute for human judgment. *If the tool becomes the ideology, we lose the ability to assess whether we are using it wisely.*

Vigilance, then, is not paranoia. It is responsibility. It is the recognition that open systems are always at risk of capture—not just by bad actors, but by lazy thinking, complacent assumptions, and charismatic opportunists. We've seen this before: the idealism of the internet gave way to surveillance capitalism; the promise of social media devolved into disinformation and polarisation. Crypto, if left unexamined, could follow a similar path—not because of its technology, but because of its users' passivity. *The defence against capture is not code. It is culture—specifically, a culture of continuous questioning.*

Humility must accompany this vigilance. The deeper one studies crypto, the harder it becomes to sustain any singular narrative. Is it revolutionary or reactionary? Empowering or extractive? A tool of liberation or a tool of speculation? The answer, invariably, is: it depends—on context, implementation, governance, and adoption. Black-and-white frameworks collapse under scrutiny. The best analysts of crypto are not maximalists or detractors. They are *students of complexity*, willing to embrace contradiction and dwell in nuance.

Consider the Ethereum Merge. A technological triumph, yes. But also a decision to centralise certain staking mechanisms in the name of efficiency. Or look at Bitcoin: the original decentralised asset, now increasingly dominated by a few mining pools and held as a speculative asset rather than transacted as a currency. These are not signs of failure—they are reminders that no protocol escapes trade-offs. Each step forward carries costs, and those costs must be measured not just technically but morally. *Sovereignty always has a shadow side.*

This is why critical thought must remain central. Not cynical thought—not knee-jerk contrarianism or dismissive critique—but *disciplined scepticism.* The willingness to ask: what assumptions underlie this design? Who benefits from this tokenomic model? What power asymmetries does this governance system conceal? What blind spots are embedded in this whitepaper? These are the questions that separate ideological adherence from intellectual integrity.

And perhaps most importantly, we must hold space for failure. Not every DAO will succeed. Not every protocol should survive. Failure is not only inevitable in experimental systems—it is necessary. It is how we learn, iterate, and refine. What matters is not how often projects collapse, but whether the ecosystem *remembers what they taught.* Crypto is often critiqued for its short attention span. If it is to mature, it must develop a memory—not just of its breakthroughs, but of its missteps and excesses.

To live with radical uncertainty is not to despair. It is to recognise the stakes, embrace the unknown, and contribute with eyes open. Crypto is not destiny. It is *a set of evolving possibilities, shaped by design choices and value commitments that remain ours to influence.* Whether it leads to emancipation or consolidation, pluralism or monopolies, genuine participation or engineered illusion, depends on how seriously we treat the responsibilities it demands.

We do not need blind faith. We need *informed stewardship.* We need a culture that can celebrate innovation while critiquing its excesses, that can hold optimism and caution in the same hand, that can build while questioning the blueprints. The most enduring experiments are not the ones that promise certainty. They are the ones that teach us how to think, choose, and adapt. Crypto—at its best—is exactly that. And the experiment is only just beginning.

# About the Author

Evelyn Hartstone is a thoughtful explorer at the intersection of technology, ethics, and society—with a keen eye for the profound questions that cryptocurrencies provoke. Drawing on years of interdisciplinary research and interviews across diverse crypto communities, she crafts deeply reflective narratives that go beyond hype and jargon. Evelyn approaches digital money not merely as code, but as a cultural and philosophical experiment about trust, power, and autonomy. Her writing invites readers into a space of curiosity and critical thought, guiding them toward a clearer understanding of where crypto fits within our shared future.

www.ingramcontent.com/pod-product-compliance
Lightning Source LLC
Chambersburg PA
CBHW031343230926
51848CB00002B/357